AFRICAN HOLOCAUST

The Story of the Uganda Martyrs

From an original painting in the Minor Seminary, Salisbury, Southern Rhodesia

An artist's impression of the Holocaust at Namugongo, 3 June 1886

AFRICAN HOLOCAUST

The Story of the Uganda Martyrs

by

J. F. FAUPEL

of St Joseph's Society for Foreign Missions, Mill Hill

P. J. KENEDY & SONS
NEW YORK

Nihil obstat Nicolaus Ferraro
    S.R.C. Adsessor
    Fidei Sub-Promotor Generalis
Nihil obstat Joannes M. T. Barton, S.T.D., L.S.S.
    Censor deputatus
Imprimatur E. Morrogh Bernard
    Vic. Gen.
Westmonasterii, die 14a Martii, 1962

Library of Congress Catalog Number : 62/18003

To

the memory

of

RENÉ LEFÈBRE
(White Father)

whose indefatigable research made this
work possible

CONTENTS

LIST OF ILLUSTRATIONS

INTRODUCTION

The author wishes to acknowledge his special indebtedness to two works in particular : *Black Martyrs,* by J. P. Thoonen (Mill Hill Father), and *Monagraphies sur les bienheureux martyrs de Ouganda,* by René Lefèbre (White Father).

African Holocaust was started as a revision of *Black Martyrs,* published by Sheed and Ward in 1941, which has been out of print for many years. However, thanks to the kindness of Archbishop L. J. Cabana in making available to the reviser the results of Fr Lefèbre's painstaking research, it has been found possible to fill in some of the lacunae in the former work, to present a more connected story, and to correct some errors which would undoubtedly not have found their way into print had not the author been prevented by the invasion of Holland from seeing his work through the press. Although based upon *Black Martyrs, African Holocaust* may claim to be a new attempt to make the martyrs of Uganda better known, and their heroic courage and steadfast faith better appreciated.

Detailed references to sources have been omitted, although every care has been taken to ensure that the account is as accurate as possible, and all suppositions have been clearly indicated as such in the text or notes. Footnotes have not been included, but the few notes considered necessary or useful are gathered at the back of the book for the benefit of those readers who may wish to consult them. In the account of the Namugongo holocaust itself, portions of two separate accounts by Denis Kamyuka have been combined in order to produce a more complete and connected narrative, and translations from Luganda have been more freely rendered than in *Black Martyrs.*

Many of the African names may appear, at first sight, formidable in the extreme to a non-African reader. The observance of a few simple rules should ensure that an almost correct pronunciation is achieved without difficulty. Luganda words should be pronounced syllable by syllable without stress on any particular one, remembering that each syllable ends with a vowel. The final 'e' is always sounded, and the vowel 'i' is always short. Thus Kabaka, Balikuddembe, Nyonyintono, Kiriwawanvu, would be pronounced Ka-ba-ka, Ba-li-ku-dde-mbe, Nyo-nyi-nto-no, Ki-ri-wa-wa-nvu. The prefix *Bu* is used of a country, Buganda, Bunyoro; *Mu* (plural *ba*) is used of a person, Muganda, Musoga, Baganda, Banyoro. The prefix *Lu* is used for the language, Luganda, Lunyoro, Lusoga etc. Adjectives take the same prefix as the noun they qualify : a common prefix is *Ki*. Thus Kiganda customs are those of the Baganda, the people of Buganda, who speak Luganda.

A difficult problem faces any biographer of the Catholic martyrs of Uganda, that of introducing no less than twenty-two principal characters, attempting to show them to the reader as persons and not merely names, and fitting them into the background story of the persecution. In this work, the characters have been presented in the alternate chapters, three, five and seven, and the story of events leading up to the persecution is told in the remaining chapters. It is to be hoped that the patience of the non-African reader will not be too sorely tried by the biographical details of clans and relationships, which are of considerable interest to Africans and to those who know the continent. It would indeed be tragic if any reader were to allow himself to be discouraged by these and fail to continue with the story of courage and achievement which, however inadequately it may be told, can hardly fail to thrill.

Grateful acknowledgements are made to Fr Thoonen for his help, advice, corrections and suggestions; to Archbishop Cabana for the loan of Fr Lefèbre's MS and papers; to Messrs Sheed and Ward for permission to use the material from *Black Martyrs;* and to numerous others who have given help, suggestions and encouragement.

John F. Faupel

Kyambogo, Kampala, Uganda.   3 June 1961 (Seventy-fifth anniversary of the Namugongo Holocaust)

Chapter One

SETTING THE SCENE

Between 1885 and 1887, within ten years of their first knowledge of the Catholic Faith, twenty-two boys and men of Uganda laid down their lives for their religion. The story of their conversion from paganism, of their battle for Christian virtue and of their sacrifice of life itself is told in the following pages; but as all were victims of Mwanga the Kabaka, or king, of Buganda, and the majority were also natives of that country, some description of its social and political structure is needed in order that the reader may appreciate fully the remarkable change wrought in the souls of these young men through the action of grace and the teachings of Christ.

In the nineteenth century, Buganda, which later became one of the four provinces making up the Uganda Protectorate, was a fully independent African kingdom with a hereditary ruler known as the Kabaka. With its highly organized system of government and its well established traditions, this kingdom, set in the heart of Africa, on the equator and some eight hundred miles from the East Coast, provided a striking contrast to the rest of tropical Africa where generally speaking each man's hand was turned against his neighbour. The early explorers Speke and Grant, and later Stanley, after experiencing the chaos and confusion prevailing elsewhere, were so impressed by the appearance of law and order they found in Buganda that in their accounts they tended to glamorize the country and its ruler and to overlook the fundamental evil that was so closely bound up with much that was good.

The Kabaka, or king of Buganda, was an absolute monarch of the type described in Genesis 41, 44—'The King said to Joseph : I am Pharaoh : Without my command no man shall move hand or foot in all the land of Egypt'. The Kabaka had uncontested rights over all his subjects, was a law unto himself and master of life and death. The only limitations to his power lay in the sacrosanct customs established by his ancestors and handed down to him, but if these acted as a check upon the Kabaka himself, they were at the same time a motive for loyalty on the part of his subjects, over whom the Kabaka claimed absolute and complete authority—not only over their bodies but over their minds and hearts also.

Besides the Kabaka, there were in Buganda two other persons who bore the royal title : the Queen Mother and the Princess Royal. Tradition required that the Kabaka should have an official mother and an official sister. The title of Queen Mother (Namasole) was usually conferred upon the monarch's own mother but if she were dead or in disgrace he could give the title at will to another relative, usually an aunt.

As might be expected in a polygamous society, the Kabaka's wives were of no public importance and, if a hostess were required, the duty was always undertaken by the Princess Royal : a tradition which endured until the death of Kabaka Daudi Chwa, in 1939. The Princess Royal (Lubuga or Nalinya) was chosen by the Kabaka from the princesses of the blood, an important body of women, often very numerous, who were until more recent years forbidden to marry and prohibited from having children. This was to ensure that the line of succession should be continued through the princes, who were encouraged to marry and produce heirs in the male line. The Princess Royal was usually a favourite sister of the Kabaka, not necessarily the eldest. Custom allowed both Queen Mother and Princess Royal to hold courts of their own, and even conferred upon them some administrative power.

In the government of the country, which is thought to have had at that time (c. 1860) a population of about three millions, the Kabaka was assisted by a number of chiefs, appointed or deposed entirely at his own pleasure and caprice. Ten of these were county chiefs, governing in the Kabaka's name the ten counties which then made up the Kingdom of Buganda. Each had his own official title, each was assisted by a number of district chiefs, also appointed by the Kabaka, and these, in turn, had under them a number of sub-chiefs. Each chief acted as a local magistrate, having his own council-chamber and court-house. With their assistance the county chiefs kept a firm hold over their people and were kept informed of what was going on.

Although appointed by the Kabaka, the county chiefs were so powerful in their own areas that the Kabaka had constantly to be on his guard against their usurpation of his own rights. To this end a number of safeguards had been established. No county chief could remain indefinitely at his own county-seat. He had to maintain an establishment adjoining the royal enclosure, and various personal duties at Court ensured that he would be present there, under the eye of the Kabaka, at certain times of the year. Even in his own county the chief was not entirely free from supervision; everywhere the Kabaka's liege-men were established, liberally endowed with land, slaves and women, owing no allegiance to the chief and expected to keep an eye on the interests of their master, the Kabaka. Religious worship, which was under the direct control of the Kabaka, and also the authority of the clan leaders provided further curbs upon the power of county chiefs who might hanker after independence.

The clans of Buganda play an important rôle in the social structure of the nation. Each is a family-group which traces its origins to a common ancestor and has common totems, mostly animals, held sacred by all its members. They are exogamous; that is, no man may marry a woman of his own clan. Thirty-six clans have been traced but, owing to the absorption of some of the smaller ones by the larger, the actual number is twenty-six. Each clan had its family estates, to which it acquired a prescriptive right when three or four generations of a family had been buried there : after this, not even the Kabaka disputed its inalienable right to the land. The clan heads, who existed independently of the Kabaka and the chiefs, had considerable influence and jealously guarded their rights and privileges against any encroachments. The Kabakas, recognizing in the clans a curb upon the power of the chiefs, never attempted to undermine their position, although they did from time to time take action against individual clan leaders. It was indeed the set policy of the older Kabakas to maintain their own position by playing one section of their subjects off against another and even religion was pressed into service in pursuance of this policy.

The evils of this abuse of religion for political ends did not show to the full whilst there was only one religion in the country, but with the advent of Islam and then of Christianity, both Catholic and Protestant, the policy bore bitter fruit in the politico-religious wars of the late nineteenth century.

The ancient religion of the Baganda, before the importation of the Sesse Islands' gods, was monotheistic. They worshipped the Creator of all things under various titles : Katonda, the Creator; Mukama, the Master; and Seggulu, the Lord of Heaven. Every morning, his blessing was invoked by the master of the house on all members of the family, particularly on those who were absent. Also, having a firm belief in the immortality of the soul, the Baganda venerated the spirits of their ancestors. These beliefs seem to have been brought to Buganda from the North by Kintu, the Father of the Baganda, and his followers, probably about the fifteenth century. The legend of Kintu and Nambi is closely reminiscent of the story of Adam and Eve, and there are also traces of the story of the Redemption in the legends of the Baganda.

The worship of Katonda, the Creator and Lord of Heaven, was

3

in the early days the basis of public and private morality, and the ancient Baganda are said to have been remarkably honest and loyal in their dealings with others, and to have had a strict moral code which frowned on polygamy and even forbade immodest talk.

Probably about the sixteenth century this worship of God the Creator was largely superseded by the cult of the Lubale, the descendents of Kintu, who had succeeded in getting themselves accepted as tribal gods by the Sesse Islanders in Lake Victoria.

Once the gods of the Sesse Islands had established a footing on the soil of Buganda, the Kabaka entrusted them to the clans of the realm, and turned them into an instrument of government. The clan heads, the natural representatives of the ancient cult of ancestral spirits, still functioned in the shadow of the ancient tombs but, by their side in the bosom of the clan, rose up also the Guardians of the Lubale.

The word 'Lubale', which at first meant a tribal god, gradually widened its significance to include also the relics or fetishes to which the gods' spirits were believed to be attached. Veritable courts, modelled on the royal court, were set up around these objects and, distinct from the temple-officers who were members of the guardian clan, there grew up a body of men calling themselves mediums or mouthpieces of the new gods.

Once launched into idolatry, the Baganda soon invented new gods to add to the descendants of Kintu, such as Walumbe the god of death, Musoke the rainbow, Kiwanuka the thunder, Kawumpuli the plague, etc. Since the mediums of all these deities could, with the consent of the Kabaka, demand human sacrifices on a large scale, these false gods quickly acquired a much greater importance in the everyday lives of the people than Katonda, the Creator, a fact clearly expressed in the Luganda saying, 'Katonda tatta—God the Creator killeth not' i.e. 'does not demand human sacrifice'. Thus, although belief in the Creator was never entirely extinguished and a shrine to him still existed at Butonda in Kyaggwe County in the eighteen-seventies, his worship was almost entirely superseded by the cult of the Lubale.

From the outset, the worship of the descendants of Kintu and of the other gods was under the immediate control of the Kabaka, and was used as an instrument of government, to protect the monarch and the state. Although the Kabaka himself paid the cult lip-service, sometimes consulting the gods, 'sending them gifts and listening to their mediums or priests, yet at the same time he alone possessed the right, if angered or offended by them, of looting their temples or estates. So it becomes clear that at any given moment, there was in Buganda but one God and one King, the reigning

4

Kabaka. For all practical purposes, he was the God of Providence since he alone controlled all that Katonda had created'.[1]

The reigning Kabaka when the first Europeans visited the Court of Buganda was Mutesa I, otherwise known as Mukabya. He has been described, more or less enthusiastically, by all the explorers who visited his court. Roscoe calls him the greatest of all the kings of Buganda, and Apolo Kagwa gives the following description :

> Mutesa is said to have been very tall and dignified. He had a Roman nose, beautiful eyes and a well-balanced neck. He was very well-loved by his subjects. Because he was unusually intelligent, his Katikiro, Kayira, called him Mutesa which means the-one-who-is-wise-in-council. He was also known as Mukabya, the-one-who-makes-others-cry.[2]

The missionaries, who had more and longer contact with Mutesa than the explorers, were less enthusiastic about him. The Rev C. T. Wilson, the first Protestant minister to reach his court, refers to him as a 'murderous maniac'. Père Girault, a Catholic missionary, accuses him of practising himself, and encouraging his subjects to practise, the vice of homosexuality, and Ashe, a Protestant, who knew him well, says, 'there was much that was good and lovable in him but his education had been a training in cruelty, brutality and lust'.

Attached to the Kabaka's court were a number of chiefs and officials who ruled over no districts but who were liberally endowed with land and property. Two of these took rank above the ten county chiefs already mentioned. They were the Katikiro and the Kimbugwe.

The Katikiro was, after the Kabaka, the most important person in the kingdom. To translate the title as prime-minister, as most writers do, is likely to give the reader a completely false idea of his functions during this period of history. He was the Kabaka's chief administrative officer, answerable to no-one but his royal master, acting as chief administrator of justice with the power of life and death and, if the Kabaka so wished, chief adviser to His Majesty. His functions approximated most closely to those of the Grand-Vizier of the fairy tales, but in this work he will henceforth be referred to as the Chancellor.

The Chancellor of the realm throughout the period with which this work is concerned was a man named Mukasa, of the Musu (edible, or cane-rat) clan. A ruthless and unscrupulous man, he was to play an important rôle in the history of the martyrs of Uganda. Like most of the chiefs, he had started his political career as a royal page and during the reign of Kabaka Suna had managed to rise to the position of Kauta, Domestic Chamberlain to the royal court, and to ingratiate himself with Prince Mutesa, the future Kabaka.

When Mutesa succeeded to the throne, Mukasa, looking for further advancement, arranged with the connivance of the new Kabaka the murder of the great warrior Namunjulirwa, chief of the rich county of Buddu and father of the martyr Bruno Serunkuma. He sold into slavery those of his victim's family he could lay his hands on, and became county chief in his stead. A few years later, in 1872, Mukasa achieved the summit of his ambition, becoming Chancellor of the realm. He then contrived to render his position almost unassailable by means of a blood-pact with Mutesa, which made him both blood-brother to the reigning monarch and 'father' to his future successor.

Although the explorer Stanley may have been over-enthusiastic about the character of Mutesa, he was not slow in discerning the true character of this evil genius, as the following extract from *Through Darkest Africa* shows.

> I told the Katikiro that it would take a year to finish such a work (building a dam a hundred feet wide to Ingira Island in order to dislodge the enemy Bavuma), but if he would limit the width to ten feet, and form the people into rows, he would have the satisfaction of setting foot on Ingira Island without danger. But though the premier and first lord of Uganda lost none of his politeness and never forgot that Mutesa, his master, was pleased to call me his friend, I was not slow in perceiving that he would not accept friendly advice from a stranger and foreigner.
>
> It was not by words, or even a hint of unfriendly gesture that the fact was betrayed, but simply by inattention to my advice. The most courtly European could not have excelled the Uganda premier. He offered in the same friendly manner a gourdful of honey-sweet plantain wine, talked sociably upon various matters, invited verbal sketches of European life, and smiled in an aristocratically insolent manner. Nevertheless, under this urbane mask I detected a proud spirit, unbending as steel. With such an unruffled, composed, smiling patrician of Uganda, what could I do but groan inwardly that good, brave, excellent Mutesa should be served by such men? At the same time I could not help smiling at the diplomatic insouciance of this man who, indeed, represented in only too perfect a degree the character of these Waganda chiefs.

Second in importance to the Chancellor, although of no great significance in the story of the martyrs, was the Kimbugwe, holding an office peculiar to Buganda, that of Guardian of the reigning

6

monarch's umbilical cord. The Baganda believed the afterbirth and umbilical cord to be a sort of second child, the double or twin of its owner : it was carefully preserved by the mother, because the health and welfare of the living child were thought to be closely bound up with those of the double. The twin was even given a name by its owner : Kabaka Jjunju, for instance, named his Tawutta, he-is-not-in-his-dotage, to signify that a Kabaka never became senile : whatever he said must be accepted with respect and acclaim by his subjects. At every new moon, the cord was presented to the Kabaka by its Guardian and given due reverence by the Kabaka himself and the assembled courtiers. An entry in the Rubaga Mission Diary for 25 July 1880 describes the scene on one such occasion : 'His umbilical cord is presented to Mutesa. He rises from his seat to touch the precious talisman solemnly with his royal hand. All the assistants rise : those with swords unsheathe them and brandish them, and the soldiers present arms.'

On the death of a Kabaka a new guardian was appointed to guard the twin of the new monarch, the former one retiring with his precious charge, which he continued to guard and reverence. Both Chancellor and Guardian of the Cord had enclosures outside but adjoining the royal enclosure, and both had the right of access to the Kabaka at all times.

Numberless other officials were attached to the Court. Some have already been mentioned; others included the chief in charge of the royal cattle, the majordomo in charge of the private quarters of the palace, the treasurer who guarded the royal stores of ivory, cowrie-shells and gunpowder, the guardian of the sacred fire, and the chief executioner. Hundreds of page-boys also attended upon the Kabaka, his numerous wives and the multitude of princes and princessess. It was this body of pages that provided the majority of the martyrs who died in the persecution of 1886.

One further institution is worthy of note, that of the royal legate. No stranger was permitted to travel in the Kabaka's dominions unless accompanied by a legate appointed for the purpose by the Kabaka. It would seem that, in the absence of written documents, the legate acted as the traveller's passport and as an indication to the public that the stranger was under the Kabaka's protection.

Such then was the well-organized kingdom in the heart of Africa which so impressed and astonished Speke and Grant, who discovered it in 1862, and Stanley who followed them some twelve years later. Needless to say, Buganda with its unified rule was well able to keep most of its neighbours either in subjection or under tribute. Only to the north-west did it meet with a worthy opponent in the Kingdom of Bunyoro. The borderland of the two countries was constantly the scene of pitched battles, forays and raids in which men were slaughtered, cattle looted and women and children carried off as slaves. To the north and to the south the kingdom was protected by lakes : Lake Kyoga to the north and the vast expanse of Lake Victoria Nyanza to the south. To the east, across the Nile, lay Busoga, kept firmly in subjection and regularly looted of cattle, women and children. On the western shore of Lake Victoria, to the south of Buddu County, Kiziba and Koki were both subjugated, and due west, the pastoral country of Ankole, though never conquered, sent large presents of cattle from time to time to allay the cupidity of its powerful neighbour.

Slavery, though fairly widespread in Buganda, was not practised on a large commercial scale, since the Baganda did not as a rule cultivate large plantations. Even the slaves sold to the Arabs were probably only in sufficient number to transport their purchases of ivory to the coast. Most slaves were obtained by means of raids or levies on the surrounding tribes, although some were Baganda who had been kidnapped as children, or sold into slavery by relatives who had got into debt.

Generally, slaves were treated with consideration, often even as members of the family, by their Baganda masters, no distinction being made between the children of slave-wives and the children of others. Even the wives, slave and free, seem to have been on an equal footing, both being equally the chattels of their lord and master. Even at the royal court no distinction was made between the pages who had come there as slaves and those presented by the chiefs, often their own sons. Both had equal opportunities for advancement to positions of responsibility. This is not so very surprising when one remembers that the Kabaka regarded all beings as created for his own personal use and pleasure and all equally as his slaves, body and soul.

Such was the political, social and religious heritage of Buganda when first Islam and then Christianity made contact with its court.

Chapter Two

The Impact of the Outside World

Shortly before the middle of the nineteenth century, Buganda's isolation from the outside world was broken by the visit of the first Arab, the Sheik Ahmed-bin-Ibrahim, who was graciously received by Kabaka Suna. Other Arabs followed, and trade between Buganda and the Arabs of Zanzibar and the coastal areas began to develop. For guns, powder, beads and cotton-cloth the Kabaka, who controlled all the wealth of the country, bartered ivory, both white and black.

During the reign of Kabaka Mutesa I, who succeeded his father in 1857, Arabs continued to come to the Court of Buganda, where they acquired considerable influence. Their religion, the tenets of which were simple and easy and implied no censure upon the customs of the Baganda, gained a number of adherents. At one time Mutesa himself seemed to incline towards Islam, but the horror of mutilation or disfigurement of any sort, for which, amongst the tribes of East and Central Africa, the Baganda were almost unique, made him loathe circumcision. He did not, however, raise any objections to his subjects becoming Muslims unless their religion led them to question his own absolute authority.

The accusation has been made that the Arabs introduced into Buganda a vice which was completely unknown before and for which no word existed in the language, the vice of homosexuality or sodomy. Sir Apolo Kagwa writes : 'These Arabs introduced into our country, along with numerous disorders, an abomination which we had never practised and which we had never heard spoken of.' Père Lourdel, one of the first Catholic missionaries to Buganda, writing in 1879, says much the same : 'If we are to accept the statements of trustworthy people, the Baganda had more normal and simple customs before the coming of the Arabs and their followers. It is they who initiated these poor people of Central Africa into their infamous practices, and taught them to disregard the lives and property of their fellows.'[1]

Whether the Arabs were solely responsible for its introduction or not, homosexuality seems to have been rife at Mutesa's court. Père Girault has already been quoted as saying that Mutesa himself indulged in the vice and encouraged his subjects to do so. His son

9

Mwanga was also an addict long before he succeeded to the throne.

From a purely natural viewpoint therefore one would hardly expect that the Royal Court of Buganda would prove fruitful ground in which to plant the seed of Christianity.

The first Europeans to reach Buganda were the explorers, Speke and Grant. They crossed the Kagera River into Buganda on 16 January 1862 and on 19 February arrived at Mutesa's Court, then situated at Banda, where they remained as guests until 7 July. The people gazed with wonder at the first white-men to visit their land and, in due course, the western world read with interest Speke's account of the remarkable kingdom which he had discovered in the heart of Africa.

For a time the event made little difference to Buganda. Arab traders continued to come with strange new things for sale and to go away with ivory and slaves in exchange; for twelve years no further Europeans appeared.

The interest which the explorers and traders took in his country at first flattered Mutesa and he joyfully accepted the presents they brought. Before long, however, he began to grow uneasy about the military posts being established by the Egyptians close to his frontiers. There is reason to believe that he was behind the fierce encounters that Baker, founder of the Equatorial Province, had with the King of Bunyoro : what could the shrewd Kabaka desire more than to have his hereditary enemy weakened by the Turks, who at that time ruled Egypt, whilst making use of him against this threat to his own independence?

In July-August 1874, Colonel Chaillé Long, an American, visited Buganda as an envoy of Colonel Gordon, Baker's successor as Governor of the Equatorial Province. Before the excitement caused by this second visit of a white man had died down there arrived, in April 1875, the dynamic Henry Morton Stanley, to be followed, a few days later, by E. Linant de Bellefonds, a Frenchman in Gordon's service. The two astonished white men shook hands in the Kabaka's great audience hall.

Because Mutesa was at war with the inhabitants of Buvuma Island, Stanley was detained at the capital where he made full use of his opportunities for describing to the interested Kabaka the wonders of civilization and the benefits of Christianity. In Christianity and in the power he associated with it Mutesa thought that he saw an answer to the Muslim threat to his dominions from the North; so, calling together his chiefs, he made them promise to accept the Christian religion when it should be preached to them. 'It is ... clear,' says Gale, 'that Mutesa's first purpose in toying with Christianity was to give colour and support to his opposition to Islam, and to make it clear that he would have no dealings with Egypt. His second purpose was confusedly connected with the power which Stanley the man had displayed, and which belonged somehow, he surmised, both to England and to Christianity.'[1]

Stanley, unaware of the true reasons for Mutesa's astonishing enthusiasm, told him the simple story of Christianity without any particular doctrine, translated some portions of the Bible, and wrote his famous appeal for a Christian mission to be sent to Buganda. This appeal, taken back through Egypt by de Bellefonds, was published in the *Daily Telegraph* of 15 November 1875 :

I have, indeed, undermined Islamism so much here that Mtesa has determined henceforth, until he is better informed, to observe the Christian Sabbath as well as the Muslim Sabbath, and the great captains have unanimously consented to this. He has further caused the Ten Commandments of Moses to be written on a board for his daily perusal—for Mtesa can read Arabic—as well as the Lord's Prayer and the golden commandment of our Saviour, 'Thou shalt love thy neighbour as thyself'. This is great progress for the few days that I have remained with him, and, though I am no missionary, I shall begin to think I might become one if such success is feasible. But oh! that some pious, practical missionary would come here! What a field and harvest ripe for the sickle of civilization! Mtesa would give him anything he desired, houses, lands, cattle, ivory, etc.! He might call a province his own in one day. It is not the mere preacher, however, that is wanted here. The bishops of Great Britain collected, with all the classic youth of Oxford and Cambridge, would effect nothing by mere talk with the intelligent people of Uganda. It is the practical Christian tutor, who can teach people how to become Christians, cure their diseases, construct dwellings, understand and exemplify agriculture, and turn his hand to anything, like a sailor—this is the man who is wanted. Such a one, if he can be found, would become the saviour of Africa. He must be tied to no church or sect, but profess God and His Son and the moral law, and live a blameless Christian, inspired by liberal principles, charity to all men, and devout faith in Heaven. He must belong to no nation in particular, but to the entire white race. Such a man or men, Mtesa, Emperor of Uganda, Usoga, Unyoro, and Karagwe —an empire 360 geographical miles in length, by 50 in breadth— invites to repair to him. He has begged me to tell the white men that, if they will only come to him, he will give them all they want. Now, where is there in all the pagan world a more promising field for a mission than in Uganda? Colonel Linant de Bellefonds is my witness that I speak the truth, and I know he will corroborate all I say. The Colonel, though a Frenchman, is a Calvinist, and has become as ardent a well-wisher for the Waganda as I am. Then why further spend needlessly vast sums upon black pagans of Africa who have no example of their own people becoming Christians before them? I speak to the Universities Mission at Zanzibar and to the Free Methodists at Mombasa, to the leading philanthropists, and the pious people of England. Here, gentlemen, is your opportunity—embrace it! The people on the shores of the Nyanza call upon you. Obey your own generous instincts, and listen to them; and I assure you that in one year you will have more converts to christianity than all other missionaries united can number. The population of Mtesa's kingdom is very dense; I estimate the number of his subjects at 2,000,000. You need not fear to spend money upon such a mission, as Mtesa is sole ruler, and will repay its cost tenfold with ivory, coffee, otter skins of a very fine quality, or even in cattle, for the wealth of this country in all these products is immense. The road here is by the Nile, or via Zanzibar, Ugogo, and Unanyembe. The former route, so long as Colonel Gordon governs the countries of the Upper Nile, seems most feasible.

This appeal to Christendom to evangelize Buganda met with an immediate and enthusiastic response. Within three days of its publication, the Church Missionary Society received from an anonymous benefactor an offer of five thousand pounds for a mission to the Great Lake. Smaller donations kept pouring in, followed, on 29 November, by a second gift of five thousand pounds. By 23 November, eight days after the appeal was published, the Committee of the Church Missionary Society had already decided to undertake the Uganda Mission.

Almost as readily as gifts came offers to serve in the new mission, among them that of Alexander Mackay, who was to play a leading and not always happy part in the early history of the Uganda mission.

Born at Rhynie in Scotland on 13 October 1849, the son of the local Free Kirk minister, Mackay, after a brilliant course at the Edinburgh Free Church Teacher Training College, followed his bent for mechanics, first at Edinburgh University and later in local engineering works. In 1873 he secured a good post as a draughtsman in Berlin, from where, in the following year, he wrote to his sister that he proposed to go to Madagascar as an engineering missionary. When it became clear that Madagascar was not sufficiently developed to afford scope for his capabilities, Mackay offered his service to the Church Missionary Society and was accepted for the mission to Lake Victoria, in January 1876.

Mackay was one of the well-equipped party of eight, under the leadership of Lieutenant Shergold-Smith, that sailed for Zanzibar later that same year. On the way inland from the coast of Africa he was seriously injured in an accident to the wagon he had built. He was first cared for at the Catholic mission of Bagamoyo and later sent back to the Coast. Meanwhile, after appalling hardships had further reduced the numbers of the party, two of the survivors, Shergold-Smith and the Rev. C. T. Wilson, the only ordained minister of the original caravan, arrived at Mutesa's Court, then situated at Rubaga, on 30 June 1877.

A further calamity then befell the English mission and delayed the start of any serious attempt to evangelize Buganda. Mr. O'Neill, who had been left at Kagei with the mission goods, and Shergold-Smith, who had gone there to fetch both, were murdered on Ukerewe Island in Lake Victoria, in December 1877. Wilson, left on his own at Rubaga, decided to leave for the South and, except for a short visit that he made in the middle of the following year, there was no missionary in Buganda until he returned with Mackay in November 1878.

Work began under difficulties. Kabaka Mutesa had been ailing since the autumn of 1877 and he had grown very suspicious of all Englishmen since the visits of Edward Schnitzer (later Emin Pasha) in 1876 and 1877, which had re-awakened his apprehension about Egyptian designs upon his kingdom. In spite of these obstacles, Mackay quickly won the Kabaka's approval, if not confidence, by his display of mechanical skill and, having gained a working-knowledge of Swahili during his enforced stay at the Coast, he was able to conduct Sunday services and resume the Bible-reading classes inaugurated by Stanley. The Kabaka and therefore also his courtiers were willing to listen to Mackay's teaching; by the end of the year, Mackay was able to write: 'The King and I are great friends, and the chiefs also have confidence in me.'

Mackay lost no opportunity of 'putting to confusion the pretensions of the Arabs'. On Sunday, 26 January 1879, his discourse was so impressive that the Kabaka said to Sengura, one of the Arabs present: 'This is the truth I have heard to-day. There can be only one truth. . . . Your religion is different from the truth, therefore it must be false.'[1] A few days earlier, Mutesa had remarked to his people, 'Isa (Jesus)—was there ever anyone like him?'

In February, Mackay wrote out the Lord's Prayer in Luganda. He had been astonished to find so many copies in use of the one written in Arabic at Stanley's dictation. 'The eagerness to know and possess the truth,' he wrote at this time 'is much more deeply seated among the chiefs than I expected'.

On 14 February Mackay and Wilson were greatly cheered by the arrival of reinforcements, the Rev. G. Litchfield, C. W. Pearson and R. W. Felkin, who had made a successful journey by way of the Nile.

They were less agreeably surprised when, only one week later, they learned that two French Catholic missionaries had set foot on the soil of Buganda. To Mackay, the news was especially displeasing. With his Calvinist upbringing he had an immense distrust of any sacerdotal or sacramental form of religion in general, and an intense hatred of Catholicism in particular. After visiting a Catholic church in Malta, on his way out to Africa, he had written : 'We go to plant Churches of the Living God in Central Africa. But we go sowing the good seed, knowing only too well that thy hand will soon come and sow tares among the wheat. The good meal will soon be leavened by thy stealthy hand, till the whole be one vile mass, corrupted by thy Mary worship and thy Mass worship.'

The new party of C.M.S. missionaries had come through the Sudan with every assistance from Colonel Gordon whose forces, so near to his Northern frontier, were a constant source of apprehension to Kabaka Mutesa. The missionaries attempted to allay his anxiety on this head by assuring him of Gordon's pacific intentions towards his kingdom, and making it clear that this change of heart on the part of Gordon was largely due to pressure exerted by the Church Missionary Society. Although momentarily relieved, the wily monarch was quick to perceive the obvious corollary : that if these foreigners in his country had sufficient influence to hold Gordon back from molesting it, they could also, if it suited their purpose, use that same influence to call Gordon's forces down upon his kingdom. The well-intentioned efforts of the new arrivals to win Mutesa's confidence had just the opposite effect, and the fact that the two Catholic missionaries, who had now set foot in his kingdom, belonged to another nation, coupled with Mackay's unconcealed hostility towards them, was quite sufficient to ensure their welcome by Mutesa, who loved nothing better than to play off one party against another.

The coming of the White Fathers to the Court of Mutesa aroused great resentment in Protestant missionary circles, in which it was generally assumed that, by sending them, the Catholic Church 'deliberately set herself to oppose Protestantism rather than heathenism and, with eyes open and with solemn protests sounding in her ears, commenced that career of aggression which was to bear such bitter fruit in the days to come'.

This entirely erroneous view of the Catholic Church's missionary activity seems to have been based on the assumption that she had made no attempt to evangelize Central Africa until the Anglican Church showed her the way. How false that assumption was is amply borne out by the facts.

In 1840, thirty-five years before Stanley's appeal for missionaries for Buganda, the Maltese priest, Casolani, had submitted to the Sacred Congregation of Propaganda in Rome a plan for the establishment of missions beyond the Sahara. The plan was approved, except that the Nile route was chosen instead of the Sahara, and put into operation in 1846. The Jesuit, Ryllo, who was in charge, died soon after his arrival in Khartoum in 1846, and was succeeded by Knoblecher, under whose direction the missionaries, one of whom was Casolani, pushed rapidly southwards. By 1850 they had established the Holy Cross mission station at Abu Kalu, south of Gondokoro on the White Nile, at the very gate of Uganda. Gondokoro is some 1800 miles as the crow flies from the mouth of the Nile, and about 280 from the boundary of Mutesa's Buganda. It was at one time the frontier post of the Uganda Protectorate.

Further southward progress was frustrated by the appalling death-rate amongst the missionaries. Of ninety-five who went out between 1846 and 1863, forty-four died, three remained to staff the Khartoum station, and the remaining forty-eight returned home, mostly broken in health.

One of the survivors, Daniele Comboni, undaunted by his experiences, was determined to continue the project. For this purpose, he founded at Verona an Institute of Missionary Priests for Central Africa. This Institute, which originally recruited volunteers who were already priests, later developed into the Foreign Missionary Society usually known as the Verona Fathers.

In 1872, Comboni—now a bishop—and his Verona Fathers took over the Sudan mission from the Franciscans, who had held the fort for eleven years, but in spite of his eagerness to push further southwards, never, up the time of his early death in 1881, did he have sufficient resources or manpower at his disposal even to make up the ground that had been lost.

Other hands were, however, preparing to take up the standard which death and disease had wrested from those of the earlier missionaries.

The avowed purpose of the White Fathers, at that time known as the 'Society of Missionaries of Our Lady of the African missions', a society founded by Bishop (later Cardinal) Lavigerie at Algiers in 1868-9, was to establish missions in the Sudan, which in those days stood vaguely for all Negro Africa. Finding his work in Muslim North Africa thwarted, the founder began to look for more promising fields of activity for his Society. The work of the explorers had focussed the attention of the world on Central Africa and, in consequence, there had been founded, in 1876, the 'Association Internationale Africaine de Bruxelles' under the patronage of King Leopold of the Belgians. The Association planned to open up Africa to Science, Commerce, Education etc. Bishop Lavigerie followed its proceedings with great interest, and realizing that it was likely to do little to promote the spread of Christianity, himself drew up, parallel with the Association's project for scientific exploration, an elaborate scheme for the evangelization of the newly discovered lands.

Lavigerie's proposals envisaged the creation of four Vicariates covering the whole of Equatorial Africa, each with its headquarters in the vicinity of one of the stations the Association of Brussels was planning to establish. The first of these Vicariates was to cover the region between Lakes Albert and Victoria; the second, the states of Mwata Yamvo in the south-west; the third to be based on Ujiji in Tanganyika, and the fourth to embrace the region between the great lakes and the Gulf of Guinea. He suggested that Bishop Comboni's missionaries should take charge of the two northern Vicariates, and his own White Fathers the two southern ones.

This plan, submitted to Cardinal Franchi, the Prefect of the Sacred Congregation of Propaganda on 2 February 1878, was so favourably received that its suggestions were, for the most part, ratified by a decree of 24 February. As Bishop Comboni's missionaries were not yet able to play their part, the White Fathers were ordered to shoulder the whole burden, beginning with those districts that could be reached from the East Coast, namely those of the Great Lakes.

The Catholic mission to Buganda was, then, not a 'wanton intrusion' but part of an overall plan for the evangelization of Central Africa, and the continuation of an enterprise, begun long before, which disease and death had retarded but never halted entirely. That Bishop Lavigerie should refuse to alter his arrangements at the request of the Church Missionary Society is easily understandable to any Catholic, who believes with complete assurance that Christ founded but one Church and to that one Church only gave his divine command to teach all nations. It would therefore have been impossible, contrary to Christ's explicit command, for the Catholic Church to neglect what seemed one of the most promising mission fields in the whole of Central Africa merely because an 'unauthorized' rival had got there first. It seems clear, also, that but for the accident of Stanley's impassioned appeal and the immediate response and enthusiasm it aroused, Catholic missionaries would almost certainly have been in Buganda well in advance of any Protestant enterprise.

The new missions assigned to them were joyfully accepted by the White Fathers and within two months four priests, Pères Livinhac, Girault, Lourdel and Barbot, and one lay-brother, Amans, were on their way to the Nyanza mission. On the same steamer were five

White Fathers making for the mission of Lake Tanganyika. Although Père Livinhac was the superior of the Nyanza group, it fell to Père Lourdel to play the leading part in the history of the martyrs.

Siméon Lourdel was born in France on 20 December 1853, at Dury in the Pas-de-Calais, and grew up on his father's small farm, tall and strong, full of life and high spirits. Early in life he made up his mind to become a priest and missionary, but for a time his high spirits made his superiors at the seminary at Arras doubtful of his vocation and he was sent to another college. There the young Lourdel embarked on the campaign of self-conquest which was to end in victory, and a retreat at the seminary of Arras, where he had been allowed to rejoin his former companions, confirmed his vocation.

A few months later the visit of a White Father to the seminary turned his thoughts to Africa and he determined to go there. To fit himself for the life he had chosen, he practised hardship and mortification without, however, losing the gaiety which made him universally popular. He joined the White Fathers in 1874 and was ordained priest on 2 April 1877, at the early age of twenty-three. He was a man of powerful frame, rugged features and an iron will, determined to do great things for Christ. After a short but useful period of missionary work at Metlili in the Sahara, he was appointed to the Nyanza mission.

The group of White Fathers destined for Uganda reached Zanzibar on 30 May 1878. From there they crossed over to Bagamoyo on the mainland and, on 17 June, started on their long tramp to the great lake, Victoria Nyanza. On the long journey, Père Lourdel made considerable progress with the Swahili language and when, after many hardships, the party reached the shores of Lake Victoria on 30 December, he was entrusted with the delicate mission of crossing to Buganda to inform the Kabaka of their presence and obtain permission for mission work in his dominions. In one canoe and with the minimum of luggage, Père Lourdel and Brother Amans set out on 20 January and reached the port of Entebbe on 17 February 1879.

Unaware of Mackay's hostility to Catholicism, since the Holy Ghost Fathers at Bagamoyo had spoken very highly of him, Père Lourdel, on arriving in Buganda, wrote to him informing him of the Catholic missionaries' intention to work in the country and asking him to speak on their behalf to the Kabaka. Mackay, on receiving the note, at once tried to persuade Mutesa to forbid the French priests to settle in Buganda. The Kabaka, although disturbed by the arrival of more Europeans, was intrigued by Mackay's evident hostility towards them and decided to make further enquiries about the strangers. During the night, he sent for Toli, a native of Madagascar who had accompanied the Sultan of Zanzibar on his visit to France in

1875. Toli assured him that the French were very good people, and advised him not to believe what Mackay had said about them. Accordingly the newcomers, who had been assigned quarters at Kitebbe, between Rubaga and the Lake, were granted a public audience at which Mackay was also present. After explaining the reasons for his coming, Père Lourdel said, 'For the rest, you can address yourself to Mr. Mackay. Having passed several weeks with the Catholic priests at Bagamoyo, he knows quite well what they are and what they do; as he speaks Swahili better than I, he will explain matters more fully'.

On being asked by the Kabaka what he knew of the visitors, Mackay 'told him very fully what they were and what doctrine they taught, especially Mariolatry, prayers to saints, image worship and obedience to the Pope'. Here Père Lourdel interrupted the tirade and told the Kabaka that he would dispense with the services of such an interpreter, and explain himself as best he could.

Mutesa was not sorry to see at his Court white men of a different nationality and different religion from the English and when in the course of the audience Mackay threatened to leave Buganda if the new arrivals were allowed to stay, retorted, 'Go if you want to, but the white men who have been announced shall come'.

During the months that elapsed before the return of the canoes which the Kabaka had sent to fetch the other Catholic missionaries, the popularity of the Protestant mission did not increase. There were further encounters between Mackay and the Muslims, and the Kabaka grumbled that the English would make nothing for him, although Stanley had promised that they would make all manner of things. Petulantly, he complained that he knew how to read before Mackay and his companions arrived, he knew the Bible, and he did not want two religions in his country, meaning Islam and Christianity. Mackay replied that he had little fear of Mutesa's turning Muslim, but that he would have two religions when he had Roman Catholics and Protestants together; to which Mutesa retorted that the religion of the Frenchmen might well be the true one.

With the waning of Mackay's popularity, Lourde's increased. On 8 June 1879, he had the satisfaction of hearing Mutesa sum up his teaching by saying, 'Then Jesus Christ is God, and his doctrine as taught by Mapèra (Lourdel) is true'. On this occasion the priest was also able to convince him that Catholics do not adore the Blessed Virgin, but honour her because of her dignity, in much the same way as the Queen Mother is honoured in Buganda. Hearing this, Mutesa remarked, 'Then Mackay has deceived us !' and brought the audience to a close with the words, 'Mapèra shall instruct us'.

The fleet of twenty-four canoes, sent to the south of the Lake to fetch Pères Livinhac, Girault and Barbot, returned to Entebbe on 17 June and a few days later the missionaries were received in audience in the royal enclosure. In order not to be mistaken for Arabs, the priests had exchanged the burnous (Arab cloak), which forms part of the White Fathers' habit, for a black overcoat. This apparent trifle contributed not a little to the favourable impression they made on the Kabaka, because, as one of the witnesses in the Process of Beatification explained :

> Long ago Kabaka Mutesa was already acquainted with the 'Our Father'. The Arabs spoke to him about it. This prayer pleased the Kabaka very much and he enquired who they were that taught it. Then an Arab, whom the Baganda call Salei, said to him: 'Those who teach this prayer dress in a black robe which goes down to their feet; if you wish to pray like them, you have only to call them in.' When the priests arrived in Buganda, wearing over their white habit this black robe, the Kabaka said to himself that these must be the ones of whom the Muslim had spoken, and received them with joy.

At the audience several courtiers spoke in favour of the new missionaries and Toli, the Madagascan, who seemed to consider the Frenchmen as his own protégés, asked the Kabaka to supply men and materials to build a large house for them. After granting this request, Mutesa brought the audience to a close with the customary gesture of the hand. Père Lourdel's impressions, expressed in conversation with his confrères and in a letter to his Superior General, were that Mutesa, though suspicious of all Europeans, had been kindly though reserved; that the great chiefs were definitely inclined to be hostile; and that the Arabs and coast-men seemed friendly enough towards the French but bitterly opposed to the English missionaries. The *Church Missionary Intelligencer,* in a postscript to letters from the missionaries written about this time, says :

> There seems to be distinct evidence that the influence of the French priests was unfavourable to our Mission, as might be expected, though in what precise way is not clear. Mr Felkin, in one letter, acquits them of personal hostility and unfairness; and it may only be that Mutesa seized the opportunity of playing off one against the other, with a view to squeezing more out of both. But the experience of three hundred years forbids us from putting any confidence in the good faith of Jesuits (sic). . . .

On 29 June another clash occurred between Mackay and Lourdel. It arose out of a request by Mackay to the Catholic priests to kneel down during the prayers he was about to recite. The priests demurred and, after the prayer, Père Lourdel explained to the Kabaka that they had not knelt because Catholics were forbidden to take part in a Protestant service. Mutesa then called upon Lourdel to read something and the priest read the first few chapters of the Swahili catechism of the Holy Ghost Fathers. When he had finished, Mackay was asked by the Kabaka what he thought of it. To the delight of His Majesty, a spirited discussion took place which, Mutesa seems to have judged, went in favour of Lourdel, because the following day he said to some of his intimates, 'The religion of the English is hard and heavy : I want no more of it'. He also added that he thought that a religion which took its stand on authority preferable to one which had for its basis the free interpretation of the Scriptures. Mackay himself seems to have recognized that he had behaved badly for, meeting Lourdel shortly after, he said, 'If you want anything, tell me. I will get it for you with pleasure'. Indeed, as Père Livinhac testifies, Mackay, apart from his religious intolerance, was a perfect gentleman.

In the second half of 1879, Mutesa seemed to become even more wavering and undecided, showing leanings first towards one religion and then towards another, and confusing each with political issues.

In July he sent for Pères Livinhac and Lourdel to attend a private audience, at which he confided to them his uneasiness about the Turco-Egyptian advance in the North and intimated to them his intention of sending one of the priests back to France at the head of a deputation which was to place Buganda under the protection of the French Government. Completely taken aback by this proposal, Père Livinhac replied that, for the moment, none of the priests could return to France and that, having come out as missionaries only, they had no authority to treat of political questions; all they could do was to inform the French consul at Zanzibar of the Kabaka's request.

Taking the French priests' reply as a refusal of French protection, Mutesa decided to send his envoys to England with Wilson and Felkin, who were about to return there by the Nile route.

Although in July and August Mutesa had been assiduously attending Lourdel's religious instructions, in September he told Mackay that he, together with his chiefs, wished to be baptized by him. In October, he asked Père Lourdel to baptize him and in November it became clear that he was still toying with Islam. This was very puzzling to all concerned, especially as this apparent indecision seemed to be alien to Mutesa's character. An eminent Muganda, who was at Court at the time, offers the following explanation :

> When Mutesa saw the three religions which had arrived in his country, he fixed his eyes and his heart on them to examine them more closely; then he gave his impressions to all his chiefs assembled in public session, saying, 'The true religion is that which is taught

by those men from France, clad in long robes, but our wealth in women kills us (i.e. is an insuperable obstacle). My friends, what shall we do?' The reply of the chiefs, though disconcerting, was not unreasonable. 'Master,' they said, 'begin by sending away your women; perhaps we shall then follow your example.'

A more probable explanation of Mutesa's apparent indecision would seem to be that, although academically interested in the tenets of the three religions and attracted by those of Christianity, he had no serious intention of abandoning his pagan ways and pagan customs. For political reasons only was he prepared to become a nominal Christian of either variety or to make his subjects adopt Islam. In his own kingdom, religion had been for so long an instrument of politics that he was unable to distinguish between the two. Nor was his confusion of the new religions with political issues entirely groundless : Islam had always been a political as well as religious force, and both Stanley and the C.M.S. missionaries had unwittingly given him cause to believe that Christianity had similar political affiliations—Stanley by talking in the same breath about the might of England and the religion of England and, almost certainly, at least by implication, conveying the traditional view that England's rise to greatness was a result of her adoption of Protestantism; the English missionaries by bringing with them letters from the Foreign Secretary and the Queen, and also by claiming to stand between him and interference from Egypt.

Mutesa was seeking a political alliance which would safeguard his independence from Egypt and was under the impression that religion was a bargaining factor in securing such an alliance. There were three possible allies at hand, the Arabs who had supplied him with arms in the past, and who might be expected to have some influence with their Egyptian co-religionists; the English, who were clearly more powerful than the Arabs, but who had so far ignored his many requests for arms and were suspect because of their affiliations with Egypt; and finally the French. If, as seemed to be the case, the acceptance of the religion of one of these groups was a condition of military aid, he was ready to give that religion a nominal allegiance. The French refusal of aid, in spite of his ostentatious interest in their religion, puzzled him completely and, as altruism was outside his experience, he began to suspect them of deeper and more sinister reasons for coming to his country.

Towards the end of 1879, Mutesa showed clearly that he was at heart still committed to paganism when he called in the mediums of the tribal gods to cure him of a disease which he had contracted. Mackay, evidently believing that the interest in Christianity shown

21

by the Kabaka had been sincere, tried to prevent them coming and got into serious trouble over it. Relations became so strained that the English missionaries proposed to leave the country. This, however, did not suit Mutesa, who feared that if the English left the Egyptians might come, and was determined to keep them as hostages. Several incidents made it clear to the French priests that they were in the same position.

It was perhaps fortunate for the missionaries that Mukasa and his fellow-gods were unsuccessful in their attempts to cure His Majesty; and the medium of another god, sent for post-haste from the Bunyoro border, also failed miserably and decamped on the evening of 31 December.

Chapter Three

IN QUEST OF GOD

Mutesa's wavering attitude towards the new religions brought about a revolution in the minds of many Baganda, especially amongst the youth of the country, a revolution that was to have far-reaching consequences in its effects upon their religion itself and, eventually, upon the political structure of the country. For almost the first time in the history of Buganda, the Kabaka failed to give a lead and appeared unable to come to a decision, with the result that the young men at Court, trained from their earliest youth to obey their Kabaka's wishes without question, and left now without royal guidance, began to think for themselves and to make up their own minds about the problem that faced them.

Towards the end of November 1879, Père Lourdel listened for the first time to a tale which he was to hear often again from others. It came from a boy named Nalubandwa, the son of Nyika who became Guardian of Kabaka Mwanga's umbilical cord.

> The religion of the Muslims appeared first and I began to practise it a little. According to them, one may commit the greatest crimes and then, just by washing oneself with water or sand, regain innocence. The Protestants arrived after the Muslims and I began to learn their words; they say, 'Sin, but believe'. I found nothing with either to set my heart at rest. They cannot have the truth: I believe they are wrong.[1] That is where I stood when the Catholic priests arrived.

Père Lourdel at once gave the boy a catechetical instruction. The next morning he returned bringing with him one of his friends. Two other boys had meanwhile applied to Père Girault, and the first catechism classes were started.

Many Baganda made contact with the Catholic Mission when they were ordered by the Kabaka to build houses for the priests. The first house was built in July-September 1879, and a chapel was ready by the feast of the Immaculate Conception, December 8th. Attracted by the kindness of Lourdel and his companions, or merely out of curiosity, people began to visit them and listen to the instructions they gave. Some were so attentive and intelligent and showed themselves so much in earnest about their religious duties that the priests felt

23

justified in baptizing four of them on 27 March, and four others on 14 May 1880.

It was in this year that four of the future martyrs first enrolled themselves as catechumens. Two, Joseph Mukasa and Andrew Kaggwa, were royal servants and two, Matthias Kalemba and Luke Banabakintu, were retainers of the county chief of Ssingo.

Joseph Mukasa was born in Mawokota County, the central county of the five that bordered on Lake Victoria, a county that has some of the finest and most typical scenery and most fertile soil. In the old days, several Kabakas had built their capitals in Mawokota, and all the clans had family estates there. On one of those estates lived, in the eighteen-fifties, a family of the Giant-Rat (Kayozi) Clan. Its head, the guardian of its property, was Mazinga, one of whose eight wives, a Munyoro woman named Kajwayo, bore him a son. Later, following a practice not uncommon in a polygamous society, she had relations with Mazinga's cousin, and bore a second son, the future martyr Joseph Mukasa. Mazinga was displeased and his cousin was obliged to flee to Gomba, where he died.

The child, born about 1860, belonged by common law to Mazinga, to whom Kajwayo bore three further children, two girls and a boy named Bamukinye. In due course he received his personal name, after one of his ancestors, and later, with special ceremonial, his clan name Mukasa, chosen from the dozen or so names current in the clan.

The little Mukasa, at first carried around on his mother's back as she went about her household and garden tasks, would later crawl or stagger in the dust around his mother's hut, naked but for a string of beads round his hips and bangles of bells round his ankles. When he grew older he would be given a goat-skin or a piece of bark-cloth to wear.

A common practice amongst the Baganda was to send even very young children away from home to be brought up by an uncle or other relative. A boyhood spent in the household of a more influential relative provided better opportunities for advancement and also usually better discipline. When Mukasa was about six he entered the household of a man named Kabadzi, not apparently a close relative but a man with whom Mukasa's legal father had once been involved in a lawsuit. James Miti, the son of Kabadzi, repudiates the suggestion that Mukasa was handed over by way of compensation. He says that Mukasa first came to them on a visit, to play with children his own age and, on expressing the wish to stay, was accepted into the family by Kabadzi who had grown fond of the little boy and treated him as one of his own children.

24

One may assume that Mukasa's boyhood resembled that of any Muganda boy at that time. He would have been required to perform light tasks, running errands and herding the cattle and goats of his patron—the heavier work of cultivation and water carrying was left to the women; he would have received instruction in the history of the kingdom and its Kabakas, in the customs and traditions of the Baganda, the story of his clan and of his own ancestry. The instructor, to train his pupils to remember the names of the many historical personages, would cut a number of wooden pegs to represent them. When any particular peg was pointed to, the pupil was expected to name the person it represented and give his history. By this means, memory was developed and the history of the clan and country preserved without any written record. For recreation there would be wrestling, the stick-throwing and reed-piercing contests and the less strenuous but complicated game of mweso, the 'board-game', so popular in many parts of tropical Africa.

Mukasa grew up healthy, bright and intelligent, tall for his age, very handsome, and noted for his skill and prowess at sports and games.

In those days, the surest road to success in life was service in the royal household and, at the age of about fourteen, Mukasa was presented to Kabaka Mutesa, to become one of his many pages. This must have taken place about the year 1874, when the Court was sited at Nabulagala (or Kasubi), a site now occupied by the royal tombs.

Wherever it was situated, and the impermanent nature of its buildings made frequent changes of site necessary, the royal enclosure, called the Lubiri, was always constructed on the same traditional pattern. Surrounded by a fence of vertical untrimmed reeds, a feature peculiar to a royal fence,[1] Mutesa's enclosure, oval in shape, contained five hundred and eighty-four buildings, many of which were huts occupied by his eighty-four wives and thousand concubines. Its total population was about three thousand. Only about a quarter of the whole enclosure was accessible to the public, the rest being reserved to the Kabaka and his women. The public part, within and to the right of the main gateway, was divided by fences into a number of successive courtyards, each devoted to some particular purpose and each accessible only through a single, guarded gateway. Although the perimeter fence had in it eight other and smaller gateways, the use of these was very strictly reserved to particular persons, or groups. Each was kept closed and guarded and only opened to allow the entry or exit of persons entitled to use that particular gateway.

Two small buildings, one housing the Sacred Fire and the other serving as a charge-room, stood outside the main gateway (Wankaki) to the Kabaka's enclosure. Immediately within it was a spacious court in which were the mosque or prayer-house and houses for a few of his principal wives. Beyond this lay a second court which led to a third, the court of the stores. This contained three storehouses for the royal treasure, mainly ivory, cowrie-shells and gunpowder, as well as waiting-rooms for distinguished visitors who were seeking an audience. Beyond the court of the stores lay a fourth, where justice was dispensed by the Chancellor. This was known as the Ores because it was studded with rough pieces of iron-stone, or iron ore, over which unsuccessful litigants were dragged. Beyond the Ores came the court of the great audience hall.

The audience hall was the largest building in the enclosure, being nearly sixty feet wide, but though impressive in size, it possessed none of the architectural features to be found in the buildings of the coastal areas. It was mainly an enormous beehive-shaped roof of grass thatching supported on four somewhat irregular rows of wooden posts, with walls of wattle and daub. There was no carved woodwork and no ornamental stonework or masonry of any kind; the only ornamentation was provided by the reed-and-thong work which, though beautiful in its way, was not durable. The court in which it stood, about two-hundred-and-twenty by one-hundred and-forty feet, also contained the drum houses, among which was that of 'Ntamivu', the giant drum which was beaten at intervals, day and night, to reassure the people that their Kabaka was still alive and well.

From the court of the audience hall a gateway gave access to the Ivory Court, so called because it contained a smaller private audience hall in which the Kabaka used to sit with his feet resting on a large tusk of ivory, probably for much the same reason that the English Chancellor sits upon a woolsack. The Kabaka's own living quarters occupied the next, and seventh, court which was divided into two by fences running from the side-walls of his dwelling-house to the side fences. In the forecourt was his beer house and a house for his brewer, and in the rear a house for the women in attendance, and the royal closet.

In these surroundings Joseph Mukasa spent the last eleven years of his short life, and many of the other martyrs their last years also.

After being presented to the Kabaka, the young Mukasa was handed over to the Majordomo, at that time a man named Kaddu, who assigned him to the group of pages under his own immediate command. These looked after the court of the great audience hall, the Ivory Court, the Kabaka's own quarters and also the private part of the palace enclosure. The rest of the four to five hundred pages were attached to the outer public courts and were under the command of the courtier-in-chief, head of all the royal servants.

Once accepted as a page, Mukasa received the cane necklet worn by all the Kabaka's servants and his wardrobe was augmented by a piece of white cloth, to be worn toga-wise over the right shoulder. An older page was appointed to take care of him and instruct him in his duties, which were to clean and sweep the building to which he was assigned and its surrounding courtyard, to run errands and make himself generally useful. He slept on the back verandah of the audience hall or in the building itself and, in the evenings, took part in the wrestling and other contests so popular at Mutesa's court.

Mukasa gave complete satisfaction to the Majordomo, who soon began to employ him in the Kabaka's private apartments, where extra neat and intelligent work was expected. He was also very popular with his fellow pages, though his greatest friend was Andrew Kaggwa, one of the royal drummers, a youth about five years his senior.

Unlike his friend Mukasa, who had a Munyoro mother but Muganda father, Kaggwa was a pure Munyoro, a native of Buganda's long-standing enemy, the Kingdom of Bunyoro. At an early age, Kaggwa had been captured and carried off as a slave by a party of Baganda raiding the border county of Bugangadzi and, being a handsome, well-built boy, presented to the Kabaka as part of his share of the spoils. He was placed amongst the royal pages, where his cheerfulness, willingness and kind-hearted disposition soon made him a general favourite both with his fellows and with his elders, who used to refer to him jokingly as 'that Munyoro'. How long he served as a page is not known, but he was still one when Stanley visited the Court of Buganda.

It was Stanley's visit and the visits of Colonel Gordon's various envoys that indirectly gave Kaggwa a change of occupation. Kabaka Mutesa had taken a great fancy to the European drums carried by the escorts of these visitors to his kingdom and, before long, had begged or bought about a dozen of these instruments for himself. He then picked a number of his older pages, among them Kaggwa, and sent them for instruction in the art of drumming to Toli, his general factotum. Leo Kyagwogera, one of Kaggwa's fellow pupils, says that it was here, in Toli's compound in the Arab quarter on the slopes of the Natete Hill, that he first met Kaggwa and lived in his company for about four months. 'At the time,' he says, 'we were both Muslims,' as was, of course, their instructor Toli. Apparently Kaggwa was quick to learn and completed his course of instruction before Kyagwogera, who says, 'When I returned to the town, my friend Andrew had taken up the Catholic religion, which he then started teaching me'. He describes Kaggwa as 'an exceedingly kind man. He was of slight build, dark colouring, squint-eyed and a very good bugler. He had also learnt to shoot and was renowned for his courage. He was a friend of persons of every class.'

James Miti (foster brother to Joseph Mukasa) also pays tribute to Kaggwa's good-nature and popularity. He says, 'I think Andrew must have been very young when he was brought to Buganda, for he had neither cuttings on his body, nor gaps in his teeth.[1] He had become a complete Muganda. He was handsome, dark, short and thin; his nose was long and rather sharp : Bahima from Ankole have such noses. He was very sociable and used to joke a lot, so that he always kept us amused.'

It seems likely that Kaggwa first came into contact with the Catholic priests through his instructor Toli, who frequently went to see the Fathers and lent them valuable aid as a carpenter. Certain it is that, after serving his apprenticeship as a bandsman, he lost no time in enrolling himself as a catechumen and, having himself found the pearl of great price, at once wished to share it with his friends. None was closer than the page, Mukasa, so that it was to him that Kaggwa first confided the news that he had found the Messias.

Scarcely had Mukasa and Kaggwa begun to receive instruction in the Catholic religion when their faith was put to a severe test. On 1 June 1880, detailed instructions about the reception of converts reached the missionaries from Bishop Lavigerie. All those under instruction were to be divided into three classes, postulants, catechumens and faithful : all converts must spend two years in the first class, and two in the second, before being admitted to Baptism which, in circumstances when any misgivings about the perseverance of the convert were entertained, must be deferred until the candidate was dying, or in danger of death. It was also to be made clear to those seeking instruction that they must be prepared to lay down their lives rather than deny their faith. The two friends were therefore called upon, at the very outset of their conversion, to make their choice; either to go away sad, like the young man in the Gospel, or to begin a long and weary following of Christ. They chose to follow.

Both the new catechumens received promotion at this time. Kaggwa, now about twenty-five, became Master-Drummer in command of all the other drummers, about fifteen in number, who were required to play on all festive occasions such as levées or receptions for distinguished visitors. In course of time he became chief bandmaster, in charge of all the instrumentalists, drummers, buglers and cymbals-players, and was given a plot of land at Luguja crossroads near Natete. Here he built his house, to which he later brought his bride, Clara Batudde.

Joseph Mukasa, now about twenty, was also chosen for a position of trust and importance. He became the Kabaka's personal attendant, a post that, now Mutesa was frequently ailing, called for tact and endurance. The young man had to be with or near his royal master day and night, ready to take messages or to lift and rearrange his patient's tall frame more comfortably on his couch. For this task Mukasa was well fitted. Tall and powerfully built, he showed exquisite gentleness, refinement of character, and a readiness to help in any way he could.

Whenever their duties allowed, both friends were assiduous in following the instructions at the Catholic mission. Here they became friendly with an older fellow catechumen, Matthias Kalemba.

This most remarkable man was a Musoga. Born about 1836 in Bunya County in Busoga, the country lying across the Nile from Buganda, he, together with his mother, was captured by a raiding party of Baganda belonging to the Otter Clan and, at a very early age, carried off to Buganda as a slave.

His captors sold him to a member of the Edible-Rat Clan, named Magatto, an uncle of the Chancellor Mukasa, who seems to have treated the little fellow as a member of the family rather than as a slave. As often happened in such cases he was, as he grew up, gradually treated as a member of the clan and as a free man. Possibly it was in recognition of this that he changed his name from the original Wante to Kalemba.

After the death of his adopted father, Kalemba remained for a time with Magatto's brother, Buzibwa, but, on attaining manhood, he left and took service with Ddumba, the county chief of Ssingo. In this service he displayed such loyalty and trustworthiness that Ddumba came to rely upon him more and more until he became, in fact if not in name, head of the chief's household and supervisor of all the other servants.

On the death of Ddumba, his brother Kabunga who succeeded to the chieftainship seems to have realized the treasure he had in Kalemba, for not only did he confirm him in his many duties but gave them official recognition by creating for him the post of Ekirumba, so called in memory of Ddumba. As holder of this office, Kalemba became known as the Mulumba.

Matthias Kalemba, the Mulumba, was of fairly large stature and rather light colouring. His face, somewhat longer than the average and adorned with a small beard, an unusual feature amongst Baganda, was slightly pock-marked. He was immensely strong, quite fearless and endowed with a powerful voice, a joyous disposition and a passionate love for the truth. His search for the truth led him first to the Muslim faith, which appealed to him by its obvious superiority to the paganism that surrounded him. When the Protestant missionaries arrived, he was at once attracted by Christianity and began to attend their instructions; but before he had made up his mind to ask for baptism he came, in the course of his duties, into contact with the Catholic Fathers. It was the traditional duty of the chief of Ssingo to erect and repair the buildings of the royal enclosure, so that when Kabaka Mutesa undertook to build houses for the Catholic missionaries he naturally commissioned this chief to build them. The chief in turn placed his trusted headman, Kalemba, in charge of the work. The rest of the story is best told in Kalemba's own words to Père Livinhac :

My father (almost certainly Magatto, his father by adoption) had always believed that the Baganda had not the truth, and he sought it in his heart. He had often mentioned this to me, and before his death he told me that men would one day come to teach us the right way.

These words made a profound impression on me and, whenever the arrival of some stranger was reported, I watched him and tried to get in touch with him, saying to myself that here perhaps was the man foretold by my father. Thus I associated with the Arabs who came first in the reign of Suna. Their creed seemed to me superior to our superstitions. I received instructions and, together with a number of Baganda, I embraced their religion. Mutesa himself, anxious to please the Sultan of Zanzibar, of whose power and wealth he had been given an exaggerated account, declared that he also wanted to become a Muslim. Orders were given to build mosques in all the counties. For a short time, it looked as if the whole country was going to embrace the religion of the false prophet, but Mutesa had an extreme repugnance to circumcision. Consequently, changing his mind all of a sudden, he gave orders to exterminate all who had become Muslims. A good many perished in the massacre, two or three hundred managed to escape and, with Arab caravans, made their way to the Island of Zanzibar. I succeeded with a few others in concealing the fact of my conversion, and continued to pass for a friend of our own gods, though in secret I remained faithful to the practices of Islam.

That was how things stood when the Protestants arrived. Mutesa received them very well; he had their book read in public audience, and seemed to incline to their religion, which he declared to be much superior to that of the Arabs. I asked myself whether I had not made a mistake, and whether, perhaps, the newcomers were not the true messengers of God. I often went to visit them and attended their instructions. It seemed to me that their teaching was an improvement on that of my first masters. I therefore abandoned Islam, without however asking for baptism.

Several months had elapsed when Mapèra (Lourdel) arrived. My instructor, Mackay, took care to tell me that the white men who had just arrived did not know the truth. He called their religion the 'worship of the woman'; they adored, he said, the Virgin Mary. He also advised me to avoid them with the greatest care. I therefore kept away from you and, probably, I would never have set foot in your place if my chief had not ordered me to supervise the building of one of your houses. But God showed his love for me.

The first time when I saw you nearby, I was very much impressed. Nevertheless, I continued to watch you closely at your prayers and in your dealings with the people. Then seeing your goodness, I said to myself, 'How can people who appear so good be the messengers of the devil?'

I talked with those who had placed themselves under instruction and questioned them on your doctrine. What they told me was just the contrary of what Mackay had assured me. Then I felt strongly urged to attend personally your catechetical instructions. God gave me the grace to understand that you taught the truth, and that you really were the man of God of whom my father had spoken. Since then, I have never had the slightest doubt about the truth of your religion, and I feel truly happy.

Kalemba's actual enrolment as a catechumen seems to have taken place on 31 May 1880. The construction of an extra building, to house the orphans which the Fathers had taken under their care, had been started at their mission at Kasubi in March of that year. On the last day of May, the Mukwenda, county chief of Ssingo and Kalemba's master, was present at the mission, possibly for the opening of the new house or possibly invited for the renewal of the dedication of the Uganda Mission to the Blessed Virgin Mary. He then asked for himself and his household to be enrolled as catechumens. To the chief himself, this was probably no more than a gesture of politeness, which ceased to have any significance when he learned that he would be expected to get rid of all but one wife. To his assistant, Kalemba, however, it was a deliberate and serious step : having put his hand to the plough, there was for him no turning back. Within a week he had complied with the conditions and set his affairs in order. Père Lourdel's diary has the following entry for 7 June 1880 :

Yesterday, a young man among our catechumens, an overseer of the slaves of a great chief called Mukwenda, an ex-disciple of the Protestants and owner of a large number of women, sent them all away except one, and then came to ask us to baptize him.

It was not, however, until two years later that Kalemba received the sacrament he so ardently desired. It was only then that, taking advantage of the permission given by Bishop Lavigerie to make some exceptions to the rule of the four years' catechumenate, Père Lourdel baptized four on 30 April 1882 and Père Girault four more on 28 May. Both priests had the great privilege of baptizing two future martyrs, Père Lourdel baptizing Joseph Mukasa and Andrew Kaggwa, and Père Girault having in his group Matthias Kalemba and Luke Banabakintu.

Kalemba was baptized on the feast of Pentecost. After their baptism, he and Luke and the other two neophytes were confirmed by Père Livinhac and then, at the High Mass sung by Père Levesque, made their first Holy Communion. Profoundly impressed by at least one of those he had been privileged to admit into the Church, Père Girault wrote :

> Among those who have been baptized this morning there is one in whom the action of Grace has been truly apparent, namely the Mulumba, a man of about thirty to forty years of age (actually nearer fifty), who throughout his whole life has had a fervent desire to know the true religion.

Before admitting Kalemba to baptism, the mission superior, Père Livinhac, had asked him whether he was resolved to persevere and intimated that, if not, it would be better for him not to receive the sacrament. 'Have no fear, Father,' was the reply. 'It is two years now since I made up my mind, and nothing can make me change it. I am a Catholic and I shall die a Catholic.'

Naturally of a haughty and violent disposition, Matthias Kalemba began to school himself in Christian humility and meekness, even in the smallest details of his daily life. Agricultural work, for instance, was done exclusively by women and a free man felt himself disgraced if seen working in a plantain grove or potato plot; but Matthias, a man of standing and influence, was bent on following Christ's teaching and not ashamed of manual labour; he was often seen handling the hoe and helping his wife Kikuvwa, the only one of his three women whom he had retained on becoming a catechumen. When travelling, also, he carried his own belongings and would not make use of the porters to which his rank and position entitled him. To those who reproached him for thus demeaning himself, he replied, 'Am I not a slave, the slave of Jesus Christ?'

On one occasion, his simple dress and humble bearing let him in for some rough treatment which a display befitting his rank would undoubtedly have spared him. Walking along, carrying the bark-cloth that served both as a blanket and hold-all, like any simple peasant, he encountered a party of royal servants which was escorting some of the Kabaka's women from Rubaga to Kasubi. To prevent passers-by from gazing at the royal ladies, the attendants, as usual, went along laying about them with their sticks. Matthias received his share of the blows with composure and made no effort to protect himself or escape. As he was picking himself up, he caught a glimpse of a fellow-Christian, a friend of his, hastily removing himself from the path of the royal party. When he met the friend again, he teased him over this, saying with a hearty laugh, 'The other day, I saw you making off whilst I was getting a beating. If you run away from such a little suffering, what are you going to do in Purgatory?'

It was certainly not cowardice that made Kalemba meekly submit to the blows. Among the many stories told of his prodigious strength and courage is one of him overpowering and capturing a baby elephant while in every danger of attack from its mother. It is also related how one day, charged by a buffalo as he walked along peaceably smoking his pipe, instead of taking to his heels he stepped forward to meet it, dealing it such a blow with his stick that it reeled and made off. This is regarded as a marvellous feat, because the buffalo is a ferocious beast without fear of men. Hunters of all nations, in fact, generally regard the buffalo as the most dangerous of all game animals.

At times, Kalemba had to accompany his chief on war-raids against the Banyoro but, although he showed himself a brave warrior, he had no stomach for these raids and refused to take part in the looting of cattle, goats, women and children, which was their invariable accompaniment and, indeed, main object.

Kalemba also began to cultivate a remarkable detachment from worldly things. He lived very humbly and, while still under instruction and not obliged to do so, fasted throughout Lent. In his position and with his opportunities he could have amassed considerable wealth. Instead, like St Paul, he chose to earn what he needed by his own labour. He took up pottery and tanning in partnership with, or as a pupil of, his friend and tenant, Noe Mawaggali. As the Mulumba he would have received from the chief a grant of land, but no regular salary, it being understood that, like the publicans of old, he could enrich himself by exactions from those under him. Kalemba had every opportunity for doing this, especially when called upon to deputize for his master in the administration of justice, when it was usual for all litigants to make presents to the judge in the hope of influencing his decision. Even before his baptism, Matthias always strove to be quite fair and impartial in his judgments and never accepted even the smallest bribe. On becoming a Christian, he asked

33

to be relieved of this duty, afraid of unwittingly doing anyone an injustice and unable to bring himself to charge the high fees or to impose the exorbitant fines called for, not by the gravity of the offences, but by the need or rapacity of the judge, or of his employer. 'What am I to do,' he confided to his friends, 'when the Mukwenda calls upon me to hand over to him the proceeds from the court cases? I get nothing out of them. How then am I going to satisfy him?'

The Mukwenda acceded to his request but retained him in his other offices and, probably about this time, also put him in charge of the daily distribution of meat to his retainers and dependants. This had previously been left to the chief's Muslim butchers, who were found to have been stealing large quantities of the meat. By making the Mulumba responsible, the chief could be quite sure that every ounce would be accounted for and distributed according to his instructions.

Around this singular man, there grew the only sizeable Christian community away from the capital, to which the missionaries were confined. Mityana, the headquarters of the chief of Ssingo County, was twelve hours' journey from Rubaga, and although some of the chief's servants came into contact with the Catholic priests when they were building houses for them, many of the inhabitants had never even seen a priest; but Matthias Kalemba was indefatigable in teaching Christianity to all who would listen. His house became a centre of Christian instruction and, twice a month, one of the more intelligent catechumens was selected to go to the capital to follow carefully and memorize the instructions given by the priests so that he could repeat them to his fellows on his return.

When the persecution broke out in 1886, this community of Christians and catechumens numbered about two hundred, and provided three martyrs, Matthias Kalemba himself, Luke Banabakintu and Noe Mawaggali.

Luke Banabakintu, also in the service of the county chief of Ssingo, was enrolled as a catechumen by his master at the same time as Kalemba, 31 May 1880. Like Matthias, he had received some instruction from Mackay but had not been baptized by the Protestants. He received the sacrament with Kalemba and two others from Père Girault on the feast of Pentecost, 28 May 1882.

Banabakintu belonged to the Lungfish (Mamba) Clan. This the most numerous of all the clans is divided into two branches, the Eel and the Frog, and members of the two branches intermarry as though they were not related. Banabakintu belonged to the Eel branch. He was born at Ntolomwe, a hamlet in Gomba County, about 1851 or a little later. His father Mukwanga, a direct descendant of Gabunga, had several wives and thirty children of whom Banabakintu was the eldest, the son of his first wife, Kusubiza of the Seed (Nvuma) clan.

When Banabakintu was about sixteen, his uncle Jjagwe came to Ntolomwe on a visit and, at the youth's own request, took his nephew away to live with him at Mityana where the youth entered the service of the county chief. In this service he did well, receiving promotion and, eventually, a small fief called Kiwanga, which carried with it the duty of supervising the servants who lived outside the chief's enclosure, the wood-cutters, porters and cooks. One of the witnesses at the Apostolic Process stated that Banabakintu was unmarried. The clan-chiefs, however, contradict this and give his wife's name as Bazalawaluggya.

Luke Banabakintu is described as being clever and honest, of medium height and dark colouring, with a deep but cheerful voice and a round face, bright and alert but commanding respect. Living as he did close to Matthias Kalemba and attending instructions with him, first at the Protestant and later at the Catholic mission, he developed a great affection for his zealous fellow-Christian. He assisted Matthias in the instruction of catechumens, taking over from him when the latter's duties called him away to the capital and, as regularly as he could, himself made the twelve hours' journey to receive the sacraments of Penance and the Eucharist. At the time of his martyrdom he was between thirty and thirty-five years old.

The third of the martyrs from Mityana was Noe Mawaggali, son of Musazi and a member of the Bush-Buck (Ngabi) Clan. He was, unlike the other two, a native of Ssingo County, having been born at Nkazibaku about 1850. Mawaggali was an expert potter, turning out all manner of articles such as earthenware dishes, water-pots, cooking-pots, jugs, bowls and pipes. He became by appointment potter to the county chief, who greatly admired his work, and lived for a time in the chief's household. Later, he built a simple house for himself on the land of Matthias Kalemba, a move that seems to have been prompted partly by friendship for the Mulumba and largely by the desire to remove himself from the pagan atmosphere of the chief's court, because it was about the same time that the zeal and example of Matthias won him over to the Catholic Faith. He was not, however, baptized until the Feast of All Saints, 1885.

As well as making pots, Mawaggali used to tan hides and, unlike his fellows who spent most of their time visiting and taking part in the interminable beer-parties, was known as a steady and industrious worker, quiet and unassuming in manner. He was tall and slender, with a head that narrowed towards the crown. He never married and was scrupulously correct in his moral behaviour.

After the death of his father, Mawaggali took his ageing mother and his young sister to live with him and provided for them. His mother Meme was later baptized, taking the name Valeria. His sister Munaku, about eighteen years his junior, suffered cruelly and heroically in the persecution and was later, after her freedom had been purchased by the missionaries, baptized Maria Mathilda. She lived to the age of seventy-six, devoted to prayer and good works, and is the source of much of the information about her brother.

(Although Noe Mawaggali became a catechumen considerably later than the other four martyrs mentioned in this chapter, he has been included here in order to complete the picture of the Ssingo group of martyrs.)

Chapter Four

PROGRESS AND UNCERTAINTY
(1880—1884)

After the failure of the mediums of the tribal gods, called in by Mutesa at the end of 1879, to cure his sickness, the Kabaka seemed once again to veer towards Christianity. In January 1880 he said to his chiefs, 'Why are you not going on with instructions? You are only living for this world and trying to amass riches. Here are white men who have come from Europe to teach you religion. Why do you not learn?' Then, calling in all the pages and other servants, he asked who could read and who could not. 'Several,' said Mackay, 'have since been here asking for alphabets etc.'

In April, however, the Kabaka again showed how steeped he was in paganism, when without warning he ordered the arrest of all those found to be wearing their bark-cloth in a certain way. The purpose of this edict, making this particular fashion a crime overnight, was to collect the number of victims required by the gods for a funeral ceremony and at the same time to pretend, by a legal quibble, that innocent persons were not being sacrificed. The funeral ceremony in question was the inauguration of a new ornamental hut over the grave of Kabaka Suna, and the tale of victims demanded by the gods was ninety-nine men, cows, goats, sheep and chickens, as well as an offering of ninety-nine eggs and bunches of plantains. A ritual execution of this nature, the number of victims always being a multiple of nine, was supposed to benefit the Kabaka and, in his person, Buganda, so that even the victims (so it is said) accepted their fate without protest.

Towards the end of May, Père Lourdel cured the Kabaka of dysentery and was warmly acclaimed by the chiefs as the saviour of Buganda.

In June, Mutesa leaned again towards Islam and, a month later, proclaimed it the state religion, at the same time leaving everyone to believe as he pleased. Still he continued the old game of coquetting with Catholics and Arabs alternately, trying to play one off against the other. Meanwhile, he was almost starving Pearson, who had been left alone at the Protestant mission after Mackay and Litchfield had left for the South of the Lake.

Early in December, Mutesa announced to an astonished audience that he wished to go to England; yet at the end of the month, Mackay, who had just returned and asked permission to teach, found himself virtually a prisoner, taunted by the chiefs with, 'Who asked you to come?' Lourdel, discussing the situation with Mackay, suggested that Mutesa himself was not really hostile to the English, but thought it politic to countenance the Arabs' hatred of them. Both missionaries agreed that their royal host 'had the heart of a tiger'.

The hostility of the Arabs towards Mackay was due partly to their suspicion that he was under the protection of the British Consul at Zanzibar and present in Buganda as an agent and spy of his government, and partly to his outspoken attacks on the slave-raiding and other vices to which many of them were addicted. Thus Mackay wrote in 1881 :

> I alone have been able to address the king and court directly in language they could understand. Hence it is that I am branded as a disputer and raiser of rows. Of course I had to open my mouth at times against murder and adultery, and cruel raids for slaves on a big scale, and even worse sins—so bad that one cannot tell about them in black and white.

In February 1881, the missionaries were horrified to learn that yet another ritual execution was to take place, on the advice of the medium of Mayanja, the god of the river, to hasten the recovery of the Kabaka. People were to be slaughtered on several of the hills around the capital, and for days the executioners would lie in wait for innocent people on the roads leading to it. 'Some of them,' wrote Mackay, 'will have their throats cut, while others will be tortured to death—their eyes put out, nose and ears cut off, the sinews of their arms and thighs cut out piecemeal and roasted before their eyes, and finally the unhappy creatures burnt alive. Others again are tied hand and foot, dry reeds and firewood heaped over them, and then the whole ignited.' It is not clear whether this particular execution actually took place, or whether Mackay and Pearson's letter, begging the Kabaka not to allow these innocent people to be put to death, had the hoped-for success.

In March, Christianity seemed once more in the ascendant when Mutesa gave orders for the Christian Sunday to be observed, as well as Friday, the Muslim day of worship, but in September a serious crisis looked like undoing all the work of the Christian missionaries.

This seems to have been precipitated by some rash remarks of the Reverend Philip O'Flaherty which gave the Arabs a handle for stirring up Mutesa's suspicions and distrust of the Europeans. O'Flaherty, in whose company the royal envoys had returned from

England, replaced Pearson at the Protestant mission in March 1881 and soon, because of his ready wit, became quite a favourite with the Kabaka. One of the returned envoys, Sabaddu, had already given the Court a glowing account of British wealth and strength, saying that Zanzibar, the Arab stronghold, was but a flea in the great lake, that the Coast all belonged to the British and that the Arabs were little more than their slaves. O'Flaherty saw fit to enlarge upon this account of Britain's might and, one day in July, told the Kabaka that, at the head of a hundred men, he could easily conquer Buganda and that a gun would soon settle its brave warriors.

The Arabs were not slow in making capital out of these foolish remarks. They spread rumours that the white men were preparing to conquer Buganda and were training their followers in the use of arms. Even the thirty or so children, rescued from slavery, at the Catholic mission were magnified into three hundred men being trained to use modern rifles. Having worked on Mutesa's fears, which had been somewhat lulled by the withdrawal of the Bunyoro garrisons by Emin Pasha, the Arabs urged him to declare Islam the state religion and force everyone to accept it.

Mutesa cared as little for the Koran as he did for the Bible but realized that the Arab plan would at least reveal which of his subjects were prepared to set the white men's religion even above his own royal will and decided, on the pretext of a grand review, to assemble his entire palace staff and bodyguard. Once assembled, the men were to be marched off to the mosque which had been built some time ago in the royal enclosure, and which served as a prayer-house, Muslim or Christian according to His Majesty's religious or, rather, political leanings.

Fortunately, a catechumen who heard of the project, possibly Joseph Mukasa, informed the priests of what was afoot. They had no illusions about the seriousness of the situation. At the proposed review there would be present at least a hundred-and-fifty neophytes and catechumens. They felt sure that the majority of these would defy the Kabaka's order to take part in a Muslim service and wholesale slaughter would probably ensue. After much consultation and prayer, they decided to entrust Père Lourdel with the task of trying to persuade the Kabaka not to give the fateful order.

On the appointed day Lourdel went to the Court and, by his unexpected presence, prevented the order from being given. The same happened the following day; but on Sunday 11 September the Kabaka spoke. 'You know,' he said, 'that Kawumpuli (the god of plague) ravages the country. I have been assured that this affliction will cease if we pray with the Arabs. All present will therefore leave the Court and proceed to the mosque.'

Lourdel went on his knees to the Kabaka and begged him, as a truly great king, not to force his subjects to adopt any religion. 'God,' he said, 'wants free service.' The Arabs, enraged by this opposition, began to shout that the Kabaka should not permit himself to be thwarted by anyone, least of all by an outsider. 'The white men want to seize your country! In teaching your subjects they only aim at gaining their support! Their religion is a religion of lies! There is no God but Allah, and Mohammed is his Prophet!'

Mutesa hesitated, and the situation looked so grave that the priest decided on bold measures. Rising to his feet with the Book of the Gospels in his hand, he cried, 'Since the Arabs pretend that the religion of Jesus Christ is a religion of lies, and that theirs is the true religion, let us ask God to judge between them and us. Have wood heaped up before the entrance of the audience hall and a blazing fire made. I offer to pass through it with the Gospels in my hand. Let them do the same with their Koran. He whom the fire spares will certainly be the true messenger of God.'

Mutesa was dumbfounded by this daring proposal. The Arabs refused to accept the challenge and talked about witchcraft; but Lourdel's faith won the day. The Kabaka declared that everyone should remain free to pray as he chose. On hearing of what had occurred, Mackay and O'Flaherty went to thank Père Lourdel for what he had done in defence of the Christian cause.

This chaotic situation, in which the Kabaka's favour seemed to alternate between Christianity and Islam, while he himself firmly adhered to his pagan practices, although disconcerting for the missionaries, did not impede the progress of their work. In some respects indeed it was an advantage, in so far as it kept the numbers of catechumens within instructable limits and ensured that those who persevered with their instructions were of the finest quality, youths and men of courage, prepared at any moment to face torture and death at the whim of their unpredictable and all-powerful sovereign.

The Catholic priests had baptized nine converts in 1880 and had numbers of catechumens (among them the future martyrs Joseph Mukasa, Andrew Kaggwa, Matthias Kalemba and Luke Banabakintu) all earnestly schooling themselves in the following of Christ, many of them, without obligation, keeping the full lenten fast.

The Protestants had not so far baptized any converts, but had numbers coming to them for instruction. In June 1881, Mackay wrote, 'Converts will find it hard to do right and yet obey the king. But we need not be anxious about the morrow. When God gives us converts, He will also give us the needed light for their guidance'. In another letter, dated 1 September 1881, Mackay refers to some of the future Catholic martyrs :

... My pupils continue to come every afternoon, and we get through a page or two of St Matthew every day. May the Lord, whose words these are, carry them home to the hearts of these lads. The oldest is named Mulumba, being a mutongolé (sub-chief) of Mukwenda. Litchfield taught him to read and gave him a considerable amount of instruction. The Roman Catholics got hold of him afterwards. I do not know whether or not he continues to read with them, but he seems anxious to understand the Word of God, and is quiet, and so far as I know lives up to his light. Then there are three good readers in the same class with Mulumba. One is Mukasa the 'Long', another Mukasa the 'Red', and another is called Kaggwa. Who taught these to read I don't know. I believe they picked up the art from other lads whom we taught in person. They were certainly not taught either by us or by the Frenchmen. They are quiet and respectful in their treatment of the sacred words, and I earnestly pray that they may come to the knowledge of the truth. Each is about eighteen or twenty years old.

With them comes Magali (Mawaggali), an older fellow and friend of Mulumba. A month ago he began with the alphabet, and now he has read through all the reading sheets I have to give him. If Kiswahili were his own language, he could read a book now easily. He is quiet and industrious.

On 2 October 1881, Mackay wrote :

Another of my pupils, called Mwana-wa-Kintu (Banabakintu), who has been absent for a month, has returned. To-day I gave him a solemn lesson on the parable of the rich young man who went away sorrowful ...

At first sight it is somewhat disconcerting to learn from these letters that at least four of the Catholic catechumens, Kalemba the Mulumba, Mukasa (the long), Kaggwa and Banabakintu, who had been learning the Catholic religion for a year and a half, and who were to be baptized only seven months later, were at the same time reading St Matthew's Gospel and the Acts of the Apostles under the direction of the Protestant missionary. There can, however, be no doubt that these future martyrs were acting in good faith, and one can but conclude that their Catholic teachers had not yet explained to them the difference between authorized and unauthorized translations of the Bible. Meanwhile, in their thirst for knowledge, they were making use of the facilities provided by the Protestants, such as printed copies of portions of the Scriptures in Luganda and the new Testament in Swahili, facilities which the Catholic mission was as yet unable to give them. Mackay, in fact, seems to have intended his efforts more as reading lessons than as religious instructions, because he writes, 'many ... have been taught to read here by my brethren

41

or myself. They come and go; but most learn to read fairly well before they leave, and all learn something of revealed truth'.

Entries in Père Lourdel's diary make it clear that he knew that some of his catechumens were visiting the Protestants, though he cannot have realized that they were reading the Scriptures there. He mentions one who went to teach O'Flaherty Luganda, and another who became involved in an argument with one of the Protestants on the questions of praying to Our Lady; an argument from which the catechumen emerged with flying colours. To his point that he could see nothing wrong in petitioning the Mother of Our Saviour, just as, in Buganda, one could offer petitions to the Mother of the Kabaka, the Protestant missioner had no answer but 'you are still a child and don't understand'.

Certain it is that, at the same period, these four catechumens were most assiduous in following the instructions at the Catholic mission, for the sequel shows that Lourdel had Kalemba and his friends in mind when, on 29 August 1881, he wrote in his diary :

> Many of our catechumens, on returning home, instruct any of their friends who show a desire to know our holy religion. Thus the good tidings spread from place to place and may at the moment appointed by Providence yield an abundant harvest of souls. Several young men have come to us, at one time or another, already knowing part of the catechism and thus saving the missionary much time and trouble. I believe that in Buganda we shall easily find excellent catechists. But alas! those who would be most suitable for this delicate task are not their own masters; they are either slaves or soldiers of the king or of his chiefs. They can only exercise their influence in their own circles.

Père Livinhac was also referring to the future martyrs when, in reviewing a year's work, at the end of October, he wrote :

> They generally learn without trouble the text of the catechism, believe without the slighest hesitation all the truths which we expound to them, and declare that they are resolved to renounce their vices and lead an entirely new life in order to secure eternal happiness. Some of them are endowed with more than ordinary intellectual gifts, with good-will and firmness of character which astonish us and fill us with hope, and with a delicacy of feeling which we were far from expecting to meet among negroes.

Thanks to Père Lourdel's victory over the Muslims in September 1881, both missions had more catechumens. On 11 December, however, the English mission reported :

To-day very few have come to read. Those who came said that they were in no small danger, as, yesterday, the king had remarked that the lads who came to us to read were informing us of what was being said in court; therefore he would not allow them to come. . . . But 'Yes' and 'No' follow each other in such quick succession in this fickle country, that we feel no longer deeply moved by any royal expression.

On 12 March 1882, Mackay wrote :

The Roman Catholics are five against our two, and are reaping a golden harvest at present. Being so many, they are able to divide the work . . . They are thus able to encourage all comers at all times . . . Crowds of old and young are taught by them every day. They likewise have baptized very many. . . . Some tell us that they have baptized hundreds, which is probably an exaggeration.

It certainly was an exaggeration. There had been no regular baptisms since the first nine converts received the sacrament in 1880. The next baptisms, already mentioned in the previous chapter, took place in April and May 1882, when eight more were baptized. Between these dates, there would doubtless have been a number of emergency baptisms of those in danger of death, especially during the plague epidemic of 1881 and the cholera epidemic in April 1882. However, although the number of neophytes was small, their sterling qualities and the large number of catechumens were a hopeful sign for the future. The Protestants seem to have shared this hope. Four converts were baptized by the Rev. O'Flaherty in March, and the mission had a number of persons under instruction.

Superficially, also, relations with the Kabaka seemed to hold promise of better understanding. The reputation of the pagan deities received a setback when one of the witch-doctors, usurping Lourdel's place as medical adviser, gave the Queen Mother a powerful potion, which sent her into convulsions and killed her. Mackay earned the gratitude of the Kabaka by making a coffin, or rather a triple coffin, as befitted royalty, for the old lady, and Lourdel achieved the remarkable feat of pleading successfully for the life of the old chief, accused by the witch-doctor of causing the death.

Then, with dramatic suddenness, the Catholic missionaries decided to leave Buganda.

A note in *Les Missions Catholiques* of 8 June 1883 explained that the priests had left Buganda, first because of the effect of the Mahdi's successes in the Sudan on the attitude of the Arabs at the Court of Mutesa and secondly out of prudence, following orders received from their superiors in Europe. This note was followed, on 13 July, by an authoritative statement by Père Charmetant, Procurator of the White Fathers at Algiers, based, he declared, on the letters of the missionaries.

According to this statement, the rumour of the Mahdi's exploits had made the Arabs more arrogant, and had even affected Mutesa himself. The French missionaries, who had hitherto been less feared than the English—known to be fellow-countrymen of the masters of Egypt—now found themselves the object of a secret conspiracy fomented by the Arabs. They were told by some of their neophytes that they were to be massacred during the night, and that their assassins had already been selected. A careful enquiry, together with the evidence of the children they had rescued from slavery and who knew what was going on outside the mission, confirmed the Fathers in their belief that they were doomed to death if they did not leave the capital of Mutesa, at least for the time being. They therefore decided to transfer their activities to the South-West of the Lake. Here, because there were no Muslims, and because experience elsewhere had shown that work among small tribes could be very fruitful, they hoped to find a more promising mission field than Buganda, where the monarch was the centre of intrigue. In making this decision they were obeying the injunctions of their Superior General and Founder who, after the massacre of some of his Fathers in the Sahara and the murder of two priests and a lay-helper in Urundi in 1881, had placed his subjects under obedience not to expose themselves to certain danger of death if they could possibly avoid it.

Mackay, in a note printed in the *Church Missionary Intelligencer* in September 1882, wrote that the French priests had given as the reason for their withdrawal that 'the unjust nature of the country rendered missionary work impossible, especially the want of family life, and the want of sacredness of the marriage tie, combined with the fact that they could not get liberty to go about the country as they would like'. In the same note, Mackay criticized this reason and predicted that Buganda was sure to become either Muslim or Christian in a very few years.

The Abbé Nicq, in his biography of Lourdel, does not mention the threat to the lives of the priests, but stresses the danger to their followers. He says that Mutesa, despite his kindness, was still prejudiced against the priests, whose presence embarrassed him and whose motive in teaching his people he could not fathom. Seeing that Mutesa was hostile, the people began to lose their traditional respect for the Kabaka's guests, and thefts and housebreaking, probably inspired by the monarch himself with the object of driving the missionaries away, became common. When these failed to achieve their object, he seems to have decided to start a persecution and chose for it the moment of the return of a great expedition from Busoga. He ordered immense quantities of firewood to be amassed in the vicinity of the capital, meant, it was said, for the burning of Christians. The missionaries, after much prayer and thought, decided to withdraw for a time from Mutesa's dominions in order to spare the neophytes, still so young in the Faith, the terrible ordeal that seemed to threaten them. They hoped that their departure would satisfy the Muslims and witch-doctors, and avert the persecution that seemed imminent. Whilst they were still hesitating, the instructions from their Superior General came to settle their doubts.

It is clear that the Arabs, feeling that the Mahdi's conquest of the Sudan, by cutting off the English missionaries from the nearest source of British power, had removed for the time being any threat of English intervention in Buganda, now directed their venom against the French mission, which was achieving greater success and which had, through the boldness of Père Lourdel, thwarted their plan of the previous September for turning Buganda into a Muslim state.

Whether the actual danger to the Fathers and their followers was as real and immediate as it appeared to them is open to question. If it was, it is hard to explain why no rumour of it reached the ears of the English missionaries. It seems possible that the stories, reported to the Fathers by sincere but over-apprehensive young converts, were exaggerated; but it should not be forgotten that, in Buganda of those days, no atrocity was impossible or even unlikely, if the whim of an absolute and capricious monarch so moved him.

Père Lourdel announced the decision to the Kabaka, telling him that he and his confrères were all more or less in poor health and in need of many things, and would like to withdraw for a time from Buganda. Mutesa showed surprise but made no objection and promised to supply the necessary canoes. In exchange for their parting gifts, he also presented them with an ivory tusk weighing a hundred-and-forty pounds.

The White Fathers, accompanied by the children they had redeemed from slavery, left their mission station in Buganda on 8 November 1882. They arrived at Kagweye in Usukuma on 4 January 1883, and by April were settled at a new station called Kamoga (the name of the local chief) at the village of Laganeda.

Following the departure of the priests, the year 1883 was fairly uneventful in Buganda. The Kabaka was ailing, and his fears, never long absent, of British intervention had been lulled by the Mahdi's

45

successes in the Sudan. The only threat to his dominions lay in the hostility of Kabarega, the turbulent king of Bunyoro, but as this threat was endemic, it caused no great alarm. The Anglican mission, reinforced by the arrival of the Reverend R. P. Ashe in April, went on quietly consolidating its position and baptized a few more converts. The Arabs seemed to have built hopes on the coming of a new teacher of the Koran; but he, on arriving from the Coast and being favourably received by the Kabaka, proved quite friendly to Ashe and did nothing to stir up opposition to Christianity.

The Catholic neophytes and catechumens lost none of their fervour and before the year was out some thirty of them, no longer willing to bear life without the opportunity to receive the sacraments, crossed the Lake and marched to Kamoga Mission. Naturally Mukasa, Kaggwa and Kalemba could not have left Buganda even had they wished to do so, but they sent their greetings to the Fathers. Père Girault, the Superior of Kamoga, wrote on 4 May 1884:

> ... In spite of this despot, the mustard seed develops in Buganda, and will soon become a great tree. Sengoba, one of our former catechumens, has managed by sheer pluck and perseverance to leave Buganda and come here. He has brought me letters of two other neophytes, Andrew and Joseph. The writing left something to be desired, but by persevering I have managed to decipher what those dear Christians wrote. ... Here is Andrew's letter: 'Father, I send you greetings, and I beg your pardon for being still so wayward. I have baptized a sick person who was going to die.'
>
> Sengoba has given us most consoling news. He says that since our departure, not only have the catechumens behaved well, but they have gained many followers. Already the Baganda instructed in our Holy Religion are very numerous; if they knew, they said, a means of coming to join us here, they would leave home at once. The chiefs themselves say that our religion is the only true one. Even proud Mutesa has invited us to return to Buganda. 'Parvuli petierunt panem, et non erat qui frangeret eis.' They ask for the truth, and for want of missionaries we cannot go and take it to them.

The party from Buganda also brought word of a serious outbreak of bubonic plague. The Baganda were terrified of plague and formerly, whenever an epidemic occurred, either every man, woman and child would make off, abandoning the sick to their fate and leaving the corpses without burial or, if flight were impossible, they would mercilessly drive those afflicted with the disease from their midst. During this epidemic, Andrew Kaggwa gathered abandoned patients into his own enclosure, cared for them as well as he could, instructed them, baptized them and gave them decent burial. Other Christians also followed his example so that, of the eighty catechumens who fell victims to the disease, only one died without baptism.

The last days of Mutesa the First were not happy. One of his armies was cut to pieces by the Bakeddi and smallpox ravaged his country, carrying off within the space of six months some ten thousand of his subjects, including a number of members of the royal household. He himself grew steadily worse and, as the year 1884 wore on, the disease he had contracted seven years before strengthened its hold. Some Arabs said to possess a marvellous remedy were brought in, but on 19 October the Kabaka realized that his case was hopeless. 'Look,' he exclaimed to those about him, 'I am getting black.[1] I am very near to death.' He ordered everyone out of the room except his personal attendants, Joseph Mukasa and Jean-Marie Muzeyi, the Princess Royal and the Guardian of the Cord, and shortly after died in the arms of his faithful servant, Joseph.

In his life of Père Lourdel, the Abbé Nicq suggests that the Christian pages, either through embarrassment or fear to compromise themselves, did not dare to propose baptism to the dying monarch and so he died a pagan. This statement, implying a lack of zeal and courage in the Christian pages, reflects mainly upon Joseph Mukasa and Jean-Marie Muzeyi. It is, however, hardly believable that this courageous pair would have been deterred by fear of the consequences from baptizing the dying man, had he shown any signs of desiring baptism.

The general opinion of his contemporaries was that Mutesa never had any genuine desire to become a Christian and never regarded the three religions, which had come to his country, as anything but possible tools of government or means of securing a political alliance. It is thought that he might have become a Muslim—Islam being undoubtedly the most expedient of the three for an uxorious monarch—but for his horror of circumcision. He seems to have had no sincere intention of adopting Christianity, although he could not but admire the beauty of its teaching.

Appreciations of Mutesa were written by Speke, Stanley and others, all of them more or less favourable, even enthusiastic; but the missionaries, who had known him for years, as his subjects and not merely as passing visitors, speak less highly of him. They do not deny that he had many excellent qualities, kindness, a sense of justice, breadth of vision, statesmanship and courtesy, but they also impute to him some of the most abominable vices that have ever enslaved mankind. To his everlasting credit, however, must be placed the complete break with pagan tradition of his death-bed command, that his obsequies should not be marred by the customary slaughter of hundreds of innocent victims.

47

Mutesa died in October 1884 and was succeeded by his son Mwanga. But before the accession of the new Kabaka is described, it is necessary to introduce some more of the principals of this story, the Uganda martyrs.

Chapter Five

SHEEP WITHOUT SHEPHERDS
(November 1882—July 1885)

The departure from Buganda of the priests was a heavy blow to the Catholic catechumens and to the neophytes, who now numbered some seventeen, apart from those who had been baptized in danger of death. The Fathers had told them to persevere in their holy dispositions and to become apostles of their still pagan brethren.

There were four main centres of Catholic teaching; the royal palace itself with its adjoining buildings, where Joseph Mukasa became the chief shepherd and teacher, ably assisted by the catechumen Jean-Marie Muzeyi and later by Charles Lwanga; the outer courts of the royal enclosure and the environs of the capital, where Andrew Kaggwa and the catechumen Matthew Kisule carried on the apostolate; Mityana, the headquarters of the county chief of Ssingo, well served by the two neophytes, Matthias Kalemba the Mulumba, and Luke Banabakintu; and finally Kitanda in Bulemezi County, a centre about which little is known except that Charles Lwanga attached himself to it.

In the royal enclosure itself there were already about a hundred-and-fifty adherents of the Catholic mission, in various stages of instruction. Many of these were attached to the court of the great audience hall and to the private courts beyond it. These looked to Joseph Mukasa for guidance and instruction. As the Kabaka's trusted and favourite personal attendant, he was looked upon as a person of importance, destined for high office, and also he possessed the character and other qualities of a natural leader of men. All who knew him in those days speak of his sterling character and of the kindness which made him esteemed, and even loved, by all, Christians, Muslims and pagans alike. He displayed the charm and courtesy for which the Court of Mutesa was famous but, in his case, these were not merely a mask covering an innate pride and cruelty. He never lost his temper or struck any of the pages under his command and, although ready to perform the lowliest offices in and about the royal dwelling with the greatest humility, did not lose thereby any of the respect or loyalty of his charges, who loved to work under him. He in turn cared for their physical, spiritual and moral welfare, doing his utmost to shield them from danger and temptation, and gathering them together in small groups, so as not to arouse suspicion, for prayer and instruction in the truths of the Catholic faith. In this task, Joseph received the whole-hearted and valuable assistance of his companion in personal attendance on the Kabaka, Jean-Marie Muzeyi.

Jean-Marie Muzeyi was still only a catechumen, yet he displayed such intelligence and so quick an understanding of the truths propounded to him that he soon proved himself an able instructor of those less gifted. With his many other gifts, Muzeyi had a remarkable memory which enabled him to learn by heart, in the space of two days, the complete abbreviated catechism (of fourteen pages) which the Fathers had prepared in the vernacular. This, which took the ordinary catechumen about three weeks, he accomplished without the aid of a book, by having the questions and answers repeated to him a number of times.

Muzeyi, a member of the Buffalo (Mbogo) Clan, was born in the hamlet of Kisomberwa, near Minziro, in Buddu County, between the years 1852 and 1857. Muzeyi's father, Bunyaga, held a royal appointment as Shoulder-Bearer to the Kabaka for the County of Buddu. His duty was to carry the Kabaka on his shoulders when necessary during a royal progress through the county—a task that, in a country as abundantly blessed with swamps as Buganda, can have been no sinecure. Muzeyi's mother, a member of the Monkey (Nkima) Clan, was known as Mukatunzi or Nnamalayo.

Muzeyi himself seems to have been blessed with a whole series of different names. Originally called Musoke, he became known at court as Muddembuga, meaning, one is told, someone-has-refused-to-obey-you-so-go-to-the-chief-to-settle-the-matter.[1] Later, because of his prudence and maturity of judgment, and because an eye-affliction, probably trachoma, made him look older than his years, his friends called him Muzeyi, a name derived from the Swahili word mzéé, old man, grandfather. When he became a Muslim, he was known as Jamari (Good Luck). One wonders whether he himself hailed with relief the touch of genius shown by Père Lourdel in christening him Jean-Marie, so that the sound, if not the spelling, of his name might remain unchanged.

When Muzeyi was still quite young, a sub-chief named Kabega, proceeding on transfer from Gomba to a new post at Segguku, saw him herding cattle and promptly kidnapped him. On arriving at the capital, he sold the boy to an acquaintance named Bigomba who in turn sold him to the Kabaka for a piece of cloth and a gourd of beer.

Still too young to become a page, the lad was entrusted to Ttamiro, the royal fence-maker, in whose household he lived, probably for some time, since many believed Ttamiro to be his father. When he was considered old enough, he became one of the royal pages and, probably at the time when his royal master was showing leanings towards that religion, a Muslim.

When the plague epidemic broke out in 1881, Muzeyi was granted leave of absence from the Court and went to stay at Mutundwe where he got to know some Christians or catechumens who gave him his first lessons in the Catholic faith. It was probably on his return from this spell of leave that he joined the group of pages under Joseph Mukasa and quickly endeared himself to that young leader by his thirst for knowledge of the faith. He soon became Joseph's right-hand man, both in attendance on the sick Kabaka and in the spreading of Christian knowledge amongst the pages. Père Lourdel has left on record his own impressions of this young man who was to be the last of the martyrs. He writes :

Jean-Marie received baptism on 1st November 1885. He continued to be a model to his companions . . . It was he who solved for them their small questions of conscience. When they disagreed, they submitted the case unreservedly to his arbitration with complete confidence in his right judgement and in his kindness. Quite unaffected and simple in manner, he possessed, despite his youth, a gravity such as I have not met with in any other negro. In the midst of the laughter, often boisterous, of his companions, one would scarcely detect a smile on his face. His thoughts were constantly concerned with religious matters. Of a rare delicacy of conscience, he received the sacraments as frequently as he could. During the plague, he showed a heroic devotion to those stricken, exhorting them and baptizing those at the point of death. His small savings were used on the redemption from slavery of young children whom he then instructed.

Jean-Marie was always seeking an opportunity to give us pleasure. Learning that we wished to redeem a young slave who was a Christian, and that the child's master refused to let us have him, he went in search of the man and by sheer persistence and importunity got him to give way and accept the purchase price, which he himself paid. Full of joy, he then brought the child and offered him to us, without the slightest desire for anything in return.

Of marriageable age and in a position to marry advantageously, Jean-Marie chose to remain celibate.

How absurd to underestimate the efficacy of God's grace! The Creator of the world well knows how to gather lilies where He will, and sometimes He does so where it is apparently impossible, to revive the courage of the missionary, daily witness of the depths of moral decadence in which these unhappy infields are enmured.

On the death of Kabaka Mutesa, Muzeyi left the Court and was appointed to help tend the tomb of his late royal master at Kasubi. Finding the pagan rites performed at the tomb incompatible with Christianity, Muzeyi left this post and went to live with Matthew Kirevu, a fellow Christian who held a small sub-chieftainship near Bbuye. He still maintained contact with his friends who remained in the royal enclosure, visiting them and taking part in their discussions of the best method of approaching the new Kabaka about recalling the Catholic missionaries to Buganda.

There is a considerable divergence of opinion about Jean-Marie's age. Père Lourdel thought that he was twenty at the time of his baptism in 1885, and Denis Kamyuka estimated his age at between thirty and thirty-five at the time of his martyrdom in 1887. In view of the general tendency that there has been to underestimate the ages of the martyrs, and of the fact that Muzeyi first became a Muslim, probably before the arrival of the first Christian missionaries, when the Court was leaning towards Islam, it seems likely that the higher estimate is near the mark. Jean-Marie Muzeyi was baptized on 1 November 1885, in a group of twenty-two which included also the martyr Noe Mawaggali.

Other servants of Kabaka Mutesa who were to die as martyrs and who, during the absence of the missionaries, looked to Joseph Mukasa and his helper for guidance and instruction, were the four pages, Anatole Kiriggwajjo, Athanasius Bazzekuketta, Adolphus Mukasa Ludigo and Gonzaga Gonza; the page (later a soldier), Pontian Ngondwe; and the palace guard, Bruno Serunkuma.

Anatole Kiriggwajjo was a Munyoro. Although it is not known how he came to Buganda, it is safe to assume that, like the other two Banyoro martyrs, Kaggwa and Mukasa Ludigo, he had been captured by a raiding party and brought to Buganda as a slave. He is known to have been in the service of Kisomose, a former Chancellor of Mutesa, who was deposed after arousing the enmity of the Queen Mother by his rejection of her amorous advances. Kisomose had already been degraded and relegated to a small sub-chieftainship before the arrival of Speke and Grant in 1862, so it must have been much later that, possibly with an eye to regaining the royal favour, he presented to the Kabaka his Munyoro slave-boy, Kiriggwajjo. Mutesa employed the lad in his own private apartments until the end of his reign, and it was during this period of service that Kiriggwajjo first put himself under instruction. After the departure of the priests, he continued his study of the Catholic religion under the guidance of Mukasa and Muzeyi.

On the death of a Kabaka, all his servants were automatically out of employment, although they could be re-appointed by his successor. Kiriggwajjo, therefore, left the Court on the death of his master and attached himself to Andrew Kaggwa, his fellow-countryman. However, like so many of Mutesa's pages, he had been on familiar and friendly terms with the young Prince Mwanga, by whom he was recalled to serve in the court of the audience hall, although he did not again take up residence in the royal enclosure. A little later, the young Kabaka singled him out for promotion to a post of importance at court but, as this post exposed the holder to considerable moral danger, Kiriggwajjo firmly refused to accept it and, in so doing, seriously offended Mwanga. It seems likely that the position offered was one that entailed close attendance upon the many royal princesses who, forbidden to marry and starved of male society, were liable to use all their wiles, and even employ force, to seduce any male whose duties brought him into the women's part of the enclosure.

One witness estimates this martyr's age as sixteen, and another as twenty at the time of his death, but, as he seems to have served Kabaka Mutesa for a number of years before the latter's death in 1884, it seems probable that he was somewhat older even than twenty.

About the early history of Athanasius Bazzekuketta, another page who served both Mutesa and Mwanga, not much is known. He was the second of the eleven children of Kafero Kabalu Sebaggala of the Monkey (Nkima) Clan and Namukwaya of the Buffalo (Mbogo) Clan. Bazzekuketta is first heard of as belonging to the household of Sembuzzi, the chief chosen by Stanley to command his escort on his journey through Bunyoro, the same who later deserted and absconded with one hundred and eighty pounds of beads. He was known as Sembuzzi's brother-in-law although actually a nephew-in-law, one of Sembuzzi's wives, Namuddu, a sister of Ddumba, being his aunt. The name Bazzekuketta, which means they-have-come-to-see-whether-their-brother-in-law-treats-them-well-or-ill, was given him when he first joined Sembuzzi's household; there is no information about his original name, nor any certainty about the place of his birth.

It was while he was still at Sembuzzi's that Bazzekuketta caught the small-pox that left its scars upon his face and, in the throes of the sickness, was approached by Raphael Sembuya, one of his companions, with the suggestion that baptism was the only remedy for his illness. He agreed to be baptized and was taught the Sign of the Cross and other prayers but not then given the sacrament, as he began to mend. This incident illustrates the charity shown by these early Baganda Christians and their zeal for sharing the good-tidings

53

with others. It also provides an object-lesson for the complacent Christian who considers his religion to be a purely private and personal matter between himself and God.

After his recovery, Bazzekuketta persevered with the study of the Catholic religion and, on entering the Kabaka's service, evidently in a humble capacity because he was nicknamed Bisasiro (Rubbish) by his companions, he found there able instructors in Joseph Mukasa, Jean-Marie Muzeyi and, later, Charles Lwanga. He could also often be found sitting at the feet of Andrew Kaggwa in the latter's compound at Natete and, later, at Kigowa.

Bazzekuketta, who was about twenty at the time of his martyrdom, was one of Mutesa's pages re-appointed by Kabaka Mwanga. He was then put in charge of the Kabaka's ceremonial robes and ornaments, to keep them clean and polished, and also had the duty of polishing the palace mirrors.

Adolphus Mukasa Ludigo, the third of the Banyoro martyrs, was a tall, slender, dark-skinned young man, whose forehead bore the tribal marks of his people. He was about twenty-four when he perished in the flames at Namugongo and, like his compatriot Andrew Kaggwa, had been carried off by Baganda raiders when still a young boy and presented to the Kabaka. James Semugoma, a witness in the Process of Beatification, tells how Mukasa Ludigo once claimed to be a descendant of the princes of Bunyoro. The independent testimony of others suggests that this claim was well founded. One, for instance, said that when, many years later, he was a catechist at Butiti, in the land of Mwenge, he was struck by the remarkable resemblance of the people there to his martyred friend, Mukasa Ludigo. 'The entire appearance of Ludigo,' he declared, 'was that of the people who inhabit that part of Mwenge which is called Bufunjo or Myeri.' Another witness referred to the scars on Ludigo's forehead, which, in his opinion, marked him as a man of Butiti in the land of Mwenge. 'We call those people Balindi,' he added, 'because they both resemble the inhabitants of Ankole and bear the scars, or fire-marks, after the manner of the Banyoro.'

Père Gorju confirms the fact that the land of Toro-Mwenge was the royal county of the Kings of Bunyoro, the land flowing with milk and honey, where their wives used to await the hour of their delivery. Nowhere more than in this county is the traveller struck by the light-skinned, oval-faced, well-built figure, characteristic of the Muhima, the shepherd-kingly race of Central Africa. If Bugangadzi, Andrew Kaggwa's birthplace, was the county of the royal burial grounds of Bunyoro, Mwenge, Mukasa Ludigo's country, was the home of its nobility.

Adolphus Mukasa Ludigo started to follow instructions in the Catholic religion about 1881, when the Court was at Nabulagala and the Catholic mission very close to it at Kasubi. He continued his lessons after the departure of the priests both at the palace and, when his duties allowed, at the home of his well-loved fellow-countryman, Andrew Kaggwa. Here when, as so often happened, there were large numbers of Christians and catechumens, Ludigo, in whose veins ran the proud Muhima blood, would ignore custom for the sake of charity and cheerfully lend a hand at the women's work of peeling and cooking plantains.

Another foreign page, Gonzaga Gonza, was a Musoga, who, like his fellow-countryman Matthias Kalemba, had been seized and carried off as a slave by a raiding party of Baganda. His original name is unknown, the name Gonza having been given to him because he was captured from a Musoga chief of that name who belonged to the Lion Clan and lived in Bulamogi County.

Gonza was first in the service of one Tegusaga who started as a palace firewood-cutter and rose to the rank of corporal of the guard. By Tegusaga, Gonza was presented to Kabaka Mutesa who employed him in the private section of the royal enclosure. Here he lived in quarters known as the House of Eunuchs,[1] the occupants of which had the duty of delivering supplies, such as firewood and salt, to the houses occupied by the Kabaka's women. Menya, another Musoga, was in charge of this section, assisted by Namulabira, and it was these two who first taught Gonza the Catholic prayers, which they had written on the back of a wooden tablet inscribed with Muslim prayers in Arabic.

The outbreak of plague which, no respecter of persons, carried off one of the Kabaka's women in February 1881, drove the Court from Rubaga back to the old site at Nabulagala and thus put the three friends in close proximity to the new Catholic mission buildings at Kasubi. Joyfully they made use of the opportunity thus afforded them of attending the instructions given by the priests. Menya, however, caught the plague and Namulabira hastened to the mission to ask for medicine and help for his sick friend. As the priests themselves could not enter the private section of the enclosure, they told Namulabira to baptize Menya and showed him how to do it. Menya died and Namulabira succeeded him as head of the section. After the death of Menya, the two survivors, Gonza and Namulabira (or Kiyenje), persevered zealously with their instructions in the Catholic faith and tried to spread the good tidings amongst their companions. One of these, won over and introduced to the priests by Gonza, was Louis Masimbi, who has left on record the story of Namulabira; a

55

story which throws light on a little known aspect of palace life, and also reveals something of the kindness and Christian charity of the martyr who led him to the faith.

In June 1881, Namulabira was accused by the Kabaka—and therefore judged guilty—of trying to set fire to the hut in which he lived and also of buying food from one of the women security officers. These women formed a sort of female Gestapo charged with the task of spying on the Kabaka's women and on his pages, and reporting to him any signs of familiarity between the two. They used to dress in skins, or male attire, and listen outside the huts at night, and were thus a considerable danger to the Christians who gathered secretly for prayer and instruction. The charge of attempted arson seems not to have been entirely without foundation, because the occupants of the House of Eunuchs were in the habit of manufacturing soap to exchange for food and may easily have endangered the hut in doing so. This was a serious matter in a compound of grass-thatched houses, through which fire could sweep with terrifying speed. The other charge, that of familiarity with the woman, Nankya, was, according to Masimbi, groundless. Both the accused, Namulabira and the woman, Nankya, had their feet placed in the same fire. Masimbi does not explain whether this was by way of punishment or by way of trial-by-ordeal, but the outcome was that Nankya's feet were burnt away almost to the ankle, and Namulabira's emerged almost scatheless, a circumstance which caused considerable wonder but did not appease the Kabaka. Although perfectly recovered from his ordeal within a few days, Namulabira was kept in prison pending the next ritual executions. It was then that Gonza showed his courage and devotion. He stood by his fellow-page in trouble, bringing to the prison water and food which he had cooked himself. He seems to have baptized Namulabira immediately the crisis arose, because Père Lourdel, visiting the Court on 12 June, was told by one of the pages that Namulabira was in bonds but had been baptized during the night. On at least two occasions, Gonza went so far as to offer himself as a hostage for his fellow-page, allowing himself to be locked up in the prison for the night while his friend went to the Catholic mission, on one occasion for instruction, and on another, when his execution seemed imminent, to receive Communion.[1]

Gonza was one of the pages of Mutesa recalled into the royal service by Kabaka Mwanga. He was then posted to the court of the great audience hall where he served under Charles Lwanga. He was not baptized until after the martyrdom of Joseph Mukasa, when he received the sacrament from Père Lourdel and with it the name

Gonzaga, obviously suggested by his own name Gonza. He was about twenty-four years old at the time of his death on the road to Namugongo.

Of the two other ex-servants of Kabaka Mutesa to suffer martyrdom—Ngondwe and Serunkuma—Ngondwe was the older and had already left the Court itself before the death of his royal master.

Pontian Ngondwe, dark and slender, with high cheek-bones, was between thirty-five and forty when he was martyred. He was born at Bulamu in Kyaggwe County and belonged to the White Egret (Nyonyi) Clan. His father, Birenge, was in fact head of the clan when he presented his son to the Kabaka. Ngondwe's mother was Mukomulwanyi of the Buffalo (Mbogo) Clan. A number of royal appointments were traditionally held by members of the White Egret clan. These included the posts of Kabaka's medicine-man, coffee-maker, and keeper of the sacred fire, which was lit at the beginning of a new reign and kept burning until its close. It was the Keeper's duty to maintain the fire throughout the reign, first offering to the Kabaka the fuel to be used to feed it, according to a traditional ritual, with the words, 'Here is firewood for the Sacred Fire. When you go to war, smear your face with the ashes and so obtain victory.' The post of official Keeper, though one of honour, was not without its occupational hazard, because when the fire was extinguished on the death of a Kabaka, the Keeper used to be 'extinguished' with it. Doubtless a Kabaka could be sure that at least one of his subjects would sing with real sincerity the Luganda equivalent of 'Long live our gracious King'.

After serving Kabaka Mutesa for some years as a page, Ngondwe was drafted into the militia and given a plot of land at Kitibwa, later called Kigowa. Probably already interested in the Catholic religion, he found there a Christian named Cyprian Kamya, baptized with Kalemba and Banabakintu, to continue his instructions. Kamya has left it on record that Ngondwe often came to his house at dead of night for religious instruction, and also that, 'when Ngondwe was not yet a Christian, he had a spiteful and vindictive character, but later he became a changed man and got on well with everybody'. When, on the accession of Mwanga, Andrew Kaggwa was given Kigowa as a fief, he found Ngondwe already living on the hill, and the latter obtained a new instructor, guide and friend.

About the parentage of Bruno Serunkuma there are a number of contradictory statements, but Amoni Bazira, assistant-head of the Sheep Clan to which Serunkuma belonged, and Sabbiti Kityo, deputy-head of the Busamba lineage, state positively that he was the son of Namunjulirwa. Stanley, in *Through the Dark Continent,* relates some of the exploits of this mighty warrior, whom he calls 'The Achilles of Africa'. Because of his courage and prowess, Namunjulirwa was a great favourite of Kabaka Suna who made him county chief of Buddu and, on one occasion, said of him in open court, 'Truly Namunjulirwa is brave, there is none like him in Buganda'. Such fulsome praise from the Kabaka naturally aroused jealousy in the hearts of other ambitious men, and it was probably this motive that inspired Mukasa, the future Chancellor, to arrange the murder of Namunjulirwa after the death of his patron, Kabaka Suna.

It is thought that the murder was arranged with the connivance of the new Kabaka, Mutesa, who certainly appointed Mukasa as the new county chief and allowed him to seize and sell into slavery those of his victim's family whom he could lay hands on. One of these was Majwala, the youngest son of Namunjulirwa, 'the little boy who alone watched the last hours of Dr Livingstone'. Majwala was rescued from slavery by Stanley and served him, then Livingstone, and finally Stanley again, on their travels through the heart of Africa. Fr Lefèbre, whose painstaking enquiries into the parentage of the martyrs were made largely through the Clan Leaders, the most likely and most reliable source of information at that late date, 1932 to 1944, lists the names of eighteen children of Namunjulirwa and suggests that Serunkuma and Majwala are two names for one and the same person, the eighteenth child.

Unfortunately, it seems impossible, at this late date, to establish the identity beyond question. All that one can say is that none of the evidence so far uncovered renders it impossible, and some seems to suggest that it is not unlikely. The difference in names has no significance either way, because it is quite usual for a Muganda boy to change his name, adopting one of the other clan or family names as he grows up.

In support of the theory of the identity of Majwala and Serunkuma, one may cite the conformity of parentage and of age. With regard to age, Majwala is described by Stanley as a 'little boy', in 1871. He was yet old enough to hold his own with full-grown men over thousands of miles of arduous travelling and must have been at least in his early teens. Fifteen years later, when Serunkuma died in the holocaust at Namugongo, he was said to have been about thirty years old. With regard to parentage, Stanley states that Majwala (or Majwara) was the son of Namunjulirwa, sold into slavery by his father's murderer, Mukasa; and the Clan Leaders, whose testimony about relationships may be taken as reliable, say that Serunkuma was the son of Namunjulirwa. Earlier enquiries about Bruno Serunkuma's parentage produced a large number of different suggestions. An examination of these reveals that all of those mentioned as being his father were in fact close relatives of Namunjulirwa who would naturally, according to Kiganda custom, be known as fathers of the warrior's young son, the term being used loosely to describe an uncle, a guardian, a patron, the head of the family or even an elder brother.

Of negative value, at least, is the fact that whereas nothing is known of the early history of Serunkuma, the same is true of the later history of Majwala who is last heard of at Zanzibar in December 1877, when he was presented with the medal struck by the Royal Geographical Society in recognition of the services of those who were with Livingstone on his last journey. Sir John Milner Gray, in an article entitled 'Livingstone's Muganda Servant' published in the *Uganda Journal,* September 1949, describes this presentation and adds, 'I have been unable to trace Majwara's after career....'

In the same article, Sir John mentions Stanley's visit to Buganda, in the course of his journey from the East to the West coast of Africa, 1874 to 1877, when Majwala was received in audience by Kabaka Mutesa. The Kabaka received him graciously, welcomed him back to Buganda because of his parentage, and presented him with a wife. Although Majwala continued with the expedition on this occasion, he must naturally have considered the possibilities of settling down in his homeland, and it would not be surprising if, after seven years of tramping backwards and forwards through the heart of Africa, he decided to return there and take service with the Kabaka, who had shown himself well disposed towards him.

Whether indeed this courageous youth who so faithfully served both Livingstone and Stanley and, in the course of seven years, 'tramped close on ten thousand miles up, down and across Africa under conditions which had severely tested even the most able-bodied of full-grown men' (Gray, *loc. cit.*), did in fact return to his native land and take service with Kabaka Mutesa under the name of Serunkuma, there seems to be no means of knowing for sure. One would like to believe it was so, and that a life of faithful service to three human masters was crowned by a supreme act of fidelity to the Master of all. If Majwala was in fact the Serunkuma who perished in the flames of Namugongo, he was indeed *faithful to the end,* the words engraved upon the medal presented to him by the Royal Geographical Society.

According to Alexis Ssebowa, who was county chief of Kyaggwe at the time of the persecution and, later, county chief of Buddu, Serunkuma's mother was named Ndibaliza. He says that after the death of her son he himself looked after her and took her with him when he was transferred to Buddu. Unfortunately, she died of plague before she could be traced by the Fathers and questioned about her martyred son. Bruno Serunkuma, who belonged to the Sheep (Ndiga) Clan, was born in Buddu when his father was chief of that county. In 1882, he was a palace guard, but lived outside the royal enclosure at Kitebi with the Protestant martyr, Alexander Kadoko, said to be his brother, although in reality his nephew, or half-nephew, the son of Mbugano who was Namunjulirwa's eldest child.

About Bruno Serunkuma's character there seems to be general agreement that before he became a Christian he was violent, over-bearing and cruel, loose-living and improvident. His servant complained of daily beatings without cause, and two children, who called at his house for a meal on their way to visit another relative, both had cause for tears before they continued their journey. One witness attributes these bad habits to his calling, and, rather delightfully, suggests that policemen generally, unless they keep a close guard upon themselves, develop bad characters.

After he became a catechumen, Serunkuma strove manfully to master his temper and control his passions. He became kind and considerate to his fellow-Christians but was still not above giving a rude answer to pagans who dared to criticize his religion in his hearing. At the time when Mwanga succeeded to the throne, or a little later, Bruno left the household of his nephew Kadoko, and took up residence in the royal enclosure in one of the hide tents provided for soldiers and guards. This move was prompted by his desire for closer association with his Catholic friends and instructors, Charles Lwanga and others, and also by the necessity of removing himself from the proximity of the two Basoga slave-girls, given him by the Kabaka. Bruno was baptized by Père Giraud during the night of 15 November 1885, after the martyrdom of Joseph Mukasa.

Within the royal enclosure, the little parish that looked to Joseph Mukasa for guidance and instruction after the departure of the missionaries was restricted to the court of the great audience hall and to those in the vicinity of the royal residence. During the illness of the Kabaka, Joseph could never move far from the side of his royal master. However, the outer courts and the environs of the capital were well cared for by Andrew Kaggwa and Matthew Kisule.

Kaggwa, the royal bandmaster, has already been introduced. Although he lived near Natete, his duties frequently brought him to the Court and gave him the right of entry to the outer courts of the enclosure. Similar facilities were enjoyed by Matthew Kisule, the Kabaka's gunsmith, who set a wonderful example of Christian charity and zeal for the spread of the Gospel. His house at Natete, like that of Andrew Kaggwa, became a popular meeting place for Christians and catechumens. He received baptism on the second night after the death of Joseph Mukasa, and, during the persecution, proved a tower of strength to his fellow Christians, although he was not called to martyrdom. He was not present to meet the first demented outburst of Kabaka Mwanga's rage, when his life might well have been in danger, and later his specialist knowledge and skill, so valuable to the Kabaka, was his safeguard against molestation.

One of Andrew Kaggwa's converts was James Buzabaliawo, the son of the royal bark-cloth maker, Sebikejje, of the Colubus-Monkey (Ngeye) Clan. Buzabaliawo was the third of eight children and was born at Tabazimu in Mawokota County between 1856 and 1861. His eldest sister, Tagusenda, had been presented by their father to Kabaka Mutesa who had one child by her, the Princess Namukabya. Buzabaliawo was brought up in the household of his royal niece and from there naturally entered the Kabaka's service, first as a page and later as a bandsman and guard. As a bandsman he came under the command of Andrew Kaggwa who taught him to play the big drum and also instructed him in the Catholic faith. He became Kaggwa's chief assistant, not only as bandsman but also as teacher of the catechism. In this capacity he was often sent by Kaggwa, who had considerable influence over the young Prince Mwanga, to put the latter through his prayers and catechism. When after the accession of Mwanga, Kaggwa became Bandmaster-General, he took Buzabaliawo with him to Kigowa but, though normally resident there, Buzabaliawo was frequently at Court, either on duty or paying visits to the Kabaka and his former companions amongst the pages. He was not baptized until the night after Joseph Mukasa's death on 15 November 1885.

The third Catholic centre, the Christian community at Mityana, has already been described. It had most zealous apostles in Matthias Kalemba the Mulumba, and Luke Banabakintu, and was nearly two hundred strong. During the absence of the White Fathers from Buganda, the main burden of instruction was born by Banabakintu, since Kalemba's duties kept him at the capital for almost the whole of this period.

The group of Christians at Kitanda in Bulemezi County is known only through its association with Charles Lwanga; but this alone is sufficient to give it an honoured name in the history of Christianity in Buganda. It was formerly thought that Lwanga began his service at Court in the reign of Kabaka Mutesa, but Charles Buza, his relative and for many years his companion in the service of Mawulugungu, is quite positive in stating that Lwanga entered the royal service only upon the accession of Mwanga.

Charles Lwanga belonged to the Bush-Buck (Ngabi) Clan, but at Court passed as a member of the Colubus-Monkey Clan, that of his former master and patron, Mawulugungu. Members of his own clan were not allowed at Court and were debarred from the royal presence because they were recognized as being of royal blood and therefore as possible rivals. Because of this relationship to the royal family, women of the clan who became wives of the Kabaka were not allowed to rear a male child : if one were born, it was strangled at birth. In actual practice, this rarely happened in more recent times because, by a legal fiction, a woman of the Bush-Buck Clan who became a wife of the Kabaka was allowed to pass herself off as a member of the Monkey Clan. Charles Lwanga was not, as some have suggested, incorporated into the Bean Clan. This belief seems to have arisen from his close friendship with Louis Kibanyi of that clan, which led some to conclude that the two were closely related.

About Lwanga's parentage there are a number of conflicting reports. Melanie of Bukalasa, who claimed to be a relative, said that he was born in Ssingo County, the son of Musazi and Meme. This would make him a younger brother of Noe Mawaggali, and it becomes difficult to explain why Noe's sister, Munaku, who lived until 1934 and was thoroughly questioned about her brother Noe, never so much as mentioned her relationship with Charles Lwanga. It is, of course, possible that she never knew Lwanga who, if born in Ssingo, was certainly sent to Buddu at a very early age to be brought up by Kaddu, probably, in that case, an uncle. Cyprian Mutagwanya and Charles Buza, a relative who knew Lwanga from his early youth, both say that they always understood that Kaddu was the real father of Lwanga, and mention their similarity of colouring, a chestnut-brown rather than a black. At least it is certain that, whether born there or not, Lwanga spent his early youth with Kaddu at Kalokero, in Buddu County.[1]

As to Lwanga's age, Père Lourdel thought that he was about twenty at the date of his martyrdom but, as Europeans are often far out in their estimates of the ages of Africans, it seems safer to accept that of Cyprian Mutagwanya who alone, of all the witnesses, relates his estimate to a known historical date. He says that he and Lwanga were of the same age, and that he himself was fifteen when he took part in the war against Nakalanga in 1875. This would mean that Charles Lwanga was approximately the same age as Joseph Mukasa, and about twenty-five or twenty-six at the time of his martyrdom. In support of this one may cite the testimony of Denis Kamyuka and Aleni Nganda; the first to the effect that Lwanga was about the same age as Adolphus Mukasa Ludigo, between twenty and twenty-five, and the second, independently, giving Ludigo's age as twenty-four. The fact that Lwanga, on entering the Kabaka's service, was at once given a position of authority and responsibility also suggests that he was already well out of his teens.

About August 1878, his father (or adopted father) Kaddu placed Lwanga in the service of Mawulugungu, the 'Maour-Ougoungou' described by Stanley in *Through the Dark Continent*, who was then chief of Kirwanyi with his headquarters at Kyato. Among Lwanga's companions in this service were his cousin Charles Buza, Musoke and James Semugoma, all of whom accompanied their chief when he was transferred, in 1879, to the chieftainship of Kitesa, in Ssingo County. In 1880, Lwanga made what was probably his first visit to the scene of his future labours when, together with Buza and Semugoma, he formed part of the chief's retinue on an official visit to pay homage and give thanks to the Kabaka for the new chieftainship. After his return to his headquarters at Nakwaya, the chief made a regular practice of sending the Kabaka gifts of beer, plantains, chickens, goats and cows. Semugoma and Musoke were entrusted with the task of delivering these and thus became frequent visitors to the capital, where they got to know the Catholic missionaries and began to attend their instructions. With the zeal so often displayed by the catechumens of those days, they began to look around for others to share with them the good tidings, and soon had their companion Charles Lwanga interested in their faith.

The two amateur catechists used to hold their meetings in secret for fear they should come to the ears of their chief and were, at first greatly dismayed when their superior, Buza, surprised them at their prayers. However, instead of reporting them to the chief, as they feared, Buza began to ask questions about their faith and was soon won over. He himself describes how, on getting Semugoma to introduce him to the priests, he was so terrified at his first sight of Père Livinhac that he nearly took to his heels. Having mastered his initial panic, he became a fervent catechumen, going to the mission for instruction whenever his duties allowed, and frequently staying overnight with Andrew Kaggwa to obtain additional instruction from the genial Munyoro bandmaster. He was also able to arrange time off for Lwanga and Semugoma to attend classes at the Catholic mission each fortnight.

When Mawulugungu died in December 1882, the members of his

retinue dispersed. As the priests had already left the country, Buza attached himself to Andrew Kaggwa, with whom he could continue his study of the faith; and Lwanga and Semugoma went to Kitanda, in Bulemezi County, where they joined a group of recently baptized Christians, praying with them, learning from them and helping them to instruct others. Here they stayed until the death of Kabaka Mutesa in 1884.

On the accession of Mwanga, Charles Lwanga went to the capital where he entered the Kabaka's service. It says much for the personality of this young man that he was at once given a position of authority in command of the pages who served in the court of the great audience hall, and immediately won the confidence and affection of his charges. His physical prowess at the wrestling contests, so popular at Court, made him something of a hero to his younger charges, but they also, as well as his equals and superiors, recognized in him qualities of leadership, gentleness and nobility of character.

To Joseph Mukasa, his immediate superior, Lwanga's arrival at Court was quite literally a godsend, filling more than adequately the gap left in the Christian ranks by the departure of Jean-Marie Muzeyi. More and more did Joseph come to rely upon Lwanga in the instruction and guidance of the pages and in the increasingly difficult task of shielding them from the temptations that beset them at Mwanga's court. He also appointed Lwanga one of the overseers of the task, entrusted to him by the Kabaka, of excavating the small lake at the foot of Rubaga Hill, known as the Kabaka's Lake. This lake seems to have been something of an obsession with the young Kabaka because four years later he was to force a number of chiefs and senior officials themselves to take an active part in the filthy and menial labour of enlarging it, and so infuriated them that none remained loyal when he was deposed. On the occasion of its first excavation also, he seems to have pressed into service some of the officials who would normally have been exempt from such menial work : Senkole, Guardian of the Sacred Fuse, was in the group under the command of Charles Lwanga, and had to be fined by the latter for absenteeism. In this way did Charles incur the lasting enmity of the man who was to be his executioner.

With leaders of the calibre of Joseph Mukasa, Andrew Kaggwa and Matthias Kalemba, and with numbers of devoted and zealous catechumens, Catholicism in Buganda, far from declining during the absence of the missionaries, grew in strength and self-reliance.

The stalwarts of the old pagan beliefs and practices, led by Mukasa the Chancellor, were disturbed and foresaw the ultimate destruction of the whole pagan social system that they valued. Had there been a strong ruler, bloodshed might have been avoided, but with one of Mwanga's weakness of character an explosion was inevitable, and the first outburst, of which the Protestants were the victims, was not long delayed.

Chapter Six

THE NEW KABAKA

When Kabaka Mutesa died, the Chancellor, who was away in the country at the time, hastened back to the capital and took measures for guarding it pending the choice of a successor to the throne. Meanwhile the sacred fire was extinguished and the whole country plunged into mourning.

It was a custom of the Baganda to have no fixed heir to the throne, a custom designed to lessen the risk of plots against the life of the reigning monarch. The choice of a successor was made by the Chancellor in consultation with the Guardian of the Cord, the Kasujju or Guardian of the Princes, and the Mugema or Titular Father of the Kabaka. Their nomination was only made after the approval of the greater chiefs had been obtained, but the choice was restricted to one of the sons of the deceased Kabaka.

Kiwewa, the eldest son of the late monarch, was traditionally ineligible, and another son Kalema, who had shot one of his brothers in a quarrel and generally shown himself unsuitable, was also passed over in favour of Prince Mwanga. This choice was in accordance with the dying wish of the late Kabaka, which carried great weight with the chiefs. Mwanga was accordingly proclaimed Kabaka, and arrangements put in hand for his installation and for the burial of his father.

Mutesa's body lay in state for five days before it was buried. Native carpenters were ordered to make coffins such as Mackay had made for the Queen Mother. When they failed in their attempts, the chiefs asked Mackay to show them how to do it : in other words, the work was once more entrusted to him. He did it to everyone's satisfaction, and the late Kabaka was buried in a grave dug in one of the largest houses of the royal enclosure on Nabulagala Hill.

As the new Kabaka was not allowed to live in the enclosure in which his father had been buried, a temporary new residence was erected for him near Budo, a few miles from Mengo. There the new monarch was enthroned with all the traditional ceremonies; the new Sacred Fuse was lit and from it the new Sacred Fire, which was entrusted to the new Guardian. The Fuse itself, made from bark-cloth and lengthened as need arose, was, like the Sacred Fire, kept burning or smouldering throughout the reign, and from it were lit, not only

66

the Sacred Fire itself, but also any pyres for ritual executions ordered by the Kabaka. The Guardian or Keeper of the Fuse was a man named Senkole.

The newly installed Kabaka was some eighteen years old, in appearance very like his father, but shorter and with more of the negro about him. He was considered very handsome, with rounded eyes and, later, 'a beard of extraordinary quality'. Fifty years earlier, Mwanga's career as Kabaka might have been unexceptional but, unfortunately for him and for his people, he became Kabaka at a time when Buganda had ceased to be an isolated kingdom and when increasing contact with the outside world inevitably produced great changes. As T. B. Fletcher of the Church Missionary Society wrote :

> To steer a straight course through a time when such radical changes were taking place needed a man of a strong character, a firm will and wide vision. Those characteristics Mwanga did not possess ... He was nervous, suspicious, fickle, passionate—a man whose one desire and object was to live his own life to the full. Self in all its many and varied aspects was his guide ...

Of even greater interest, because written before the event, is Mackay's shrewd estimate of the character of the young man now called to the throne. Shortly after Mwanga's accession in 1884 Mackay wrote of him :

> It would be very hard to describe Mwanga's character. I have perhaps had more opportunity of knowing him than my brethren have had. He knows how to behave with dignity and reserve when the occasion requires that; but he soon throws off that assumed air, and chats familiarly. ... But none can fail to see that he is fitful and fickle, and, I fear, revengeful. One vice to which he is addicted is the smoking of bhang (hemp). ... This being so one cannot place much confidence in Mwanga's stability. ... Under the influence of the narcotic he is capable of the wildest unpremeditated actions. Recently I have had reason to find him guilty of such. But generally the young fellow is amiable.

Archdeacon Walker's impression of Mwanga, formed on meeting Mwanga for the first time in 1888, was no more favourable. He describes the Kabaka thus :

> A man with a weak-looking mouth, and a rather silly sort of laugh and smile; he raises his eyebrows very high, and twitches them in surprise, or in giving assent to a statement. He looked a young and frivolous sort of man, very weak and easily led; passionate and, if provoked, petulant. He looked as if he would be easily frightened, and possessed of very little courage or self-control.

67

Even before his accession there were evil reports current about the young Prince's conduct which, Ashe says, shocked even the pagans whose standards of morality were far from high. Ashe refers of course to the practice of homosexuality, a vice repugnant to the Baganda, in which the Prince was encouraged by many of his Muslim companions. To make matters worse, he had also taken to heavy drinking and to hemp-smoking, which habits often left him half stupified. His elevation to the throne at less than twenty years of age tended to bring into prominence whatever there was of pride and vanity in his nature. His father, Mutesa, for instance, had always allowed the Chancellor and other honoured guests to sit with him within the great audience hall, but Mwanga had them stationed in the doorway. At one time, in order to watch his guests unobtrusively, Mwanga had a large mirror set up before him and held a smaller one in his hand. Dr. Junker, the Russian explorer who arrived in Buganda during the persecution, describes the audience he had with Kabaka Mwanga in 1886 :

> Mwanga was dressed simply in bark-cloth clasped on one shoulder toga-fashion and without any ornaments. He was a young man of about one or two-and-twenty, of large and powerful frame, with large, prominent eyes, and animated, intelligent expression, but with a childish habit of constantly laughing aloud with wide-open mouth ... Advancing to the centre of the hall, I exchanged the usual Arab salute with the king, and followed Mackay to the left, where we took our places on the chairs we had brought with us, near the king and the French missionaries. Mwanga pointed to me and made some undignified jocular remark to the prime minister, which I cut short by thanking him for permission to enter his country ... He never asked me a single question and constantly interrupted me, so that on a hint from Mackay I refrained from urging Emin's business, reserving it for a private audience.

These contemporary impressions give an indication of the character of the new monarch, whose vices and irresolution were to contribute so much to the sufferings of his people.

It seemed for a time that Mwanga intended to continue the policy pursued by his father of showing favour first to one religion and then to another, but whereas Mutesa seems to have done this with deliberation, his son, moved by fickleness and caprice, ended by alienating all groups, Catholics, Protestants, Muslims and pagans alike.

During the period of mourning for the late Kabaka, which lasted until all the elaborate and protracted funeral rites were ended, there were state-affairs to occupy the attention of the new monarch. All appointments made by his predecessor ended with his death, so that new appointments, or re-appointments had to be made, and the new Queen Mother and Princess Royal to be officially inducted. As Kati-kiro, or Chancellor, Mwanga chose to re-appoint his father's choice, the wily Muhima-blooded Mukasa. It was quite usual for a new Kabaka to retain the services of his father's Chancellor and, although Mwanga must have known Mukasa for the cruel and cold-blooded intriguer that he was, he could not at the beginning of his reign afford either to deprive himself of the help so shrewd and far-seeing a man could give him or to incur the enmity of one who had acquired parental rights over him through the blood-pact with his father. Of the other principal appointments, the new Guardian of the Cord was Nyika, the adopted father of the martyr Kizito, and the new Army Commander was the Muslim, Kapalaga Sabaddu, the same miser-able Sabaddu who had proved such a coward and miscreant in his dealings with Stanley.

Amongst those re-appointed as royal servants were Joseph Mukasa, Andrew Kaggwa, and the pages, Bazzekuketta, Gonza, Mukasa Ludigo and Kiriggwajjo, the last three all being transferred to the court of the great audience hall where they came under the command of the newly-appointed page-in-charge, Charles Lwanga. Other new recruits to the corps of pages were Achilles Kiwanuka, Ambrose Kibuka, Gyavira, Mukasa Kiriwawanvu and Mbaga Tuzinde to the court of the audience hall; Kizito and Mugagga to the private part of the enclosure; and Ssebuggwawo to the Kabaka's own quarters.

Joseph Mukasa was not only retained as the Kabaka's personal at-tendant, a duty he had performed to the satisfaction of the late Kabaka for four years, but was also made Majordomo. Mwanga further showed his confidence in Joseph by consulting him on matters of state and, it is said, by giving him permission to administer a reproof whenever he thought the Kabaka guilty of conduct un-worthy of his rank.

Andrew Kaggwa also received a special mark of the royal favour. A new office, called Kigowa, was created and Andrew became the first Mugowa, or holder of the rank. The post, equivalent to Band-master-General, carried with it the command of the entire militia from which the royal bandsmen were drawn. The name Kigowa was adapted from the Swahili, Ki-Goa, because the only other European-type band known in East Africa was that of the Sultan of Zanzibar, which had Goan personnel. With the new commission, Andrew received a grant of land on Kiwatule Hill, not far from Kigowa (formerly Kitibwa), the encampment of the royal bands-men. Andrew Kaggwa had always been on friendly terms with

Prince Mwanga : now their relations became even more cordial, and Mwanga constantly called upon the Munyoro to accompany him on hunting and boating trips.

The Christians and catechumens were delighted at these marks of royal favour shown to their two leaders. In Andrew's enclosure at Natete they had practised their religion more or less in secret : now secrecy was at an end. In a very short time Kigowa became a Christian centre, and a number of catechumens became retainers on Kaggwa's estate. Among them were two of Mutesa's ex-pages, Pontian Ngondwe who was already established there, and Buzabaliawo who went there as Andrew's second-in-command.

Both Catholics and Protestants had high hopes for the new reign. As Prince, Mwanga had shown himself well-disposed towards Christianity and had even himself attended instructions given by Andrew Kaggwa, for whom he had a great admiration. Sometimes Andrew had sent his assistant, Buzabaliawo, to put the Prince through his prayers and catechism, not with any great success : Ashe, who was trying to teach the Prince his letters at that time, says that he was wayward and flighty and seemed unable to concentrate his attention on one thing for any length of time. Nevertheless, Mwanga had said in all sincerity to his Christian friends, 'If ever I become Kabaka, I will allow religion to spread throughout my country'. On another occasion, he had been asked by the Anglican missionaries about his attitude to religion if he became Kabaka and had replied, 'I will like you very much, and show you every favour'. Père Lourdel also, to whom the Prince had sent numbers of his servants for instruction, believed him to be favourably disposed towards the missions and had said to him privately, when the Catholic missionaries were about to leave, 'As soon as you are Kabaka, we shall return to Buganda'.

There seemed every reason to believe that Mwanga was sufficiently well-intentioned to allow the missionaries freedom to teach and his subjects freedom of conscience, even though he himself did not appear to take his own instruction very seriously. It was not long before these hopes were rudely shattered.

The first indications that all was not well came when the English missionaries, Ashe and O'Flaherty, at that time the only white men in the country, attempted to pay their first courtesy visit to the newly installed Kabaka. When they arrived at the audience, after the chiefs and courtiers had been admitted, they found themselves shut out, and had to return home. By this discourtesy, they thought, Mwanga was trying to flaunt his newly acquired importance, and they decided not to risk another rebuff until Mackay, who was away repairing the mission boat, was able to join them. However, when they learnt that their enemies were spreading rumours that Mackay was raiding and pillaging along the shores of the Lake, they decided to put in an appearance at Court in order to refute the slander. Mwanga received them smilingly and told them that they had 'Kyejo', a word that may mean anything from unconscious self-complacency to downright insolence : their 'Kyejo' consisted in their not having come to see him earlier. During the audience Mwanga was deliberately provocative, speaking highly of the Arabs, the bitterest enemies of the English missionaries, talking about asking the French priests to come back and proposing that the Englishmen should fetch them in their boat, asking Ashe whether he knew how to sew and to make guns, and suggesting that they should build for him a house and a boat.

When Mackay returned, he and Ashe went together to pay their respects to Mwanga who, in the meantime, had moved to another temporary enclosure on the slope of Nabulagala Hill. During this audience, Mackay was commissioned to bring three more English-men to Buganda, obviously for building, because Mwanga was dis-playing no interest in their missionary activity. Mackay agreed to go to the South of the Lake, where there was an Anglican mission station, but there was some unpleasantness about the legate who was to accompany him. Mwanga was inclined to be self-willed and rude, while Mackay remained polite but firm. Eventually, the Kabaka gave way and appointed as legate the Protestant page, Micah Sematimba. After some further desultory talk, the audience ended, and the two Englishmen left with a not very favourable impression of their new ruler.

Mackay was unsuccessful in obtaining recruits and returned in December 1884 without any additional personnel. Mwanga was disappointed but said little at the time. Then, in January 1885, his ill-will towards the Englishmen erupted into violence and the first shedding of Christian blood.

To explain this change from friendliness to hostility, one must try to understand the mind of the young Kabaka and the various in-fluences working upon it.

It seems clear that both Mutesa and Mwanga had a completely false idea of why the English missionaries had come to Buganda; and for this misunderstanding Stanley must be held responsible. A sent-ence in his famous appeal—'It is the practical Christian tutor, who can teach people how to become Christians, cure their diseases, con-struct dwellings, understand and exemplify agriculture, and turn his hand to anything, like a sailor—this is the man who is wanted'—

suggests that Stanley himself did not distinguish between the spiritual benefits of Christianity and the material benefits of one particular Christian civilization, and he undoubtedly managed to confound the two in the minds of the Kabaka and his chiefs. The Kabaka wanted the material benefits described to him by Stanley and, as is clearly implied in the famous appeal, was prepared to pay for them in ivory, skins and cattle. The missionaries came out to preach the Gospel, believing that they had been invited for that purpose; the Kabaka thought that they had come to work for him and complained bitterly that they would make nothing for him, although Stanley had promised him that they would make all manner of things. Thus the two parties were at cross-purposes from the beginning, and the belief was soon established that the Englishmen had obtained admission to the country under false pretences. That Mwanga was under the same impression as his father had been seems clear from his enquiries, made to Ashe and O'Flaherty, about building, boat-building, sewing and gun-making. How deeply-rooted in the Kabaka's mind this idea was, is shown in Mackay's report of the audience of 11 November 1885, when the Anglican mission had already been seven full years in the country. Mwanga then repudiated Mackay's claim to be a teacher, saying that he was an artisan, who had come out to make guns for the Kabaka. He granted that Ashe was a teacher, but then, no one had asked Ashe to come to Buganda. Mackay, on the other hand, had been invited to come.

When the missionaries first arrived and showed no readiness to work for him, Mutesa was puzzled. When they began to expend their energies on teaching his subjects, without asking for payment, he was suspicious but, although he gave credence to the Arab allegations that the missionaries were agents of their government, he was sufficiently well-balanced and fair to wait for evidence of treachery before passing judgment.

Mwanga lacked the balance and judgment possessed by his father. He was merely a boy, still in his teens, brought up without discipline and surrounded by evil counsellors who, taking full advantage of the Kabaka's youth and gullibility, launched an intensive campaign of vilification against the missionaries. The Arabs had not given up the hope, so narrowly frustrated in 1881, of turning Buganda into a Muslim State. The greatest threat to the success of their efforts lay in the possibility of British intervention, so it was against the English missionaries that their venom was mainly directed. They constantly reiterated the charge that these men were agents of their government, an advance guard or bridge-head established in the country in preparation for its annexation by Britain.

The Chancellor and many of the chiefs, who represented the

hard-core of paganism, made common cause with the Arabs in this campaign. In point of fact they had no greater love for the Arabs than they had for the Europeans, but they recognized in Christianity especially a force that, if unchecked, would eventually destroy the pagan social system to which they clung, a system based on tyranny, slavery, polygamy and the degradation of woman.[1] They alleged that all foreigners were trying to gain control of the country by attaching to themselves numbers of followers, and pointed to the missionaries' practice of redeeming slaves as evidence supporting their contention. The baptism of a number of Protestant followers on Christmas Day 1884, and the feast that followed it, became a 'seditious gathering', and every effort was made to persuade the Kabaka to believe that the Christians would remain loyal only so long as they were a minority, but would seize power when strong enough, depose the Kabaka and—supreme horror in Baganda eyes —place a woman on the throne, just like in England.

It is not surprising to find the young and inexperienced Kabaka, unable to believe in altruism, already suspicious of the missionaries, giving credence to many of the allegations made against them.

In January 1885, Mackay asked permission to go in his boat to the South of the Lake to take some letters. The Kabaka asked whether he wanted a legate to accompany him; to which Mackay replied that he did not.[2] Mackay's impatience with what he looked on as constant surveillance is understandable : he seems not to have realized that the presence of the legate was a symbol of the Kabaka's protection. Mwanga gave the permission asked for, but at once informed his Chancellor that Mackay had refused a legate. Mukasa eagerly seized the opportunity thus offered to work upon Mwanga's offended vanity, and persuaded him to make an edict for the arrest of all Baganda found in the service of foreigners, whether white men or Arabs.

Unaware of the edict and of the danger to his boys, Mackay set off for the Lake-shore on 30 January, accompanied by Ashe and five boys, who intended to see him off and then return. The whole party was intercepted by soldiers under the command of Sabaddu and taken back in custody to the capital. There, after a stormy scene with the Chancellor, the two missionaries were permitted to return to their mission station, but the boys were detained on a charge of having attempted to leave the country. Another mission-boy, Seruwanga, who had disregarded a warning to flee, was arrested that night near the mission, and a woman named Sarah Nalwanga, the widow of another Protestant, Philip Mukasa, who had died of smallpox, was also arrested with her child for teaching Christianity to some of the Princesses.

A judicious present of cloth by the missionaries only partly appeased the Kabaka and secured the release of Mackay's personal boy. The others were taken next morning to Mpima-erebera, one of the thirteen official execution-sites, near the River Mayanja. Here, at the last moment, the two youngest boys were reprieved, and Sarah and her child set aside to be returned to prison. The other three boys, Mark Kakumba aged fifteen to sixteen, Joseph Lugalama aged eleven to twelve, and the older boy Noah Seruwanga, had their arms cut off and then, still alive, were bound to a low scaffolding under which a fire was lighted, and slowly burnt to death. The two younger lads pleaded for mercy, Kakumba appealing to the Commander who, as a Muslim, believed in Allah the All-Merciful, and Lugalama begging to be thrown into the fire without having his arms cut off. The oldest, Seruwanga, bore his torture in silence.

A witness of this horrible execution was another Protestant, Freddy Wigram Kidza, a guide in the service of Sabaddu. As they stood watching the holocaust, his chief said to him, 'Ah, are you here? I will burn you too and your household. I know that you are a follower of Jesus.' 'Yes, I am,' was the bold reply, 'and I am not ashamed of it.' The Commander did not follow up his threat but, seventeen months later, Freddy Kidza was to die in the still greater holocaust at Namugongo.

It is not surprising to find Mackay writing in his diary on this tragic day, 'Our hearts are breaking'. The previous evening, on his return to the mission, he had written, 'then we all three joined in pouring out our hearts in prayer to Our Heavenly Father, commending ourselves to His almighty protection and asking guidance. . . .' Elsewhere Mackay wrote, 'It was not a case of religious persecution pure and simple. It was a burst of fury against the Englishmen and any who consorted with them.'

Although Mackay is not incorrect, this statement over-simplifies the reasons for the massacre. The principal instigator, the chancellor Mukasa, was certainly moved by hatred of Christianity, and the Editor of the *Intelligencer* is quite justified in adding, 'The fact that the lads were taunted with their faith in the Lord Jesus Christ and died singing his praises may justly claim for them the right to a place in the noble army of martyrs. . . .' Ashe says that Lugalama 'was really condemned because his master had given him to us and not to the King or Katikiro'. Lugalama was a very handsome young Muhima boy, captured in a raid on Ankole by Sebwato, who subsequently gave the boy to the missionaries. When the Chancellor saw the youth, he wanted him, probably for his master who was already addicted to homosexuality. Ashe says, 'When we said he had been given to us by Sebwato, the Katikiro seemed displeased and vexed, but let the matter drop. At the time, we suspected nothing but we discovered afterwards that the chief was annoyed that we should receive gifts of boys as if we were chiefs, forsooth !'

On their way to execution the lads were taunted only with their belief in Jesus Christ; 'And so,' says Ashe, 'the three boys were led away to death, a mocking crowd following them. "Oh, you know Isa Masiya (Jesus Christ)," said Mujasi (the Commander), "You know how to read. You believe you will rise from the dead? Well, I shall burn you and see if it be so." . . . But the young Christians, as some reported, answered boldy and faithfully.' Seruwanga, a daring fellow, answered the taunts by breaking into the hymn, 'Daily, daily sing the praises', in which the others seem to have joined. The report that they sang in the actual flames seems to have been incorrect.

James Miti explains that the woman Sarah Nalwanga, whom he calls Sara Kitakule and her son Serunjogi, was at first condemned to the same death, but then spared because she was discovered to be a relative of the Kabaka. 'Kabaka Mwanga pardoned Lady Sarah and ordered that she should be punished only by being made to attend the burning of her fellow converts.' Apparently, however, she did not at once receive a full pardon because, a week after the death of the boys, Mackay wrote :

The king sent for his revolver. Mukasa, a confidential servant, came for it. He was once one of our pupils, but afterwards fell into the hands of the Roman Catholics. Let me confess honestly the reason why he and many of our best pupils were laid hold of by these Papists. Simply because we were unable to undertake the teaching of them all. We have ever had to grieve over the fact that the fewness of our numbers most seriously damages the work, for daily more Baganda are eager to learn than we are able to teach. But Mukasa is evidently a better Catholic than Romanist, for he not only said to-day he daily prayed God to deliver us from the hands of wicked men, but we heard from others that he had interceded for us to the king, telling him that the prime minister was seeking to kill us. . . .

We had asked Mukasa to represent to the king our unpleasant position, practically that of prisoners, the captain of the guard having stationed his spies close to our gate. . . . We had also asked him to petition the king for poor Sarah and her child, the captain wanted to burn both mother and child alive. The king, however, had ordered her to be saved, as he wanted to put her in his harem. The poor woman, though ill, was kept in the stocks. On Mukasa's representation the king had her brought before him, but instead of keeping her, sent her back to us, at the same time sending to the prime minister asking him to have the captain's men removed from our gate. The messenger came with the woman, and also a man with orders to withdraw the sentry. We felt devoutly thankful to our Heavenly Father that at last this storm had blown over; but our aching nerves had again to brace themselves to encounter another storm.

This testimony to the charity shown by Joseph Mukasa towards those of a rival religion and to his courage in approaching the Kabaka on their behalf, is the more valuable in that it comes from one who detested Catholicism so much that he was unable to refrain from displaying that animosity even in a tribute to the Catholic leader.[1]

The new storm mentioned by Mackay was a plot, organized by the staunch pagans, to kill Kabaka Mwanga and place his brother Kalema on the throne. The recent outbreak of violence against a few Christians had been too half-hearted to satisfy those who wanted the complete eradication of both Christianity and Islam and realized that Mwanga, though prevented by the strictness of its moral code from accepting Christianity, had broken with the past and was indeed liable, at any time, to decide in favour of one of the new religions and give it freedom to spread throughout his dominions.

Without a miracle of grace,—and with grace he lacked the moral fibre to co-operate—it was impossible for Mwanga to surmount the obstacles of heredity, tradition, background and upbringing. His grandfather, Suna, had had twenty thousand women (surely a world record), his father more than a thousand. He was surrounded by polygamy and promiscuity and had been taught other vices by his boyhood companions. He had never been subjected to strict discipline or taught self-control. Nevertheless, he had the intellectual ability to see where the truth lay, and the opportunity of knowing it. His unhappy career would seem to have been the result of the constant conflict between mind and will, a conflict that led him into destroying his greatest and most trusted friends.

Mwanga had nothing but contempt for the old pagan rites and, unused to hiding his feelings, displayed this openly. Only reluctantly had he agreed to go through the superstitious ceremonial attached to his enthronement and, soon after his accession, seems to have gone so far as to order his pages to beat and drive off one of the mediums of the tribal gods, who was sounding his drum near the palace. Ashe reports that one of the Christians gleefully described this incident to him, and his own reaction to the news. 'I pointed out to this young enthusiast that persecution was wrong, and what happened to the followers of the tribal gods to-day might happen to the followers of Jesus to-morrow.' An African witness in the Process of Beatification also describes what must have been the same occurrence, but

76

seems to suggest that it was Joseph Mukasa, on his own initiative, that sent the pages to drive the witch-doctor off. He says:

> A man named Balabandaga, whose business it was to make incantations to Namalere the servant of the other gods, arrived early one morning in the royal square at Mengo and began to beat his little drum. When Joseph heard him, he sent some of the Christian pages to go and beat him. They did so and, snatching from him the sack in which were the things of Satan, they tore it open and scattered the contents. There were amulets, some made of small chips of wood, others of bigger blocks, others again of horn.

It seems most unlikely that Joseph Mukasa would have given such an order unless directly commanded to do so by the Kabaka,[1] whose personal attendant he was. Apart from his own kindness and Christian charity, to which the testimony is unanimous, he was too astute a man to take a step so calculated to arouse hatred for his religion and for himself.

This attitude of the Kabaka towards the traditional religion of Buganda greatly disturbed the older pagan chiefs who wanted no change in the social structure of the country. Mwanga's momentary hostility to the English mission did not allay their fears, because he made no secret of his intention to recall the French missionaries and even hinted that, on their return, he would declare himself in the matter of religion. To none was the situation more galling than to the Chancellor, Mukasa, who despised all foreigners including the Arabs, and wanted nothing from them but guns and powder. It enraged him to hear the youth he had just placed on the throne declare that God, touched by the prayers of the Christians, had raised him to the royal dignity; to hear him recite the Our Father in the presence of the Court and to hear him talk of recalling the French priests. Even more disturbing to the Chancellor was the friendship between the Kabaka and Andrew Kaggwa, and the growing influence of Joseph Mukasa, which he regarded as a threat to his own position and even to his security.

Finding that the chiefs of the old regime shared his apprehensions, he decided to rectify the mistake he had made barely three months before, and remove from the throne the wayward and wilful monarch who would not accept his advice. Knowing well the traditional loyalty of the people to their Kabaka, the conspirators decided that he must be killed before the country would accept his brother Kalema in his place.

The coup was planned for 22 February 1885, when the Kabaka and Court were due to attend further funeral rites at the newly constructed tomb of the late ruler, Mutesa. Fortunately, a warning of the plot reached Mwanga through the Queen Mother and he absented himself from the ceremony. It was the Christians who unearthed the plot, and Joseph Mukasa who passed on the warning to the royal family; at the same time assuring the Kabaka of the loyalty of his Catholic subjects and their dependants.

On 25 February, the Kabaka acted. He sent for his Chancellor and told him that he knew everything. The accused began to weep like a child and protested his fidelity, playing his part so well that not only did Mwanga pardon him, but entrusted him with the task of deposing and disgracing his fellow conspirators. This probably accounts for the unusual clemency displayed on this occasion. Apart from Kiyega, who is said to have been killed by Mwanga's Muslim friend Lutaya, no one suffered the death penalty, although some seventeen chiefs were deposed. The Chancellor even succeeded in shielding his creature, Sabaddu, the commander who had undertaken to assassinate the Kabaka, and whom Mwanga wished to put to death.

The new appointments made by the Kabaka after this abortive rebellion left the Chancellor and his followers in no doubt as to who had been responsible for its failure. Several Catholics and a number of Protestants were promoted to positions of trust, and the Kabaka hinted that Joseph Mukasa would be his next Chancellor and Andrew Kaggwa his next Commander-in-Chief. The Catholics, on their part, took advantage of Mwanga's good-will towards them and reminded him of his promise to recall the Catholic missionaries.

The White Fathers themselves, having heard of Mwanga's accession, were actually preparing to return. Père Lourdel, who had been stationed at Tabora, returned to Kamoga in readiness for the start, but the recall to Europe of Père Livinhac for his episcopal consecration had left them short of priests. Père Girault, the superior of Kamoga, wrote to Mwanga congratulating him on his accession and explaining that he was as yet unable to send any priests to Buganda. On receipt of this letter, the Kabaka, ignoring its contents, acted with his usual precipitancy and at once ordered a fleet of twenty canoes to go and fetch the Fathers.

The canoes, manned by three hundred rowers under the command of Toli, Adolphus Nantinda and Sematimba, arrived back at Entebbe on 13 July 1885, after a prosperous voyage of only eighteen days. On board were Fathers Lourdel and Giraud (a new missionary, not to be confused with Père Girault) and Brother Amans. At Dumo, one of the halting places on the lake-shore, Père Lourdel had already been able to gather information about the actual state of affairs in Buganda. There, to their mutual delight, he met Jean-Marie Fuwuke, a young soldier who had been baptized in the group of 15 May 1880, and who was then collecting the royal taxes in those parts. From him, Père Lourdel received the following account of Mwanga's attitude :

> Mwanga is well disposed towards you; he will leave you, I think, full liberty to instruct; but, for himself, he will have difficulty in practising the Christian religion. When he feels well, he does not think of praying; but when he is indisposed, he becomes devout. Unfortunately, he smokes hemp, a habit which in course of time will dull his wits. Several neophytes have great influence over him, and help him by their advice. They are his personal servants and are always with him.

The returning missionaries received a magnificent reception. After about an hour's march from Entebbe, their party was met by a considerable crowd preceded by the royal ensign. Behind it, under a canopy, marched one of the Christians, a favourite of the Kabaka. The two parties greeted each other amid the report of fireworks and the ceremonial firing of rifles. This deputation may have been sent at the request of Andrew Kaggwa, for Père Lourdel tells how Andrew, on hearing of the arrival of the priests, hastened to show his joy by sending a deputation to greet them and to offer presents of a goat and supplies of plantains and bark-cloth.

That night the party halted in a halfway village, and on the following day made its way to Mengo. Catechumens came out to welcome them, and the Kabaka sent a messenger to bid them welcome and invite them to an audience.

Whenever a guest of importance from afar was to appear before the Kabaka of Buganda, it was customary for him to send, from early morning, relays of pages to greet the visitor and report back on his progress. So it was on this occasion. From the moment the priests arrived at the Kabaka's road, pages bringing greetings from His Majesty followed one another every two or three minutes. The boys arrived breathless, their faces bright with excitement as they bowed to the visitors and delivered their message : 'The Kabaka sends me to greet you : Come!' Then, dashing back to their master, they would exclaim, 'I have seen the visitors; I have seen them! They greet you! They are at such or such a place!' This coming and going continued until the moment of reception. On this occasion, Joseph Mukasa, the Majordomo, would doubtless have seen to it that each of his catechumen pages got his chance to welcome the priests. Kindly Père Lourdel would pat their curly heads and ask their names, for most of them were still strangers to him. Little did he think then that within a year, again on his way to the royal audience hall, he would meet some of these same swift runners, bound and marching to martyrdom.

Arriving on Mengo Hill, Père Lourdel saw more familiar faces. Almost speechless with joy, old friends clasped the hands of the priests. There was no end of greetings and, as they passed slowly through the throng, joyful applause and happy smiles welcomed them.

The missionaries were led at once to the great audience hall where Kabaka Mwanga awaited them, reclining on his couch as his father, whom he liked to imitate, had been used to do. He received them graciously and seemed genuinely happy about their return to Buganda. He repeated, in a joyful tone, the cry of his subjects, 'The priests have arrived!', and he made Père Lourdel promise never again to leave Buganda. The modest present that they brought was graciously accepted, and in return the Kabaka granted them a plot of land at Nalukolongo, on the southern slope of Rubaga Hill. The missionaries had asked for this property because it was near the high-road and at the same time only twenty minutes' walk from the royal enclosure. The Kabaka also promised to build a house on the estate and an enclosure.

Chapter Seven

MWANGA'S NEW PAGES

The enthusiastic reception given to the Catholic missionaries on their return to Buganda encouraged them to hope that they would now be allowed to continue without let or hindrance the work begun six years earlier. Before long, however, the grim truth became apparent that the Buganda to which they had returned with such high hopes was in a much more troubled state than the Buganda they had left some three years before. Almost from the moment of their return events moved rapidly towards the climax of the Namugongo holocaust.

A few days after his arrival, Père Lourdel wrote to Cardinal Lavigerie describing what he thought to be the situation. Mwanga, he said, had rejected superstition and witch-doctors and had refused to send the traditional presents to the shrines of the tribal gods. A proposal to adopt Islam as the state religion had been coldly received, and complete liberty to teach their religion had been given to the Catholics. Lourdel went on to report that, as far as he could ascertain, the number of catechumens exceeded eight hundred; that no more than five or six had gone over to the Protestants; and that there were now villages in Buganda with fifty, sixty or even a hundred adorers of the true God. Crowds of catechumens, he said, had come to see the priests and their joy at seeing them back in the country was indescribable. 'It is now one thousand and fifty-one days since you left,' one of them had said. 'How long the time appeared! We began to despair of ever seeing you back. All the same we continued to instruct our brethren and our children, and consoled ourselves with the thought that priests returning to Buganda after our deaths would at least find their teaching alive in many hearts.'

Although this young man, Matthew Kirevu, was out in his reckoning—the priests were away only nine hundred and eighty-one days—his words do reflect the spirit that inspired these early followers of Christ in Buganda.

That the joy at the priests' return was not shared by all is indicated in the concluding passage of Lourdel's letter to his Superior General. He wrote:

Some chiefs are hostile to us, especially the Chancellor. Before our return he had demanded the death of the white men, or at least of those who followed their instructions. Three men who frequented the English mission were seized by his orders and burnt alive. Our return has angered him. It was only after I had presented myself three times at his enclosure that he consented to receive me. He has not even thanked me for the present which I sent. Seeing, however that we are highly in favour with Mwanga, he has resigned himself to appearing less sulky. Yesterday he sent us a bullock in order to show that, at least for the present, he did not want to declare himself our enemy.

Although Lourdel was in general optimistic, he was not, as his letter shows, entirely at ease. The English missionaries were even less so. Earlier in the year they had experienced one outburst of active hostility and there were indications that another might be expected. One of their converts had recently been beaten and deprived of his chieftainship by the Chancellor, and there were rumours of further repressive measures to be taken against the Christians.

At the end of August, Kabaka Mwanga decided upon a royal progress through part of his kingdom and commanded Mackay and Lourdel to accompany him, the other missionaries, both Catholic and Protestant, being left at home. The royal party, which visited some of the Lake islands and the counties of Ssingo, Bulemezi and Mawokota, was away for a month. Joseph Mukasa did not accompany his master, and must have welcomed with relief this respite from the difficult and dangerous task that he had set himself, that of shielding and protecting the young pages in his charge from the solicitations of their royal master.

To gloss over the unpleasant vice to which Mwanga was addicted would be to disregard the decisive factor in the story of the persecution. True enough, there was in Buganda sufficient hatred of Christianity and all that it stood for to produce an outbreak of persecution at any time, but this hatred could never have had free rein without the consent of the Kabaka. As Mwanga was himself attracted towards Christianity, it seems unlikely that he would ever have given this consent had it not been for the constant thwarting of his unnatural passion by the Christian pages.

There can be no doubt that Mwanga turned against the adherents of the faith to which he was naturally attracted mainly because of the firm resistance offered by these young Christian pages who, according to Kiganda tradition, should have had no desire but to obey their Kabaka's slightest wish. Many of those asked to give evidence about the lives of the martyrs make this clear in their testimony. Andrew Kiwanuka, for instance, says :

At that time the Kabaka practised the works of Sodom. Muslims and pagans were prepared to do those things with him, but the Catholics absolutely refused. For that reason the Kabaka began to detest us, and deliberated with the pagans and Muslims about putting us to death, us the Catholics. With my own ears I heard him utter words of anger because the young Catholics refused to sin. I, for one, was often importuned by him, but refused. ...

The same witness says much more in a similar vein, and Denis Kamyuka repeats and corroborates his statements, paying, at the same time, a special tribute to Joseph Mukasa, whose presence alone, he says, was enough to silence the lewd talk of Mwanga and his boon companions.

Joseph did all in his power to guide and protect his charges in these difficult circumstances. He zealously instructed them in the faith, told them that they should always obey God rather than man, and urged them never, even though it cost them their lives, to give in to the evil demands of the Kabaka and his vicious companions. He even attempted, with considerable success, to spare them the importunities of their royal master. Whenever Mwanga sent for one of the younger and more handsome pages, under circumstances that appeared to him suspicious, he would send the lad scampering off to Andrew Kaggwa or to Matthew Kisule for a catechism lesson and then report to the Kabaka that the lad was absent. At other times he would countermand orders, intercept messages or sidetrack those who brought them. Also, taking his life in his hands, he would attempt to persuade Mwanga to give up his evil ways. 'O my Master,' he would plead, 'I beg and implore you, do not act like that, because God detests uncleanness. Leave my Christians alone, and rather leave to the Muslims the vileness with which Satan inspires them.'

It is not surprising that the affection and esteem in which Mwanga had held his loyal servant began to give place to anger and irritation against the man whose very presence was a reproach to one enslaved by vice.

The new pages who were recruited upon Mwanga's accession to the throne quickly succumbed to the influence of Joseph's personality and charm. They became just as devoted to him as those who had served with him under Kabaka Mutesa. Joseph, on his part, was not slow in turning to the benefit of religion the influence he acquired over them. He organized catechism classes to be given by Christians at Court, or by more advanced catechumens. Among these he found an able lieutenant in Charles Lwanga, whose arrival at Court more then adequately filled the gap in the Christian ranks left by the departure of Jean-Marie Muzeyi.

Most of the religion classes were held in the great audience hall, of which Charles Lwanga was in charge. Only occasionally, and then late at night when the Kabaka was sleeping soundly, was Joseph himself able to leave the vicinity of the royal dwelling and teach those gathered in the audience hall. His coming was always hailed with delight, for no one taught as well as he did. He was not only clever at argument, as the Protestant missionary Ashe, who had crossed swords with him, admits, but he was able to illustrate his teaching from the life and passion of Christ, from the parables, and from the history of the early Church as he had read it with Mackay in the Acts of the Apostles. At other times, when he had to remain within earshot of the Kabaka, Joseph gathered together some of the pages who served in the private part of the royal enclosure and taught them in the hut which Mwanga had built for him close to the royal dwelling-house.

There were nine future martyrs amongst the new pages. Of these Charles Lwanga has already been introduced to the reader. Serving under his command in the court of the audience hall were Achilles Kiwanuka and Ambrose Kibuka of the Scaly Ant-eater or Pangolin Clan, Gyavira Musoke and Mbaga Tuzinde of the Lungfish Clan, and Mukasa Kiriwawanvu of the Sheep Clan. Three others, Mugagga of the Leopard Clan, Kizito of the Lungfish Clan, and Denis Ssebuggwawo of the Cane-rat Clan, were employed in the private part of the enclosure.

Kiwanuka and Kibuka might be called the Boanerges, the sons-of-thunder, amongst the martyrs. Like the Apostles, James and John, they seem to be always linked together; they were brothers, in the Kiganda sense of the word, and their names were the names of tribal gods, Kiwanuka, the god of thunder, and Kibuka, the war-god who was shot down out of a cloud by the Banyoro. Although known as brothers, being of the same clan, the two were, in fact, only distantly related through a common ancestor, Kasoma, who was Kibuka's great-great-grandfather, and two generations further removed from Kiwanuka. Both belonged to the Scaly Ant-eater (Lugave) Clan, and they were of approximately the same age, Kiwanuka being seventeen and Kibuka eighteen at the time of their death at Namugongo.

Kiwanuka's father, Kyazze, the son of a former Chancellor, held a post under the chief of Ssingo County, and it was at Lulagala in that county that the martyr was born. His mother was Nassaza Talidda of the Civet-cat (Fumbe) Clan. As he grew up, Kiwanuka first entered the service of the county chief, but later became a dependant of Sabakaki, the man who presented him at Court on the accession of Mwanga.

Ambrose Kibuka Katikamu was also born in Ssingo County, at Butuzzaliso (Bunyiga). His mother was Ampera, and his father, Kisule, was a former official drum-beater to the Kabaka. Kibuka's birth must have been hailed with great joy, because he was the first male child to survive. His father, who was advanced in years and had no less than thirty daughters, had almost given up hope of a son and heir.

Kiwanuka and Kibuka entered the royal service at about the same time, together with a fellow clansman named Lubinga, and were posted to the court of the great audience hall. It was Lubinga who persuaded them to burn the amulets with which their parents had provided them and to place themselves under instruction in the Catholic faith. The old Kyazze, Kiwanuka's father, was very upset when the three friends paid him a visit and on enquiring about their amulets learned that they had abandoned their pagan beliefs. He determined to prevent his son and kinsmen from returning to the surroundings in which they had acquired such subversive ideas. The three lads, however, equally determined to continue with their instructions in their new-found faith, escaped his vigilance and returned to Court.

After the martyrdom of Joseph Mukasa, when it seemed likely that they too might, at any moment, be called upon to lay down their lives for their religion, Kiwanuka and Kibuka, together with other pages, stole by night to the Catholic mission to ask for immediate baptism. They were baptized by Père Lourdel on the night of 16 November 1885, receiving the names Achilles and Ambrose respectively. After his baptism, Ambrose Kibuka, quite convinced that the martyr's crown would soon be his, begged leave of absence and went to bid farewell to his parents. He firmly resisted all their entreaties to abandon the religion that placed him in such peril, and returned to his post to await his fate.

Gyavira, another of the pages under Charles Lwanga's command, received this name from his companions only when he came to Court. His proper clan name was Musoke. The name Gyavira, which means the-place-he-comes-from-is-feared-by-all, referred to his place of origin, Segguku (now known as Kittante), about eight miles along the Kampala-Entebbe road. Gyavira's father Semalago, a much married man with fifty wives, had been guardian of the royal children during the reign of Kabaka Suna. Mutesa had appointed him guardian of the important shrine of the god Mayanja at Segguku, near to which was Nakinziru, one of the official execution sites where, in Mwanga's time, the executioner Sebatta usually officiated. The martyr Gyavira Musoke was born and brought up at Segguku, but which of the fifty women was his mother is not known.

85

At Court, Gyavira soon became attracted to the Catholic religion, to which so many of his companions in the court of the audience hall belonged, and became a fervent catechumen under the guidance of Charles Lwanga and Joseph Mukasa. Being small for his age, about fifteen, of slight build, dark colouring and handsome features, he soon attracted the unwelcome attentions of Kabaka Mwanga. However, encouraged by the words and example of so many of his companions, Gyavira remained firm and, with a courage remarkable in one so young, persistently rejected the shameful proposals of his lord and master. When he was burnt alive at Namugongo, on 3 June 1886, Gyavira was no more than seventeen years of age.

Mbaga Tuzinde, a youth of about seventeen to eighteen at the time of his martyrdom, was known as the son of Mukajanga, the chief executioner, in whose household he was brought up and who presented him at Court. According to European ideas, Tuzinde and Mukajanga were not related in any way, but in Baganda eyes, strange as it may seem, Tuzinde was at the same time both son and father to the old man.

Although they belonged to different clans, Tuzinde to the Lungfish and Mukajanga to the Colubus-monkey Clan, their grandfathers, Kikonyogo and Salasamba respectively, had been very close friends and had made a blood-pact together. This, according to Kiganda custom, made them brothers, and also established relationship between the other members of their respective families. Thus Mukajanga and Tuzinde were blood relations (in the Kiganda and not in the European sense) and Mukajanga, because he was much older and had been entrusted with the task of bringing up the lad, was known as the father of Tuzinde. An additional relationship arose when Kikonyogo, Tuzinde's grandfather, died. Tuzinde succeeded him as head of the family and, because Mukajanga was a member of it through the blood-pact already mentioned, he became in this way the father of the old man as well as his son. This latter development created, in its turn, an additional complication in that Mukajanga's wives, having become the young man's daughters-in-law, were, by Kiganda custom, debarred from ever staying under the same roof with him.

Mbaga Tuzinde was born at Bunyonga in Busiro County. His real parents were Katamiza Waggumbulizi of the Lungfish (Mamba) Clan, who had ten wives, and Mmumanvi Bukuwa of the Yamfruit (Kkobe) Clan.[1] His clan name was Tuzinde; the name Mbaga being, in fact, a nickname which he acquired from his work at the Court. One of his duties there was to distribute the food which the Kabaka provided for his many dependants. When the meal contained no meat, a great luxury, his companions used teasingly to ask,

'What! No meat to-day?' to which his invariable reply was, 'Mbaga' (Am I the butcher?). Another of Tuzinde's duties was to carry the royal standard in the Kabaka's canoe when His Majesty went sailing or travelling on the Lake.

Mbaga Tuzinde was of medium height and well-built, chestnut brown in colour, very kind-hearted, obedient and truthful, and also good at sports. His features were somewhat marred by smallpox contracted during the 1884 epidemic. He began his instructions in the Catholic faith when he became a page at the accession of Mwanga and was still a catechumen when the persecution broke out in May 1886. He was baptized by Charles Lwanga on the morning that the pages were arrested.

Of all the martyrs, Mbaga Tuzinde had most to contend with in the way of temptations to save his life by renouncing his religion. During the week which the martyrs spent at Namugongo awaiting execution, he was separated from his companions and, deprived of their moral support, but not of their prayers for his perseverance, had to face alone the prayers, tears and entreaties of his many relatives, begging and imploring him not to throw away his young life. From this ordeal, which might well have broken the resolution of a mature man, this youth of no more than eighteen emerged with courage and purpose unshaken. With complete confidence in the words of Christ, 'He that shall lose his life for my sake shall save it', he went to his death cheerfully and manfully.

Another of the future martyrs attached to the court of the audience hall was Mukasa Kiriwawanvu, the son of Lumanyika of the Sheep (Ndiga) clan, who held, successively, a number of sub-chieftainships in various parts of the kingdom. It seems probable that Lumanyika also began his career as a page at Court, and he must in his youth have been a notable athlete, since he managed to defeat Kabaka Mutesa, no mean opponent, in a friendly wrestling bout. In recognition of his prowess, the Kabaka gave him a Musoga slave-girl called Maleokuvawo, who was the first of his wives and bore him five children. The fourth child was the martyr Mukasa Kiriwawanvu.

The youth was born, between 1861 and 1866, at Nakasawula in Kyaggwe County at a time when his father was assistant to the chief, Serumbe. Taking after his father, he grew up tall and powerful, long of limb and dark coloured, and was presented at Court by Kawulukisi, a village chief in Ssingo County, to whom Lumanyika was at the time attached as an assistant.

One of Kiriwawanvu's tasks at Court was to help in the serving of food to the Kabaka's guests, of whom there were often large numbers. Only the most important personages were invited to dine with the Kabaka himself, but hospitality was liberal and food was provided for all those who were waiting for an audience. The young man must often have served Lourdel and the other missionaries when they came to visit the Kabaka and accepted his hospitality. The meal on these occasions consisted of the golden-yellow matoke (plantains wrapped in the leaves of the plant and steamed), beef or goat meat, salt and plantain wine.

Mukasa Kiriwawanvu, the only one of the twenty-two beatified martyrs to die without the baptism of water, was a fervent catechumen but when at the height of the crisis Charles Lwanga baptized the other catechumens, he was already in prison for striking his fellow-page Gyavira. He was between twenty and twenty-five years of age when he died at Namugongo.

The three remaining martyrs amongst the new pages, Mugagga, Kizito and Ssebuggwawo, also entered the service of the Kabaka when Mwanga came to the throne but were employed in the private quarters of the enclosure and were therefore not under Charles Lwanga.

Mugagga, or Mugagga Lubowa, to give him his full name, one of the pages persistently solicited by Mwanga without success, belonged to the Leopard (Ngo) Clan. His father, Mazinga, who later became a Protestant and took the name Isaiah, had three wives. The first, Tigalya, was a great-aunt of Seddu Kakinda, the royal bark-cloth maker. The second wife, Nassubwa, was the mother of the martyr and of four other children. Mazinga, because of the relationship by marriage, through his first wife, received patronage and assistance from Seddu Kakinda who was also head of the Yam-fruit (Kkobe) Clan. Kakinda established Mazinga and his family upon one of his estates at Jjalambwa, in Mawokota County, where Mugagga was born about the year 1870. His name, which means rich or wealthy, was given to him by his mother in the hope that fortune would look kindly upon him.

Following the common Kiganda practice, Mugagga was sent, as a young boy, to the household of Seddu Kakinda, who brought him up as his own child and presented him at Court when Mwanga became Kabaka. Some witnesses suggest that Mugagga worked in the court of the audience hall, but Desiré Wamala asserts positively that he was attached to the private section of the enclosure. This seems to be confirmed by the fact that he was unable to receive any religious instruction by day, and could go to Charles Lwanga at night only. He was thus not publicly known as a Christian, and when, on the fateful morning of 26 May 1886, he ranged himself with Charles and the other Christians, the Chancellor himself tried to save him by stating that Mugagga was not a Christian. The sixteen year old boy would not accept the chance of escape thus offered to him. He had bravely resisted the shameful demands of the Kabaka during his catechumenate and now, fortified by the grace of baptism, received that morning at the hands of Charles Lwanga, was eager to die for his faith.

Although Mugagga's father became a Protestant, most of his family, including his mother who received baptism and the last sacraments when mortally ill, embraced the faith for which he laid down his life. His adopted father, Seddu Kakinda, also eventually became a Catholic, although at the time of the persecution he was so horrified at the fate of his adopted son that he drove from his home his daughter, Namirembe (later Sister Pelagia), because of her adherence to that religion.

The youngest of the martyrs, Kizito, was born at Waluleta (formerly Bukkanga) near Bbowa in the county of Bulemezi. As in the case of so many of the martyrs, there has been some confusion about his parentage and ancestry, owing to the ambiguity of the Luganda terms of relationship.

Kizito's real father was Lukomera of the Lungfish (Mamba) Clan, and his mother, who bore Lukomera nine children before she deserted him and died, still a pagan, at the age of forty, was Wangabira of the Civet-cat (Fumbe) Clan. Nyika, or Nyika-omuyonga, Guardian of Mwanga's umbilical cord, often said to be the father of Kizito, was his father by adoption only. The relationship arose from a blood-pact between Nyika's father Kiggwe and a member of the Lungfish Clan named Mitala-ekoya. Kiggwe, a descendent of Kabaka Kateregga and a member of the Leopard Clan, was county chief of Gomba when he made this alliance. Later he incurred the royal displeasure, was deprived of his office and possessions and became, because out of favour with the Kabaka, virtually an outlaw. In this time of adversity, the blood-pact stood him in good stead. Because of it, the Lungfish Clan gave him and his family asylum and aid, and Mitala-ekoya became a second father to his son Nyika.

During Mutesa's reign, Nyika managed to restore the family fortunes and rose to the position of Kangawo, county chief of Bulemezi, a position which he held when Speke, who refers to him as 'Congow', visited Buganda. As county chief, Nyika was able to show his gratitude to the members of the Lungfish Clan for their timely succour and assistance. Amongst the appointments he made was that of Kizito's father, Lukomera, to a chieftainship in the county.

Then, in 1874, Nyika in his turn lost the royal favour. He was deposed, stripped of all his property and left destitute, until the Kabaka relented sufficiently to give him the small chieftainship of

Kajongolo. It seems to have been about this time that Nyika decided to adopt one of the sons of Lukomera, who had shared in his downfall. He asked for Nsubuga (later baptized Michael) but Lukomera persuaded him to take Kizito instead.

The young Kizito's future seemed assured when first, Kabaka Mutesa restored to his adopted father the title of Namutwe, and then Mwanga, on his accession, appointed him Guardian of the Cord, a post second in importance to that of Chancellor. With a patron of such importance, the youth could expect rapid advancement and the first step towards this was taken when Kizito became a royal page. Although his prospects seemed rosy, even the most sanguine could not have foreseen that this young lad would achieve immortal fame within the short space of two years.

As a page, Kizito was attached to the group which served in the private quarters of the enclosure and not, as previously thought, to that under Charles Lwanga in the court of the audience hall. It is likely that he had become interested in the Catholic religion before entering the royal service, because Nyika, although too much attached to pagan ways and to his numerous women to become a Christian himself, was very well disposed towards the Catholic Fathers and placed no obstacle in the way of any member of his household who wished to follow their religion. Among those of his family to do so were Jean-Marie Fuwuke and Paul Nalubandwa.

Fuwuke, an adopted son, was actually a great-grandson of Mitala-ekoya, the man who had made the blood-pact with Nyika's father. He was one of the earliest Christians, being baptized on 15 May 1880.

Nalubandwa, Nyika's real son, had the distinction of being the first Muganda to place himself under instruction and was one of the first four baptized, on 27 March 1880. It was Nalubandwa who led the party of neophytes and catechumens to Kamoga in Tanganyika during the absence of the missionaries from Buganda. In 1884 he accompanied Père Livinhac, then Bishop-designate, to the coast and lost his life on the return journey. An attack of dysentry had so weakened him that he broke down during the crossing of the Mgunda-Makali desert. He insisted on his companions leaving him to die alone instead of endangering their own lives in trying to save his. After bidding farewell to the others, he bravely waited until hunger, thirst or some wild animal put an end to his sufferings.

The youthful Kizito, continuing the family tradition, became an eager and fervent catechumen, seizing every opportunity for instruction and, after the martyrdom of Joseph Mukasa, constantly importuning the priests to baptize him. He seems to have been employed largely as the Kabaka's errand boy. It was he who was sent to the Lake to order the canoes for Mwanga on the fateful day, 25 May 1886. He also used to be sent to collect, drive to the Palace and deliver to the royal butchers the cattle selected for slaughter for the royal table. Being young, cheerful and good-looking, he was also one of the objects of the Kabaka's unnatural lust. However, in this child of about thirteen the tyrant encountered a resolution and resistance to his gross passion that put him to shame. Members of his clan suggest that Kizito was about sixteen when presented at Court, but the general opinion of those who knew him is that he was no more than fifteen, at the most, at the time of his death at Namugongo. Nevertheless, despite his youth and his small size, he was sufficiently mature to understand the evils that surrounded him at Court and to understand and love the virtue of chastity.

It seems strange that with a patron so highly placed at Court Kizito should not have been spared the supreme sacrifice. Indeed Lukomera, his father, believed that Nyika could have intervened successfully on behalf of his adopted son, and reproached him for not doing so. Probably Nyika, having twice already had bitter experience of the effects of the royal displeasure and of the capriciousness of the royal favour, dared not risk approaching the Kabaka directly. He did, however, plead with Mukajanga, the executioner, to spare his adopted son, probably believing that this intervention would prove effective. In normal circumstances, the wishes of the Guardian of the Cord would certainly have carried great weight, but Mukajanga had even greater fear of the Chancellor and was, moreover, smarting at the disappointment of being unable to save his own adopted son, Mbaga Tuzinde. His words to Kizito, when placing him on the pyre, 'Did you think I would kill my own friends and spare you?' reveal this bitterness very clearly. Not that there had been any plea for mercy from the boy himself who, with his eyes on the martyr's crown so nearly within his grasp, had made no effort to placate the old man but, on the contrary, offended him by various audacious remarks, such as, 'You arch-devil! The fire that burns your tobacco will one day burn you.'

It is gratifying to note that, although Nyika remained and died a pagan, Kizito's own father, Lukomera, was inspired by his son's heroic sacrifice. One day after the end of the persecution, he asked Michael Nsubuga, another son, to which religion Kizito had belonged. Being told, 'the French religion', he urged all the members of his family to become Catholics. He himself became a fervent Catholic and a catechist, converting the whole of the village in which he dwelt. The villagers flocked to listen to his instructions and on Sunday evenings he led them and his family in the recitation of the rosary.

The last of the twenty-two martyrs to be introduced to the reader, and the first to die in the main outbreak of persecution, is Denis Ssebuggwawo of the Cane-rat (Musu) Clan. Members of this clan, to which the Chancellor also belonged, enjoyed a privileged position at Court. They had the right to enter the royal appartments at will, had their own quarters in the private part of the enclosure, and provided the personnel for the Kabaka's bodyguard, his secret police and the custodians of the royal closet. These privileges dated from the time of Kabaka Mawanda, when a member of the clan had saved the life of his mother.

Denis Ssebuggwawo was born at Kigoloba in Bulemezi County, about the year 1870. His mother, Nsonga, was a Musoga who had been carried off as a child by Nkalubo Ssebuggwawo, the martyr's grandfather. When she grew up, Nkalubo gave her to his son Kajansi, who had nine children by her, including three sets of twins. The first child, a boy, died as an infant. He was followed by the first pair of twins, the martyr Denis Ssebuggwawo (Wasswa) and Isaac Kajane (Kato), the names Wasswa and Kato being traditional names in Buganda for male twins. Not long after this event, Nkalubo Ssebuggwawo was put to death by Kabaka Mutesa, and Kajansi, his son, transferred himself and his family to Bunono, in Busiro County, where the family estates were situated. Here the rest of the children were born, and here the young Ssebuggwawo and his twin brother Kajane grew up until, on the accession of Mwanga, they were presented at Court by their fellow clansman, Mukasa the Chancellor, who at the same time gave the Kabaka his own sons Mwafu and Kasamitala.

The four lads, as members of the privileged Musu Clan, were posted to the private section of the royal enclosure, where they came under the immediate command of Joseph Mukasa, the Majordomo. The Chancellor's son, Mwafu, who was a pretty boy, quickly succumbed to the blandishments of his royal master and became Mwanga's favourite plaything. This fact, revealed by Daudi Nyondo, is of considerable significance and is the essential clue for a proper understanding of the events of 25 May 1886.

Ssebuggwawo and his twin brother became, under the guidance of Joseph Mukasa, keen and zealous catechumens and were amongst those instructed by Joseph in his hut, close to the Kabaka's residence. Of Isaac Kajane (Kato), James Miti writes :

> The latter was a great favourite of the Kabaka; he would always stay with his master during the day hours or during the night; in fact he slept by the side of the Kabaka's bed, to be always at hand and within call whenever the Kabaka would require him. He had,

however, been made chief and quitted the palace by the time of the persecution of Christians.

During his period at the palace, Kajane made desperate efforts to convert the Kabaka himself, as is clear from Mwanga's own words, quoted elsewhere,[1] and from Miti's account of his arrest.

The other twin, Ssebuggwawo, showed no less zeal. He proved an apt pupil, eagerly seized upon every opportunity for instruction, and tried to pass on to his companions whatever he had himself learnt. Far from being deterred by the death of his instructor, Joseph Mukasa, Ssebuggwawo prepared to follow him on the road to martyrdom and was amongst the pages who slipped away from Court to the Catholic mission to ask for baptism on the night of the 16 November 1885, the day after Joseph's martyrdom, when he received the name Denis, the great patron of France. Nor did the young neophyte relax in the slightest his efforts to convert his companions : indeed it was his attempt to convert Mwafu, the Chancellor's son and the Kabaka's favourite, to Christianity and a decent way of life that finally fanned Mwanga's smouldering anger against the Christians into the flame that consumed him and many of his companions.

The story of that outburst belongs to a later chapter. It is necessary first to describe some of the events that led up to it, especially the murder of Bishop Hannington and the death of the Catholic protomartyr, Joseph Mukasa.

[1]Ch. 13, p. 151.

Chapter Eight

THE MURDER OF BISHOP HANNINGTON

The letter from Père Lourdel to Cardinal Lavigerie, mentioned in the last chapter, shows that the Fathers, although hopeful, were not free from misgivings about the future. The English missionaries were even less comfortable. Only a month before the return of the White Fathers there had been a strong rumour that Christians were to be arrested, and one Protestant convert, Alexander Kadoko, the nephew of Bruno Serunkuma, had by the Chancellor's order been beaten and deprived of his chieftainship of Nanfumbambi. About the same time, Ashe had had to make four visits to the royal enclosure before he could obtain an audience. In July, therefore, the Protestant missionaries decided to let their Christians elect a Church Council so that, if they themselves had to leave the country, their followers would have an organization of their own.

The month of August passed fairly quietly except for disturbing accounts of numbers of executions ordered by Mwanga for all manner of reasons.

In September, Mackay and Lourdel accompanied the Kabaka on the royal progress already mentioned and before their return to the capital received, in the mail forwarded from the Coast, two alarming items of news. The first was a report of the German decision to occupy the port of Bagamoyo and its hinterland, and the second was the information that the newly-appointed Anglican Bishop, Hannington, intended to make his way to Buganda following Joseph Thomson's route through Masai country and through Kavirondo. The reason for the missionaries' alarm will be understood if it is remembered that the Arabs were always accusing the Europeans of being land-grabbers, and that the Baganda dreaded nothing more than strangers approaching their country through Busoga, which separated them from Kavirondo, there being an old prohecy that one day strangers entering from that direction would conquer Buganda. Kabaka Mutesa had been shrewd enough to reject the Arab charges against the European missionaries, saying, 'Let the white men alone. If they mean to swallow up the country, surely they will not begin at the interior. When I see them beginning to occupy the coast, then I shall believe your words to be true'. Mutesa had also often teased Mackay, saying, 'You white men would like to see the

94

country behind Busoga, wouldn't you? But that I would never allow'. In fact, Mutesa always spoke of Busoga as his back-door. Now not only were Europeans actually occupying the Coast, but Mackay's Bishop was on his way to Buganda through the country behind Busoga. To make matters worse, the man on the throne was no longer the level-headed Mutesa, but the excitable Mwanga, liable to panic and act precipitately.

On receipt of the news, Mackay at first proposed to break it to the Kabaka at once, for fear he might hear it from the Arabs and suspect the missionaries of being implicated in the German plans but, after discussing the matter with Lourdel, he decided not to make the news public until their return to the capital.

After their troubles earlier in the year, the Englishmen had written to the Coast, asking the Bishop and his party not to travel by Thompson's route. Unfortunately, their letter arrived in Zanzibar a fortnight after Hannington had left, and never reached him. He had, indeed, chosen that route against the advice of Thompson himself, but he believed that the Germans, who were stationed astride the usual way through Tanganyika, would obstruct this passage, and had therefore determined to find another route to Lake Victoria. There was one reassuring point in the Bishop's letter to Mackay : he had stated his intention of passing through Kavirondo, south of Busoga, and ordered the mission boat to meet him there in October. If he kept to his plan, he would at least enter Buganda in the usual way, via the Lake.

On 25 September, Mackay and Ashe went to Court with the present that was usually made when the boat arrived from the South. They broached the dangerous topic of the Bishop and the Germans by explaining that their Bishop was on his way to Buganda and had asked for the mission boat to meet him at Kwa Sundu (Mumia's) in Kavirondo : would His Majesty give permission for it to sail? The Bishop's reason for coming that way, they added, was to avoid the Germans who were in Usagara on account of a misunderstanding with the Sultan of Zanzibar. The missionaries did all they could to allay any suspicions that the Kabaka might entertain of their complicity with the German annexations.

As the missionaries had feared, Mwanga and his councillors were perturbed at the news they had received and began to cross-question the two Englishmen.

'Are the Germans white men?'

'Yes, they are.'

'Which are the stronger, the English or the Germans?'

'The Germans, especially by land.'

'Is the Bishop an Englishman?'

95

'Yes.'

'Is he bringing many goods?'

'He will not come empty-handed, but he is a chief not of this world's goods but of religion. He is a great teacher.'

'Is he coming alone?'

'Not likely; he is a great man and does not travel alone; he will have one or two assistants with him.'

At the end of the audience, Mackay asked whether the Kabaka would kindly send a legate with the boat. Mwanga said that he would and gave the missionaries a cow on leaving.

Next morning, Mwanga called a council of his chiefs, all of whom seemed to agree that the white men were all the same, and that the Englishmen were the forerunners of war, who were only waiting for the arrival of their Bishop to begin to seize the country. The chief of Bulemezi, presuming that the great man would have a large following, offered to go and fight him off. Another chief said that when you see running water you may expect more to follow; the only way to stop it was at its source. Applying the metaphor, he asserted that the missionaries were drawing the white men to the country and therefore, to stop the evil, should be killed. There was general agreement that the Bishop should not be allowed to enter the country, especially as he was trying to do so through the back door. The general tone of the meeting was one of panic, mostly genuine but, on the part of the Chancellor, probably feigned in order to further his own ends, the expulsion of the missionaries.

Kulugi, the Treasurer, seems to have been the only one of the chiefs to keep his head. He proposed that the Bishop and his party should be told to proceed first to Musalala, at the South of the Lake. From there, after the strength and dispositions of his party had been ascertained, he could be invited, if the Kabaka so wished, to come to Buganda. This eminently sane suggestion was accepted and the Protestant, Micah Sematimba, who had been nominated as legate, was instructed not to bring the Bishop direct to Buganda, but to convey him to Musalala and then to return to the Kabaka to report.

Two days later, on Monday 28 September, O'Flaherty went to Court to try to get permission to bring the Bishop straight to Buganda. With the aid of a map, he tried to convince the Kabaka that the Bishop's route did not take him anywhere near Busoga. Although Mwanga appeared to agree, he gave no fresh instructions to the legate.

On 1 October, Mackay, also using a map, tried to prove to the Kabaka that the English had nothing whatever to do with the Germans who were annexing some of the coastal areas. 'We have been accused,' he added, 'of wishing to eat[1] the country, but in all the years we have eaten nothing.' At once the cry arose, 'Who told you that we said you meant to eat the country?' Mackay replied that everybody said so, and that he could not understand their reason for alarm. After an animated conversation in whispers between Mwanga, the Chancellor and another chief, the Chancellor assured Mackay that they harboured no suspicions of the missionaries, and that Mackay had been misinformed. Thereupon Mackay again asked to have the Bishop brought direct to Buganda. Kulugi, probably realizing the danger of this insistence on the part of the Englishmen, rose and re-stated his own proposal, and the Chancellor explained to Mackay that Sematimba was to stay with the Bishop at Musalala and send his assistant to report on the party and its goods. Mackay offered to send one of the missionaries with the boat, but Mwanga replied, 'I wish you to stay where you are'.

The eagerness of the Anglican missionaries to spare their Bishop the extra delay and the long detour at the end of his already long and exhausting journey was almost certainly misinterpreted by many of the chiefs, who were unable to believe that the great man's intentions were pacific. Nevertheless, in spite of their suspicions, the tragedy that followed might have been averted if Hannington had not entered Busoga.

The mission boat was sent off that same day to meet the Bishop, and after its departure both missions settled down to the work of instruction of the large numbers that were now flocking to them.

Three uneventful weeks passed and then, on the morning of Sunday, 25 October, a Protestant page, Gideon Entanda, brought news of the arrival of two Englishmen and twenty coast-men at the headquarters of Luba, a great chief in southern Busoga.

Mwanga at once called a meeting of his councillors to discuss the situation. He himself was at first prepared to bring the Bishop and his party to Buganda, but the Chancellor and the Kyambalango, supported by other chiefs, urged him to have the intruders put to death and their goods seized. Instructions were given for a band of armed men to proceed to Busoga, and the councillors and chiefs who were present brandished their spears to signify their agreement with the decision.

Little Kasamitala, one of the Chancellor's sons who had been in attendance on Mwanga during this session, ran to tell his companions amongst the pages that the death of Hannington had been decided upon. No one was more upset at this news than Joseph Mukasa. 'Mutesa expressed a dying wish,' he said to those about him, 'that Mwanga should succeed him, because he expected him to be friendly to the Europeans. And now he decides to kill one ! But it is all due to those great chiefs urging him on. They would not have dared to tell Mutesa to put Europeans to death when they first came.'

That afternoon, Joseph went out with two young pages, one of whom was James Miti, to a property of his on Kampala Hill. Food was offered to him but he did not stay to eat and before dark he was back in the royal enclosure. There Bwewusa, one of his subordinates, told him that the Kabaka had been asking for him and, finding him absent, had shown great annoyance. 'Balikuddembe,' he had said, 'has gone to the white men to play the informer. But won't I tie him up in one hide with the white men of whom he is so fond?'

Later in the evening, after spending some time in his drinking-house with the Princess Royal and other princesses, Mwanga sent for Joseph and said to him :

'Since you have been for a walk, just tell me why you went out.' Then without waiting for a reply, he added, 'Batuka, didn't I tell you that Buganda needs ruling by force?'

'Quite so,' replied Joseph. It seems quite possible that Mwanga had been drinking to excess and that Joseph did not quite know what to make of this conversation. The Kabaka went on :

'Who are meant by him that will open and him that will shut?'

'That I cannot tell, Sire.'

'So you are asleep in the presence of your master speaking in proverbs?'

The pages who overheard this conversation were frightened at the turn it was taking, but Joseph, nothing daunted, answered promptly :

'I have understood the proverb, Sire. It suggests that he that will open and he that will shut are on an equal footing, but in fact they are not. If he that opens is a friend, there is no trouble, but if he is not a friend, there is.'

'You served my father,' the Kabaka went on, 'but did you ever see a white man entering his house by the back-door?'

'The white men come and go,' Joseph answered. 'They merely pass through. Allow that white man to come or, if you do not want him to pass through Busoga, order him back; but do not harm him.'

'Perhaps I should send you to order him back!' sneered the Kabaka.

'If you send me, I will go.'

'But would you meet my dogs before they have been let loose on your bushbuck? Those dogs of mine are strong when I have set them on to round up their prey with no one to call them off.'

The young pages listening to this interchange trembled with fear. Not so Joseph, who answered boldly :

'Your father Mutesa never put a white man to death. Why, then, should you want to kill one? Do not put him to death because of what your chiefs have said : they will applaud any decision. Do not kill that white man, for if you do, you will have to answer for it before God.'

The Kabaka was furious. 'What!' he cried. 'You have been teaching the whole of my enclosure under my eyes, and now you want to teach me as well! All right! If I have to answer for my actions, perhaps you will be appointed judge to decide the case. Now get out of my sight! Go!'

Joseph retired to his hut and spent the whole night in prayer. Next morning, he assembled his pages and warned them that the Kabaka's angry mood was likely to have its effect upon them also.

On the same Sunday, Mark Sekajija, a Protestant page, brought the news to Mackay and his companions that two Englishmen were in the stocks in Busoga. Mackay, presuming that these must be Bishop Hannington and his chaplain, decided to dismiss the Sunday congregation and seek an immediate audience with the Kabaka. Then Joseph Kasala came to tell the missionaries that the Kabaka meant to kill the prisoners, adding that one of them was lacking a thumb. Ashe immediately exclaimed, 'It is the Bishop.' He knew that Hannington had lost a thumb in an accident in his early days.

Ashe and Mackay hastened to the palace. As they passed through the gate, young Mark Sekajija came up to them and whispered, 'They have gone off to kill them.'

When the two anxious missionaries applied for an audience, they were told to explain to Kulugi, the Treasurer, what they wanted. They carefully explained to Kulugi the news that they had heard and begged him to carry their message to the Kabaka. Presently, he returned with the message, 'The Kabaka commands you to go to the Chancellor.' Their previous appeal to the Chancellor, in January, had been so unavailing that they refused, declaring that they were the Kabaka's guests and his alone. Kulugi obligingly went back to Mwanga and after some time came back with yet another evasive reply, 'The Kabaka commands you to come tomorrow, when he will give you his messenger to go and save the white men.' 'Tomorrow,' they answered in desperation, 'will be too late. Let him send now!' Kulugi generously offered to try once more, but this time found that Mwanga had slipped out of his enclosure by one of the back gates. He did not return until nightfall, by which time the two missionaries had had to leave, before the great gates were closed for the night.

Next morning, 26 October, Mackay and Ashe were back at the palace, this time with a short letter in Luganda, to be delivered to the Kabaka in case he again refused to see them. Mwanga sent out to say that he would send for the Frenchmen to come and read it to him. Knowing that this was but another excuse to fob them off, and that the Kabaka would not allow them to get near him, they left and went to Père Lourdel to ask him to intercede on their behalf for the life of the Bishop.

Lourdel, who was usually admitted to the royal presence without any difficulty, went at once and after persistent entreaties extracted from Mwanga a promise to spare the white man and simply order him away. Lourdel hurried off to tell Mackay to write a letter to the Bishop, instructing him not to use the Busoga route. Mackay had a severe attack of fever, but wrote at once, and even hastened after Ashe who according to the Kabaka's instructions was taking the letter to the palace to be sent on to Busoga. They handed in the letter and again waited around until nightfall but nothing happened, and it became evident that Mwanga's promise was insincere, and that he had no serious intention of doing anything.

The anxieties and uncertainty of the missionaries over the succeeding days are best conveyed by extracts from Mackay's Journal, published in the *Intelligencer* of 1886. For security reasons, the Editor suppressed the names of Mackay's informants.

28th October.

S—, of the king's store came early. He reports that the king and Katikiro are eager to know *who told us* of their design to murder the Bishop and his party. Many of the pages and other lads in the palace are Christians, and now they are suspected of giving us the information. They fear being all killed, but do not shrink. The devotion and courage of these young Christians are wonderful. Later in the day, S—, a page, reported that the king had at first wished to bring on the Bishop and his party, but the Katikiro and Pokino[1] persuaded him to kill them and get their goods. Mwanga complained that 'we knew all his secrets from his own pages, who regarded *us* as king and himself as Katikiro, or second in authority, while we looked on the Katikiro as only a peasant. If we were fighting-people, his pages would be rebels.' Apparently he understands that we are not fighting-people.

29th October.

No news all day. ... A few of our people about. They take a gloomy view of the situation and do not believe that the last messengers were sent to cancel the order given to Wakoli, but to confirm it, and ensure the death of the Bishop and his party. ...

After sundown we heard from various quarters that Mwanga goes to the lake to-morrow to shoot, and that he had given orders to Sebatta, one of the executioners, to catch people at our place. Probably he expects that in his absence some of the lads will come and give us news. For fear that our own boys might be arrested, we at once sent them all away to hide among our Christian friends. . . .

30th October.

After dark, Ismail came to tell us that messengers had returned from Busoga with tidings that the white men had been killed, and all their porters. . . . . Oh, night of sorrow! What an unheard-of deed of blood!

31st October.

Ismail sent word at night to the effect that some of the Arabs had been up at the court and brought back word confirming the story of last night, viz. that the bloody deed was done. It puzzles me to understand the cause of so terrible a crime. They say that they will not have the white men entering the country from *every side*. Why not then send them back? The king is said to have proposed this, but the Katikiro replied, 'Will you let their goods go also?' . . . God knows the cause and He alone knows what the consequences will be.

1st November (Sunday)

It was this day last week we heard of the arrival of our brethren. What a week of dreadful anxiety and sorrow this last week of October has been! Now is the time to actually carry out our former plan, viz. to get our Church Elders to assemble their friends in each neighbourhood, and have worship in their houses. We have now ten elders, and these could hold as many meetings simultaneously. While the present suspicion lasts, we only increase it by collecting crowds on our premises.

2nd November.

One of our people . . . heard . . . that Mwanga said he meant to ask me to build him a house like ours, with an upper story, but he feared I would refuse, as I was in anger! If he was not conscious of having done, or meant to do us a terrible wrong, why should he fear our wrath?

3rd November.

Every day several of our people spend some hours with us. . . .

4th November.

We have still some faint hope, for had Wakoli done at once the murderous deed, news would have come here quickly. This is now the twelfth day since Wakoli left. . . .

5th November.

Nine lads baptized to-day. . . . K— came in the afternoon to tell us that the page Musoke, and a man of Wakoli's, with a Musoga, had come yesterday. They went first to the Katikiro, and were sent by him to the king accompanied by a boy to see that they spoke to no one. The king sent them away again overnight, so that no one knows what news they brought. This looks suspicious. . . .

Later in the day we got letters from D— and S—, informing us that the page Musoke had let out to the boy who accompanied him from the Katikiro's to the king's, that the white men were really killed, and their whole party, while he had got orders to go and fetch the goods *by night*, that the news might not get out.

We have no hope now for the Bishop. The worst seems over. Our dear brethren are happy. We remain in the midst of death. Lord, Thy will be done.

The English[1] missionaries found it hard to give up the hope that by some outside chance their Bishop might have been spared. The Kabaka and his Chancellor, still hoping to conceal the part they had played in the massacre, kept the Englishmen on tenterhooks by spreading rumours to the effect that the Bishop was still alive. Thus, on 9 November, Mackay wrote, 'more conflicting reports. Again we are told that the Bishop and his companion are still alive : but all agree that all his Wang'wana (porters) have been killed'. However, as more details of the murder began to come in, they ceased to give any credence to the rumours Mwanga continued to spread. Lourdel had already given up hope by 1 November, when he wrote 'Hannington murdered. . . . Beginning of Mwanga's cruelties : Alas, it will not be the last!'

A few days later (after 1 November), Lourdel was told in secret that the Chancellor had stated that the three Englishmen in Buganda would also be executed, if the one in Busoga should prove to be the chief for whom they had sent their boat to Kavirondo. When, on November 5th, the death of Hannington was confirmed beyond reasonable doubt, Lourdel at once sent a note to the Englishmen to warn them of their danger. Ashe's diary confirms this, and also reports that, on the night of the 5th, a warning was sent by the Princess Nalumansi, advising them to placate the Kabaka by sending him a substantial present. Weighed down with grief and weariness and in Mackay's case fever also, the Englishmen seem to have taken no positive action until the Princess Nalumansi's advice was repeated by one of their own converts, probably Apolo Kagwa, on 9 November. Mackay's journal for that day reads :

W—, chief storekeeper under Kulugi,[2] and one of our Christians, sent us a message to the effect that in this country, when the king killed anyone, the friends of the dead man were regarded as enemies desiring revenge, unless they took the king a present to show that they had no such feelings. This was a hint that we should do so likewise. From another quarter we heard similar advice. Nalumansi, a princess baptized here, but now following the Roman Catholics, sent to say that we ought to make friends with Mwanga. We therefore held a consultation together, Ashe and myself feeling convinced that, to remove the suspicion now present in the king's mind, we ought to give him a valuable present.

10th November.
Sent off all our servants with loads to the Katikiro's. It is customary to send to him first all presents for the king, that he may have the honour of forwarding them and presenting them. The minister received his present with thanks, and at once sent a messenger with our men to take up to the palace the loads intended for Mwanga. The king, however, had gone to the lake, shooting, so the goods were left in his store. ... We sent no message with the present, but Tumah, whom I had appointed spokesman, took it upon himself to say to the Katikiro that we had no connection with the white men in Busoga. This spurious information I resolved to correct at once. So I sent Tumah back in the afternoon, ordering him to tell the Katikiro that the white men in Busoga *were* our brethren, and that we had asked them to come at Mwanga's own repeated request; but that we knew nothing of their intention to come through Masai, or via Busoga, until they actually came; that they had travelled with an Arab caravan to Baringo, and took the shortest road from there, not knowing that there was any objection here to that route.

11th November.
Tumah and Tohar went to the palace, with yesterday's present to the king. They returned in the forenoon, saying that Mwanga was in a rage. He demanded to know what the present was for. Lourdel was there, and tried to appease the king by saying that our present denoted good feeling. Mwanga denied that and ordered us to come ourselves and explain.

Mwanga's fury at the sending of the present is understandable if one remembers that he was still keeping up the pretence that he had not murdered Hannington. The two well-wishers who had advised the missionaries to send the present, according to Kiganda custom, had overlooked the fact that *officially* they were not supposed to know anything about the death of their brethren in Busoga, or even of their arrival there. Thus the sending of the present amounted to an accusation against the Kabaka that he had killed their brethren and was plotting against them. Mwanga was furious with the English missionaries, but even more furious with the person or persons who had put him into this embarrassing situation by revealing his plans.

The story of the momentous audience of 11 November is given in Mackay's own words, continued from above :

> Ashe and myself went up commending ourselves to God, ... for we little expected to return alive. We found Père Lourdel in the store. He told us that the king was eager to find out who had told us that he meant to kill us, and suspected Alexandro (Kadoko).
>
> We were all three soon called in. The king and Pokino ... then demanded the reason for the present. We replied, 'For friendship'. Had the boat come? No. Had the king come to the throne only yesterday? No. What did we mean by the present at this time?

The Englishmen's Guardian Angels must have been working hard to prevent even the forthright Mackay from blurting out the real reason for the present, which might well have been their death warrant. The Pokino attempted to put the words into their mouths, exclaiming, 'They think that we want to kill them, and wish to redeem their lives. What danger are they in? Do we kill our guests? Do we kill Baziba, or Basoga, or Arabs?' However, they resisted the temptation to tell Mwanga outright that they were well aware of what he had done and of what he had been planning to do.

> We replied that we had gone repeatedly to the court, and the king had refused to see us. We feared that he was angry with us, for some unknown reason, and we did not know that we had done anything to offend him. We had written him a letter, asking news of our brethren in Busoga, and got no reply.

At this, there was a general outcry asking who had told them about their brethren in Busoga, and the Kabaka added, 'I see that there are some double-tongued lads here, who tell you my secrets'. They were repeatedly asked who had told them of the white men's being in Busoga, but the two missionaries refused to mention anyone.

> After a deal of cross-questioning, they failed to find an answer, and then blamed some unknown Muganda for trying to frighten us by telling us that the king meant to kill us. We should not listen to such stories. We replied that no Muganda had said to us a word of the kind; we heard themselves say so now.
>
> Again and again, and yet again, they demanded who was our informant. We declined to mention anyone, saying that we did not think the king would kill his guests. 'Oh, but some Muganda has told you! Boys go to your place to learn to read, and you try to get from them the king's secrets.'
>
> Mwanga then tried passion. He would kill anyone found at our station. We were Bagwagwa (low savages), who tried to get at his

secrets. Other names of abuse he likewise called us. He would kill any chief even who came near us. He would appoint no one to watch our premises, but would hold ourselves responsible for anyone coming near us. If any Muganda were found in our ground, he would put one of us in the stocks, and then we would have to pay a fine amount to redeem him. Yes, he would put us all in the stocks; and let word of that go to the Coast; and he would challenge England and all Europe to come and rescue us. What could white men do to him? How could they come into his country unless they flew in the air? Had Lukonge (ruler of Ukerewe Island where Smith and O'Neill had been murdered) not killed white men, and had the Queen been able to touch Lukonge? Was he not still there? Had Mirambo not killed white men, and had the Queen been able to touch him?

As Mwanga's passion increased and his threats against the two missionaries grew more and more outrageous, Père Lourdel seems to have grown uneasy and apprehensive. All this talk about putting Europeans to death with impunity was dangerous and might lead to action. Lourdel interrupted the Kabaka and said, 'If you killed these white men, then I should not care to stay in your country'. 'If I killed them,' replied Mwanga, 'should I spare you? Are you not a white man like them?' However, the interruption produced the desired effect, and the Kabaka abandoned this dangerous topic.

> Then he told his boys present that none of them was to come near us. The king was not to be told upon to others. He would try his own device, and punish his own people if we heard of his doings or words. . . .
>
> Mwanga continued, that there were some people who wished to destroy our peace of mind, and frighten us with stories that the king wished to kill us, else why had we robbed ourselves by bringing him what we lived upon? He would not take my only rifle: it was old and broken. But after examining it, he ordered me to repair it, and return it to him. . . .
>
> He allowed that we refused to tell (who had informed us) because we knew that he would put to death our informant, and then we would consider ourselves the cause of that person's death. 'You do not like to kill people, do you? But what favourites you would be if you would only tell *one name* of your informants!'

This stormy audience lasted for over two hours and was exhausting to all parties. At the end of it, Mwanga dismissed his guests and, calling an attendant, said to him, 'Take these white men and give them two cows to quieten their minds'. Lourdel was called back and given a goat. Mackay concludes his account of the memorable audience:

We returned home weary, but grateful to our Heavenly Father, who had preserved us in this great danger, for we little expected to see liberty or life more. From the whole scene, coupled with the Katikiro's remark to Tumah 'that we might now sleep in peace', we could easily see that the plot to kill us had been there, and although they were ashamed of our having discovered it, their abuse of us, and determination to find out who had told us, showed their mind.

The missionaries heard later that Mwanga was in a panic at the Arabs' stories about the German annexations, and had, earlier that morning, exclaimed, 'the Germans are coming, and I shall be the last native king of Buganda. After my death the white men will take my country, but so long as I am alive I will not let them do it'. In spite of Mwanga's prohibition and threats, the Christians continued to send information to the mission and gradually the details of the massacre in Busoga were revealed. Mackay's journal for 15 and 16 November gives two of these reports.

15th November.
    Received a note from D— this morning. He had seen a lad named Kyonneka, who had been sent ... to Busoga. This lad returned to-day. He had been an eyewitness of the massacre. He reports that Wakoli (the Kabaka's gatekeeper and not the Musoga chief of that title) arrived at Luba's in the afternoon. They speared the Wang'wana (porters) first, in number about fifty. The white man begged them not to spear him, but to take his rifle and shoot him. This they did.

16th November.
    We received a letter from one of the king's storekeepers (probably Apolo Kagwa.). He got details of the murder of the Bishop and party. There were fifty-three servants, and all, except two or three boys whom Luba seized for himself, were killed. S— heard from some of his friends who had been in Busoga how the massacre took place. The army of the Baganda, under Mutesa, Sembuzi, Betege, and Masudi, first arrested the Bishop. They tied him up and put him into a wretched hovel, apparently deserted, for it was filthy and full of cobwebs. He complained for some days of being ill, and begged his captors to build him a new hut, which they did. Wakoli (the king's gate-keeper) then arrived. The white man and his men were at once taken to an open place outside the plantations, where the Wang'wana were all speared. The Bishop implored them not to spear him, but to shoot him with his own rifle. This they did, and afterwards cut off his head and his feet. They allowed six days to elapse after the massacre, and then Musoke (Mwanga's page) returned to Buganda with the intelligence that all were dead. I believe that the reason for delay before reporting was that they have

some notion that white men have a resurrection soon after death. This too explains the cutting off the head and feet probably.

The actual killing of Bishop Hannington took place on Thursday, 29 October 1885. Later reports show that he was speared to death. The story of his being shot probably originated with the rifle shot fired as a signal to commence the massacre. Possibly the shot coincided with the Bishop's going down on his knees, which might easily lead any but a close observer to think he had been shot. When the Bishop realized that he was to be killed, he asked his executioners to tell the Kabaka that he had purchased the road to Buganda with his death, and that he died for the Baganda.

The second white man mentioned in the reports was the Bishop's cook, a Goan named Pinto, who was also killed. Of the coast men who were serving as porters, three or four were kept by the Busoga chief, Luba, and one, who had been left for dead, managed to get away.

In an editorial comment, the *C.M.S. Intelligencer* remarked, 'the secular press, indeed, has not yet discovered that a martyred missionary Bishop is as important a person as a successful jockey; but that need not disturb us'. It need not indeed. The name of Hannington and of all those who gave their lives for the cause of Christianity in Buganda will be remembered long after the names of innumerable successful jockeys have passed into oblivion.

Chapter Nine

THE CATHOLIC PROTOMARTYR, JOSEPH MUKASA

From the time of their return in July 1885, until the memorable audience of 11 November 1886, described in the last chapter, the Catholic missionaries had appeared to enjoy the confidence and favour of the Kabaka, and had taken advantage of the liberty they were accorded to prepare for baptism a group of the catechumens who had been enrolled before the Fathers had left Buganda. Before the actual baptism, which took place on 1 November, the Feast of All Saints, the situation had deteriorated rapidly and although none knew what would happen next there was no doubt in the minds of the missionaries that further trials were in store. In Père Lourdel's diary, the entry for 1 November reads : 'This night twenty-two baptized. This feast will not occur again before a large number of these neophytes are called upon to shed their blood for the Faith.' The group included two future martyrs, Noe Mawaggali and Jean-Marie Muzeyi.

Even on 11 November, although Mwanga had uttered threats against the Frenchmen as well as against the English, he does not seem to have meant them seriously for when, at the end of the audience, Lourdel asked the Kabaka whether the order forbidding his subjects to go near the white men applied also to the Catholic mission, the Kabaka replied in a low voice, 'No, you people are not included'.

Almost immediately after the 11th, Mwanga developed some form of eye trouble and sent down to the Catholic mission for medicine. Lourdel brough him an eye-salve which quickly brought the patient relief. On the evening of the 13th, Lourdel visited his patient again and found him delighted with the improvement. Mwanga was most friendly, called Lourdel his father, made him promise never to leave Buganda, tried on his hat and admired himself in it in the mirror. On leaving, Lourdel left the Kabaka two opium pills, telling him, if the eyes caused any discomfort, to take one pill on retiring so that he would sleep well. Mwanga presented the priest with a beautiful goat and sent him off in high spirits, believing that the tension of the last few weeks had eased.

Next morning, Joseph Mukasa came in haste to the mission to summon the priest to the palace 'The Kabaka has had a bad night.

Could it be fever?' Lourdel went at once to the Court where he found Mwanga with the Chancellor, Kyambalango and Kulugi. His Majesty did not conceal his annoyance.

'Mapèra,' he complained, 'You gave me opium pills to make me sleep. I slept well in the early part of the night, but the pill I took after midnight has made me very sick and makes me feel giddy.'

Lourdel assured the patient that no harm would come of it, and offered to fetch something to relieve him. To this the chiefs objected on the grounds that the Kabaka's illness was due to taking the opium pill after he had been rubbed with oil; such a treatment, they claimed, was bound to make a person ill. Père Lourdel was astonished at the suggestion, but the Kabaka accepted it eagerly. He showed himself extremely annoyed that the priest had not warned him and went on as if an attempt had been made to poison him.

At about eleven o'clock Lourdel, accompanied by the Chamberlain, one of Mwanga's Muslim friends, went off to fetch some citric acid and returned to find everyone in a panic. He writes:

> On coming back, I met the Chancellor running to the Kabaka's house, and found the patient vomiting a little milk which had been given him during my absence. Poor Mwanga cried and moaned like a child and believed himself lost. The Chancellor too was wailing. I told them that fear is a bad counsellor, and that the Kabaka would be well again that night; if he died, they might kill me as well. The Princess Nassiwa, Mwanga's eldest sister, whom I had treated and cured a few days before, told the patient that she had taken not one but three pills, and persuaded him to drink a little of the citric acid. This stopped the vomiting, and at night the Kabaka's health was completely restored.

When relating the story of this incident to O'Flaherty a few days later, Lourdel said that before administering the citric acid, he had drunk some himself to show that it was not poison. He, however, had been in no small danger, because the chiefs were very suspicious of his intentions. The Kyambalango, in fact, told him later that he was on the point of stabbing him for poisoning the Kabaka but, as the antidote proved effective, stayed his hand.

That the pagan chiefs should be suspicious of all white men after the murder of Bishop Hannington is not surprising. The idea of anyone forgiving a wrong was quite alien to their code. Many of them, when they heard the story of the medicine, said openly, 'the Kabaka is a fool for taking medicine from a white man. He has just put two of his brethren to death. Naturally, the white man would take this opportunity of revenge by poisoning him.'

As to the Kabaka himself, his behaviour to Père Lourdel shows that he, at least, never seriously believed the priest capable of such a crime, but he was cunning enough to realize that the widespread credence given to the tale of an attempt to poison him gave him an excellent excuse for proceeding against his otherwise popular Majordomo, Joseph Mukasa. To Lourdel he was quite friendly and, when taking leave of him that night, asked the priest to take back to Père Giraud some goods that had been stolen from him about a month before.

When Lourdel left the palace that night, Saturday 14 November, he was under the impression that all was well again, and returned to the mission in good spirits. But Mwanga's fickle, fitful and revengeful brain—the phrase is Mackay's—relieved of worries about his own health, began to work again on the problem, left unsolved on 11 November, as to who had kept the missionaries informed of all the moves in the Hannington affair.

Mwanga's bitter resentment against the person or persons who had told the missionaries of all that was happening and being planned is easily understood. If only the Englishmen had remained in ignorance, the killing of Hannington and his party could have been passed off as the result of an unfortunate and regrettable misunderstanding but, because they knew of the arrest of the Bishop almost as soon as he did and were thus able to make representations to him before the killing was accomplished, he stood revealed as a deliberate and cold-blooded murderer. Knowing that he had been put in the wrong, he laid the blame, not on himself, but on those who had helped to reveal his actions in their true light. He was also genuinely uneasy about the German annexations and the possibility of British punitive action. To a man of Mwanga's character, it was necessary to find a victim upon whom to vent his ill-humour, and the obvious one, Joseph Mukasa, was close at hand.

Joseph had dared to tell him bluntly that he did wrong to put the European to death, and that his father Mutesa would never have done such a thing. This Mwanga chose to regard as an insult to his dignity and to the memory of his father, and to make his principal charge against his Majordomo. It was not his only grievance. Joseph had constantly shown his disapproval of his master's vices, and had encouraged the Christian pages in their stubborn refusal to accede to his shameful demands on them. These refusals were already sufficiently humiliating to a monarch who expected from his subjects the blind, unquestioning and slavish obedience which rulers of Buganda had been accustomed to receive from time immemorial, and the taunts of his Muslim courtiers, that he was no longer a king when even young boys dared to 'insult' him by refusing certain of his demands, did nothing to sugar the pill or lessen his resentment against the Christians and, especially, against their acknowledged leader at Court. Even so, Mwanga, true to type, found it necessary to work himself up into a rage before he could take action against the man he knew, in his heart, to be a true and loyal friend : so, after brooding over his imaginary wrongs, he called Joseph to him and began to upbraid him.

It is said that the session lasted all night, the Kabaka, at one time heaping abuse on the head of his devoted servant, at another threatening to exterminate all Christians. What Joseph answered to the various accusations and threats is not known, but the outcome shows that he did not do what was expected of him, did not grovel to the Kabaka and admit that the latter could do no wrong.

When the ordeal was over and morning had come, Joseph Mukasa walked down to the Catholic mission, heard Père Lourdel's Mass and received Communion from his hands. Leaving the church, the young chief was just telling a few friends that the Kabaka had been storming at him during the night, when a page, called Kafulusi, came up and told him that His Majesty wanted to see him at once.

Mwanga, meanwhile, having worked himself into a satisfactory state of fury and given himself the added grievance of a night without sleep, had summoned the Chancellor and some of the time-serving chiefs to obtain their approval and moral support in the new injustice he was about to perpetrate. James Miti gives the following account of the proceedings.

Having assembled the Chancellor and a number of chiefs, the Kabaka said to them :

> Since I have been here, I have been eating in one pit with a venomous snake. My slave (Joseph Mukasa) has long since decided on a plan to kill me; he arranged with the white men that they should find a new road to Buganda; he for his part would dispose of me in a cowardly fashion. For, surely, that white man managed to get to Busoga because someone in Buganda lit up his way.

Thereupon, the chiefs, accepting their cue, exclaimed : 'Indeed, it was he that became their guide.' The chiefs were then dismissed and Tabawomuyombi, one of the executioners, was sent to call Joseph into the royal presence.

The martyr was on his knees praying when the summons came, and he at once rose and went to the Kabaka's house. On his arrival, Mwanga began to detail his grievances to the Chancellor who was also present :

> This fellow has informed on me through Père Lourdel, by betraying our plans to the white men. He has caused obstruction, and even

insulted me by saying that it was wrong to kill the white men in Bus-oga and that my father, Mutesa, would never have done such a thing. He is also the man who attempted to poison me by asking Père Lourdel to give me the medicine which almost killed me. I have often forbidden him to practise the white men's religion, but he does not listen. He even teaches that religion to my servants here at court, and has incited them against me. They no longer do a thing that I tell them.

The Chancellor eagerly followed his master's lead.

This fellow, Mukasa, has not a grain of respect for me either. He has even taught that religion to my own children. From his attempt to poison you it is apparent that we have a sorcerer before us. Well then, since he wanted to kill you, let him precede you to the abode of death. Give him to me and I will rid you of him.

Outside the doorway, the executioners were waiting to do the Kabaka's bidding. Calling in Mukajanga, their chief, the Chancellor said, 'Tie this fellow up at once!' The Kabaka signified his assent and then, keeping up the pretence that his life had been in danger, said to his Chancellor, 'You have saved me! Now there will no longer be two Kabakas at this Court.' Then, as the prisoner knelt before him with his hands tied behind his back, he added, 'This is the fellow who always wanted to teach me, and told me to put away my charms!'

'I am, then, to die for my religion', replied Joseph.

Turning to the chief executioner, the Kabaka gave the order, 'Go to the court-house at the entrance gate and fetch firewood to burn him'. The Chancellor, making no attempt to conceal his elation, added, 'Do not let him live the night'. Then Joseph was led away by Taba-womuyombi, while Mukajanga went to arrange about the firewood.

Meanwhile, unaware of what was afoot, Père Lourdel arrived at the royal enclosure. On the way, he had heard that the Kabaka was well again, his eyes completely cured, and had been talking the whole night through. As he entered the main gate, a young page came up to him and said in a low voice, 'The other day you did not want to baptize me, yet I was right in saying that you would soon be driven out of the country'. The priest expressed surprise, and the youth continued, 'The Kabaka has been saying very bad things about you during the night. He pretends that you wanted to poison him and to place another prince on the throne, and has made up his mind to drive you away or even to put you to death'.

Continuing on his way, Lourdel read anxiety in the faces of the catechumens and neophytes. For the first time since his return to

112

Buganda, he was not admitted at once to the royal presence, but told to wait until the Kabaka should send for him. The priest sat down to wait, very ill at ease. Then, from one of the inner courts, a young catechumen, with a look of terror on his face, rushed out to tell his fellow pages that their chief, Joseph Mukasa, had just been tied up and was being taken off to execution.

Overcome with grief, Père Lourdel went home and told his fellow priest, Père Giraud, what had happened. Both realized the seriousness of the situation, but could do nothing but put their trust in God and in our Blessed Lady, and commend themselves and their flock to their protection and care.

After leaving the royal presence, Mukajanga told his assistant to remove the bonds from their prisoner. This honour, of walking unfettered to their place of execution, was accorded to chiefs; and Mukajanga, the grim old taker of lives who liked the man he was to put to death, was determined to show no lack of respect for his victim. Joseph, when Tabawomuyombi was undoing the cords that bound him, said approvingly, 'That's right. I am going to die for my religion. You need not be afraid that I will attempt to escape.' Then he stepped resolutely forward, unfettered.

On the way, which did not lead through the court of Stores, where Lourdel was waiting, a number of pages, moved with compassion for their leader, attempted to join the little procession, but Mukajanga drove them away, shouting, 'Go off! Do you want to make a king of him?' Two or three, however, persisted in following the little group, and later found themselves in trouble for doing so.

A walk of about half a mile down Mengo Hill brought the party to the valley between Mengo and Nakasero Hills through which runs the river Nakivubo, no more than a trickle except after heavy rain. Here there was a flimsy prison building and near it one of the recognized places of execution. This spot seems to have been chosen because the stacks of firewood, used to feed the Sacred Fire and kept near the main gate of the palace, made it possible to carry out the sentence without much delay.

Even so, old Mukajanga did not hurry about his distasteful task. He knew from experience that the Kabaka, especially in the case of old friends or pages, was liable to revoke or commute the sentences of death passed in anger, and he had often earned the gratitude of both Kabaka and victim by delaying an execution until the royal anger had had time to cool. On this occasion, although he had rightly assessed the fickleness of the Kabaka, he had underestimated the vindictiveness of the Chancellor. As he and his men were going about their task of building the pyre, in a leisurely fashion, a messenger was seen coming down the hill. If, at first, they thought that the expected reprieve had come, they were quickly disillusioned. To their dismay, they found that the Chancellor had sent the man to make sure that the execution had taken place or, according to another version, to order the executioner 'to burn the fellow at once before the Kabaka repented'.

Mukajanga dared not incur the enmity of this powerful and unscrupulous man by disregarding so definite an order, but he could perform one act of mercy for his victim. His orders were to burn his prisoner to death. In fact, the sentence, 'Bamwokye' 'Let them roast him', was often carried out to the letter, as in the case of Charles Lwanga, the victim being roasted over a slow fire. Mukajanga had Joseph brought to the place of execution and told him that he would have him beheaded before placing him on the fire.

The executioner's words recalled the martyr to earth, and to consciousness of the terrible wrong about to be committed. They also brought back to his mind the thought of the Kabaka whom he had served so loyally and so well, his wayward friend whom he had tried to convert to better ways. One last effort would he make to appeal to Mwanga's better nature, and to show his loyalty : 'Friend', he said to Mukajanga, 'tell Kabaka Mwanga from me that he has condemned me unjustly, but that I forgive him. However, let him repent, for, if he does not, I shall be his accuser before the judgement-seat of God.' The old executioner answered, according to one report, 'The Kabaka will shelter behind me and we shall plead our cause together.' According to another witness, Mukajanga said, 'I shall begin the defence of our cause as your opposing counsel'. The same witness goes on to point out that this actually happened, because the old man died before his master.[1]

When all was ready, Joseph Mukasa Balikuddembe was tied on a rough framework, under which fuel was heaped. Then Mukajanga gave a signal to one of his men called Lukowe; the long curved knife flashed through the air, and the life-blood of the martyr soaked into the soil of the country he had loved, and served so faithfully. The pyre was lit with a torch from the Sacred Fire, and the martyr's remains were slowly burnt to ashes.

Mukajanga and his men were still watching the fire, and feeding it with dried grass and wood, when a second messenger rushed down the hill with orders from the Kabaka not to burn Joseph, but to keep him prisoner. Mwanga had repented too late : even he had failed to realize how his ruthless Chancellor could hate.

At about five in the evening, while the smoke from the martyr's funeral pyre was still rising, Mwanga, like an earlier tyrant whom he much resembled, attempted to ease his feelings with music. He called the page Denis Kamyuka to come and play the *entala*, a kind of native xylophone, with him. Another Catholic page, Simeon Sebuta, who describes this incident, was seated nearby, and Mwanga, after playing on the instrument for a while, looked several times in his direction. Sebuta, who was mourning the loss of his well-loved leader and friend, failed to respond with the customary congratulations and thanks for his playing which the Kabaka expected. So, throwing down the sticks he was using, Mwanga went into his house, where he remarked to his sister Nassiwa, 'Sebuta is sulking because his fellow Christian, Balikuddembe, has been killed'.

It was shortly after this that the chief executioner arrived to report the completion of his task, and to deliver to the Kabaka Joseph's last message. Mwanga pretended to laugh this off, but was in fact so deeply impressed and disturbed by it that he gave orders for another victim to be burnt on the same spot, and for his ashes to be thoroughly mixed with those of Joseph Mukasa. The mingling of the ashes, over which the spirits of the deceased were believed to hover, was supposed so to mix up and confuse the spirits of the two victims that they would be unable to accuse him or take their revenge. 'How can he now plead against me?' said Mwanga.

The identity of this second victim, sacrificed to Mwanga's superstitious fears, cannot be established with any degree of certainty. Some make mention of a boy called Kuzambiza Muwanga, a pagan, but others maintain that this youth was executed on another occasion. Lourdel refers to the victim as a page, and Livinhac mentions two, or even, three, Christians. Support for the theory that the victim was indeed a Christian comes from two sources : Mackay's diary reads, 'What a day! Two fresh martyrs to Christianity . . .', and the author of *La Vie du Réverérend Père Siméon Lourdel,* who claims to have adhered closely to notes written and revised by Père Lourdel himself, mentions that the second sufferer, a page, displayed remarkable fortitude, to explain which Mwanga said, 'The white men give these children some medicine to maintain the faith in their hearts; when once they have taken it, neither torments nor sufferings can wrest faith from them'.

After the death of Joseph, men were sent to raid his property, it being the usual practice to confiscate everything belonging to a condemned man. Joseph had no enclosure of his own, having been an inmate of the royal enclosure for some eleven years, but he seems to have had a plot of land, looked after by friends or dependants, and must have received numerous gifts from his royal masters in the days when he was in favour. However, such was his generosity that the raiders probably had the same experience as many of the Prefects of Rome during the early persecutions when they found that the poor had already been made the heirs of their victims.

Action was also taken against the young men who had insisted on following the martyr to his place of execution. According to a rumour which reached Mackay, several boys were condemned to death for this. One of them, according to him, was the young page Mark Seka-jija who had brought him news of the plot to murder Bishop Han-nington. Another was Nikodemo Sebwato, also a Protestant. Catholic witnesses mention two others, Kijala and Kasokambirya, who were confined in a narrow hut called *Kabula muliro* (it never has a fire) for five days, during which cold water was poured unceasingly over them. In the end, the Kabaka pardoned them, saying, 'Release those two slaves of mine for they are my fife players'. The two boys mentioned by Mackay were also pardoned.

The reaction of the English missionaries to the martyrdom of Joseph Mukasa was sadly misrepresented by the Abbé Nicq, in his life of Père Lourdel. In the first edition of this work, he wrote :

> We have difficulty in understanding how the English preachers, in particular Mr Mackay, could, in their journal, make sport of those who had compromised themselves in order to get them out of trouble. They went so far as to say that Joseph Mukasa had been killed be-cause of some native medicine for the eyes given by him to Mwanga. Now, Mukasa never gave the king medicine, either for the eyes or for anything else. The cause of his death, as the facts prove, were his inviolable attachment to the Catholic religion, his hatred of witchcraft, and above all the reproaches he made to the king on the occasion of the death of Bishop Hannington.

In the third edition of the work, this accusation is somewhat modi-fied, and reads :

> The execution of Joseph Mukasa left them (Mackay and his brethren) fairly indifferent, because Joseph was a Catholic and because a native instructed by the French missionaries was neces-sarily, especially in the eyes of Mackay, opposed to the English occupation.

A number of references to Joseph Mukasa made by the two Eng-lish missionaries, Mackay and Ashe, which have already been quoted, show no animosity against the Catholic leader but rather admiration for his sterling qualities, tinged with some perfectly natural disap-pointment that he had gone over to the Catholic Faith. In spite of this, their accounts of Joseph's martyrdom are fair and their tributes to him generous. Ashe, for instance, wrote :

> That same day news reached us that Balikuddembe, a young chief who learned to read at our mission, but who joined the French

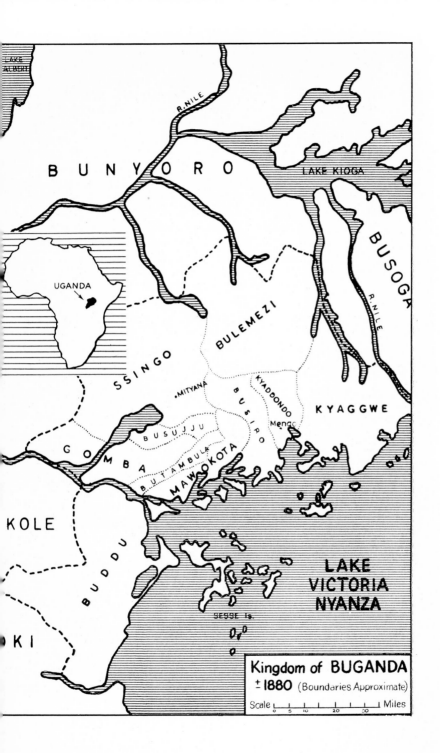

LAKE
ALBERT

R. NILE

B U N Y O R O

LAKE KIOGA

B U S O G A

UGANDA

R. NILE

S S I N G O

B U L E M E Z I

•MITYANA

KYADDONDO

B U S I R O

Menco

KYAGGWE

G O M B A

B U S U J J U

B U T A M B U L A

MAWOKOTA

KOLE

B U D D U

LAKE
VICTORIA
NYANZA

SESSE Is.

KI

Kingdom of BUGANDA
± 1880 (Boundaries Approximate)

Scale _____ Miles
        0 5 10   20   30

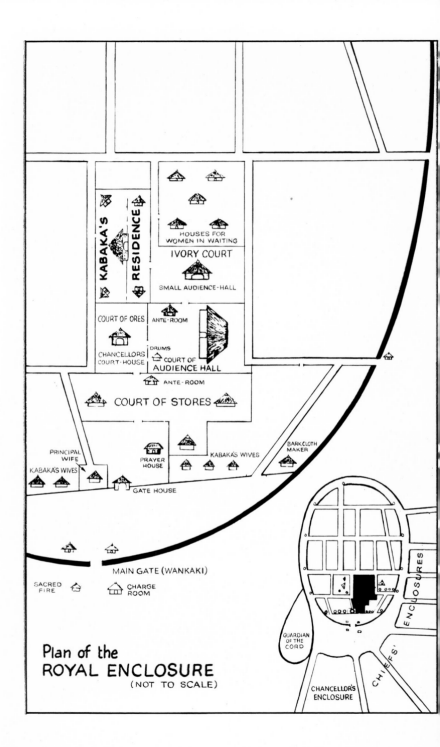

KABAKA'S RESIDENCE

HOUSES FOR WOMEN IN WAITING

IVORY COURT

SMALL AUDIENCE-HALL

COURT OF ORES

ANTE-ROOM

CHANCELLORS COURT-HOUSE

DRUMS

COURT OF AUDIENCE HALL

ANTE-ROOM

COURT OF STORES

PRINCIPAL WIFE

KABAKA'S WIVES

PRAYER HOUSE

KABAKA'S WIVES

BARK CLOTH MAKER

GATE HOUSE

MAIN GATE (WANKAKI)

SACRED FIRE

CHARGE ROOM

GUARDIAN OF THE CORD

CHANCELLOR'S ENCLOSURE

CHIEFS' ENCLOSURES

Plan of the
ROYAL ENCLOSURE
(NOT TO SCALE)

priests' pupils afterwards, had been seized, and that he was under sentence of death by fire.

That afternoon a whole troop of pages came down from Mwanga bringing 8,000 cowrie shells, as a part payment for some things which he had bought from us. One of the boys, Tito, drew me aside and told me that Balikuddembe was dead. This young hero had dared to tell the tyrant that he did unwisely to kill the white men. Mwanga immediately sent for the Katikiro. 'See,' he said, 'this fellow wants to insult me,' and forthwith the cruel sentence was passed. The chief executioner was a friend of Balikuddembe's and mercifully killed him with a sword before committing his body to the flames.

Mackay, named by Nicq as the principal offender, expresses himself even more warmly in his appreciation of the Catholic martyr. In his journal, reproduced in the *Intelligencer* of 1886, he wrote:

We had intended, some of us, to go to court to-day to teach. .... Now we think it better to remain quiet until we hear how Mwanga's eyes turn out. Any evil happening to him will certainly be laid at our door, as they believe strongly in human power to bewitch.

A force of men passed by our gate this forenoon. We hear that they are Mujasi's, and that they have been ordered to rob and burn alive the king's head page, Balikuddembe, also called Mukasa. The accusation seems to be that he informed on the king. This fine tall lad has been a faithful servant of Mwanga, ever since he became king. Formerly he read with me a Gospel and the Acts, along with Mulumba, Mwana wa Kintu and others. Afterwards the Roman Catholics got hold of all these, and since then he and Kaggwa have been leading men among the Romish converts. He has, however, continued friendly to us, and spoke well for us to the king last February when we were in deep trouble. May the Lord and Saviour, in whom he has learned to trust, be with the poor lad in this hour of horror and death and give him a joyous entrance into the happy land! ...

Poor Balikuddembe! The first report was that he had given the king some native medicine which made his eyes smart, and that he was arrested for that. Now we hear that he had said to Mwanga that it was wrong to kill the Bishop, as the white men were benefactors of the country. The king was wrathful, and when he found the occasion in the matter of the medicine, he sent for the Katikiro, to whom he said, 'This fellow has insulted me.' The order was at once given to burn him alive. It appears that the executioner meant to delay carrying out the sentence; but the Katikiro, who hated the lad because of his Christianity, sent to the executioner telling him to burn the fellow at once, before the king repented! Mwanga did repent and sent to order the lad to be merely kept prisoner, but it was too late. Already he had gone where these tyrants can no more

117

torture him. .... What a day! Two fresh martyrs to Christianity, and who knows how many more will follow? ...

When Balikuddembe was tied up, the king mocked him, saying, 'This is the fellow who was always wanting to teach me, and told me to put away my charms.' Brave lad, Mukasa! Thou hast witnessed faithfully for thy Master here below. Enter into the joy of thy Lord.

The Abbé Nicq was writing at a time, just after the religious wars in Buganda, when feeling ran high and many hard and bitter things were being said on both sides. It is a great pity, however, that he should have repeated the allegations he had heard, without first making quite certain that they could be substantiated.

One further testimony to Joseph Mukasa's character and courage may be quoted. It also comes from a Protestant source, from James Miti, the young page who had accompanied Joseph on the afternoon of 25 October 1885. Writing many years later, after his retirement from public service, when he was Kabazzi, Head of the Genet Clan, Miti says :

> As to Joseph's character, he was a staunch Catholic convert, unambitious, little in his own eyes, obedient to his superiors, kind to his equals and indulgent to his inferiors. His charity was unbounded: He loved all for God's sake and tried to consider the interests of others at all times, even at his own expense, as we find in his endeavour to intercede for Bishop Hannington, whom he had never seen, and who did not belong to his own Faith. And thus, a martyr of charity, Joseph Batuka Balikuddembe laid down his life in his endeavour to save that of an unknown (to him) European missionary.

Joseph Mukasa's claim to be counted among the noble company of Christian martyrs needs no arguing. No one, knowing the facts, can doubt that he died in defence of justice and of the sanctity of human life; in defence of the virtue of chastity; in defence of the Catholic Faith; and, immediately, because of the implacable hatred of Mukasa, the Chancellor, for Christianity and all that it represented.

Chapter Ten

DAYS OF TENSION
(November 1885—May 1886)

If, by striking at their leader at Court and by uttering threats to exterminate all Christians, Kabaka Mwanga hoped to intimidate the growing Christian community, check its progress, and, above all, reduce his pages to a state of abject servility to his wishes, he soon discovered that he had failed completely to achieve his object. The Christian pages, far from being disheartened by the death of their leader, were in high spirits, encouraging one another and saying, 'Let us remain firm! If the Kabaka wishes to put us to death, then we too shall know how to die like Joseph, our leader.' Many who were still catechumens decided to ask the priests for immediate baptism now that martyrdom seemed imminent. On the very day of Joseph's death, Père Lourdel wrote :

> This afternoon, a number of pages came in haste to the mission, saying, 'We are destined for death; give us baptism before we die!' How could we refuse them this grace, the more so as some had done several years of postulancy? 'There is no loss in our death,' they said, 'if only they will not harm you', and, having received the sacrament, they hurried back to their cruel master.
>
> At night, a dozen more came. I spent part of the night in preparing them, and then they received the sacrament of regeneration with a wonderful faith, all the more inspiring since they will, perhaps, soon seal it with their blood.

The words were to come true in the case of three of those baptized that night : Lwanga, Buzabaliawo, and Serunkuma. Did the priests give Lwanga the baptismal name of Charles—after Charles Cardinal Lavigerie, as Lourdel says—because they saw in him a similar quality of leadership? Certainly, this young man of twenty-five, animated by a new life on the night of his baptism, seized the banner that had fallen from the hand of his martyred friend Joseph, and took over the leadership of the young Christian pages, sustaining their faith and virtue by word and example and, within a few months, leading them on the way to martyrdom.

On their return to the great audience hall, Charles Lwanga and his newly-baptized companions found the rest of the pages still talking over the events of the day. Andrew Kaggwa was also there. Perhaps they were even in time to see Mukajanga the executioner enter the hall and hear him tell his story of the martyrdom. 'He also said to us,' relates one of those present that night, '"I was moved with compassion for that child." He said this because the good qualities of Joseph had pleased him immensely.'

On the following day, Mwanga did not give audience. Instead, he summoned to his presence all the pages who had served under Joseph Mukasa and gave the order for all those who did not pray with either Christian mission to rise and take their places near him. Only three responded. One of these was Mwanga's evil genius, the Muslim Bwami Kirungi.[1] All the rest, even the young boys, stayed bravely in their places.

'I will have you all put to death,' shouted the Kabaka in a fierce voice. 'Very well, Master,' came the calm reply, 'you will have us all put to death.' This answer seems to have taken Mwanga aback, for he did not then go beyond threats of killing all Christians and expelling the missionaries from Buganda.

If Mwanga flattered himself that he had at least intimidated his pages, he was very much mistaken. As had happened on the previous night, numbers of them stole down to the Catholic mission under cover of darkness and implored the priests to baptize them. At the mission, the pages found that others had the same idea as themselves. Matthew Kisule, the royal gunsmith, was there with a number of his assistants; Alexis Sebowa, chief of Kitabazi, with some of his followers; two servants of Toli; two women, the wives of Christians; and also some followers of the county chief of Ssingo, of Andrew Kaggwa and of the martyred Joseph Mukasa.

Marvelling at the splendid dispositions and constancy of these converts, Père Lourdel again spent part of the night in instructing them, and then administered the sacrament they so much desired. Evidently at a loss for names for such a large number, forty in all, the Father seems to have had recourse to an alphabetical list of saints. Abraham, Adrien, Alexis, Alfred, Alipe, Amans, Amadeus, Anselm, Antoine, Azarias, are some of sixteen names beginning with the letter A which appear in the register. The group included no less than seven who were shortly to lay down their lives for the Faith : Achilles Kiwanuka, Adolphus Mukasa Ludigo, Ambrose Kibuka, Anatole Kiriggwajjo, Athanasius Bazzekuketta, Denis Ssebuggwawo and Gonzaga Gonza. The name Gonzaga would have suggested itself because of its similarity to the African name, and that of St Denis, the great patron of France, would naturally appeal to any French priest.

The Kabaka, meanwhile, baffled by the solidarity shown by his

Christian pages, called on his Chancellor for advice. The latter urged him to carry out his threat of killing all the Christians, but Mwanga pointed out that the majority of his pages and guards were adherents of the missions, and that some five hundred men and five hundred women went to the English mission and a similar number to the French. If he were to put all these to death, it would be said that he was slaying the whole country and would give rise to discontent.

The only other event on that day was the appointment of Bwami Kirungi to the post of Majordomo, left vacant by the death of Joseph Mukasa. Bwami was one of the Muslim debauchees who surrounded the Kabaka, pandering to and encouraging his unnatural passion. His appointment as successor to Joseph left the Christian pages in no doubt about the real reason for Joseph's death.

The following day the Kabaka held court and large numbers of chiefs were present. In spite of their reluctance Lourdel, Mackay and O'Flaherty thought it politic to attend, and were fairly well received. This, after the alarming rumours of the past few days, somewhat re-assured them.

That evening more catechumens were baptized, among them another future martyr, Ngondwe the soldier, who had formerly been a page of Kabaka Mutesa. Père Giraud, who baptized this group, gave him the name of Pontian, in honour of the martyred Pope whose feast occurred two days later, 19 November.

As Père Giraud had been in the country only four months, the work of instruction and preparation for baptism devolved almost entirely upon Père Lourdel, who was kept fully occupied not only by the catechumens seeking baptism, but also by the baptized Christians who came to the mission seeking the sacraments at all hours, since they could only come by stealth. They approached the mission through the plantain groves and knocked softly on the door, giving their names, and begging for the sacrament of penance and for communion. In this way they prepared themselves for the death which, they felt sure, would not be long delayed. The priests, for their part, encouraged their children to persevere in the Faith, and reminded them constantly of the words of Our Lord, 'He that shall lose his life for my sake, shall find it'. Because of this, according to the witnesses, all remained firm and fearless of death. In the week following the martyrdom of Joseph Mukasa, no less than a hundred and five catechumens were baptized.

On 20 November, Lourdel and Mackay met again at the palace but failed to see the Kabaka. They went to call on the Chancellor at his own place and were graciously received. 'But this personage,' wrote Mackay, 'is a master of dissimulation. . . . Lourdel is very friendly at present. We are all in the same boat, he says. Affliction draws men together. Their place is deserted as well as ours, except that some call on them, as on us, at midnight.'

On Sunday, 22 November, only a few Christians managed to attend Mass and, on Monday evening at eleven o'clock, Peter Damulira, one of the first four Baganda to be baptized, turned up at the mission with twenty-nine catechumens who implored the priests to baptize them. The Kabaka was reported to have said to Bwami Kirungi that on the morrow he would catch and roast hundreds of Christians. What else could the priests do but baptize them? However, nothing happened next day and the missionaries began to believe that the catechumens, misled by false alarms, had exaggerated the danger. Consequently, they ceased to baptize, in order to instruct the candidates more thoroughly.

The last days of the month passed without further incident but, on 3 December, Mwanga, still worried by Joseph Mukasa's last message, had all the pages of the private apartments and of the court of the audience hall summoned to his presence, and said to them : 'You pretend that you will plead against me, but you insult me. Now, let those who do not pray ll me, because I do not wish, to punish them with the others.' Only four, none of them catechumens, came forward. Baffled by such persistence, the Kabaka concealed his resentment for the moment, but next day returned to the charge. He first attempted to intimidate the boys, saying, 'I know that you go on praying. You are disobedient dogs. You call Jesus your King, and look upon me as your brother, because I am black like yourselves'. Then he demanded an answer to the question : 'Do you want to continue going to the white men for instruction, or will you be content with seeing them here?' Père Lourdel happened to be waiting for an audience, so one of the boys went to ask his advice. He said that they should do what the Kabaka wished. Misunderstanding this in his excitement, the lad reported to the others that they should answer, 'Kabaka, do with us what you will', which they did. Their unanimity again gave Mwanga pause.

Shortly after this, he found an opportunity to vent his ill humour on a single victim. A young page named Paul Kiwanuka, who sat sewing near the Kabaka's house, was so intent on what he was doing that he did not hear Mwanga call to him. The Kabaka called a second time without result and then, losing his temper, already frayed by the obstinacy of his pages, had the boy's ear cut off. There was no audience for Lourdel that day.

In the evening, Mwanga, addressing himself to Charles Lwanga, said, 'I do not mind your praying if you wish to, but pray here and do not go to the white men.' The permission seemed to suggest that the Kabaka, who was for the moment taken up with political cares, was beginning to relent.

Two days later, on 6 December, the Kabaka again raised the subject, this time trying cajolery instead of threats. Addressing Charles Lwanga in a kind fatherly tone, he said, 'My friend, it seems to me that during the past few days you all approach me with a certain fear. Do you think I wish to put you to death like Mukasa? If I had him killed, it was not because he prayed to God, but because he insulted me by opposing the order to put the Englishmen to death, and because he informed the white men of my plans. I know that you do not do that; you have, therefore, nothing to fear. I do not forbid you to practise religion; only pray here, and do not go again to the white men. Besides why do you go there at all? They make you no presents; you gain nothing by going to their place. If you should still want to visit them, you would give me to understand that you are betraying me, like Mukasa. In that case I should be forced to drive away the strangers, and you with them, in order to save my kingdom. Then they will treat you as slaves; pile work upon you; make you carry stones and handle the hoe; and you will then be sorry for having disregarded my advice.'

Charles replied, 'You accuse the white men of wanting to take over your kingdom, and us of helping them to carry out that wicked design. Yet, the religion which they teach commands me to serve you loyally. Up to now you have looked on me as one of your most faithful subjects. Know, then, that I am still ready to lay down my life in your service.'

These noble words undoubtedly surprised the Kabaka, for he immediately broke off the discussion. Possibly he also reflected on the contrast between this young Catholic and his immediate superior, the Muslim Bwami Kirungi, who had that very week compromised himself with the Princess Royal. Certainly on the morning after this exchange, the Kabaka appointed another Catholic, Honorat Nyonyintono, to succeed the disgraced Bwami as Majordomo.

According to James Miti, Mwanga had been well aware of the intrigue between Bwami and his sister Muggale, and had derived considerable amusement from it. When the two were caught together, he had to take official cognizance of their crime. Even so, he was prepared to pardon Bwami for what was a capital offence. It was the Chancellor, a stickler for the old traditions, who had the youth's eyes plucked out. Mackay confirms the second part of Miti's statement in his journal:

Mwanga himself gave Lubuga (the Princess Royal) a terrible beating. Bwami he let go, and bade him go and thank the Katikiro for his pardon. The Katikiro however put him in the stocks, and since has ordered the lad's eyes to be put out and his ears to be cut off. Probably he will be killed outright when they tire of torturing him. Had he been a Christian he would have shared the same fate as Balikuddembe.

December passed without further incident. In spite of the prohibition, large numbers of men and youths went to the Catholic mission for instruction. Women also began to attend, and showed themselves no less attached to the Faith than the men. A wave of grace swept over the country. Christmas was quiet but happy and, on the Saturday after the Epiphany, the priests had the consolation of baptizing fourteen more catechumens.

The English missionaries, at this time, were very uneasy about the possible repercussions in Buganda of events taking place around it. Khartoum had fallen into the hands of the Mahdi, and Gordon had been killed. This left Emin Pasha and his force to the North of Buganda cut off from communication with Europe via the Nile. There was also a report of the approach of Dr Fischer, a German, who with an escort of two hundred rifles was looking for the missing Russian traveller, Dr Junker. When a letter arrived from Sir John Kirk, British Consul at Zanzibar, courteously begging Mwanga to give the English missionaries liberty to teach and to move about the country, as they were not political agents, and also requesting him to relieve Emin Pasha and his Egyptian officers in the Equatorial Province, the Kabaka at first showed himself very suspicious and distrustful but, eventually, much to everyone's surprise, commissioned Père Lourdel to write to both Emin Pasha and Dr Fischer, giving them permission to come to Mengo. It appears that the priest was able to persuade the Kabaka that neither had designs upon Buganda, and that assistance to Emin Pasha would do something to restore his reputation, damaged in European eyes by his murder of Hannington. The invitation never reached Fischer. Emin preferred to remain in Equatoria, but Dr Junker, who was with him, was to avail himself of Mwanga's hospitality at the most tragic moment in the history of the martyrs.

In the meantime, Mwanga continued to be civil, even to the English missionaries. He allowed O'Flaherty, who was in very bad health, to leave the country, and sent Mackay a present of ten thousand cowrie-shells, at the same time telling him that he was a 'favourite'.

The January mail brought a letter informing Père Lourdel that the newly-consecrated Bishop Livinhac would shortly arrive at Bukumbi, a White Fathers' mission at the South of the Lake. Mwanga assured Lourdel that he would be pleased to see the Bishop, and gave orders for a fleet of fifteen canoes, under the command of the Catholic, Adolphus Nantinda, to go and fetch him. Probably even more pleased at the prospect of the Bishop's presents, Mwanga continued the conversation in a friendly way, displaying a cordiality which the Father had ceased to expect from him. He asked why Christians were allowed to marry only one wife; why they paid their slaves for the work they did; and why they renounced all the joys of this world in the hope of a heavenly reward for the sacrifices made on earth. When Lourdel had answered these questions, Mwanga took him aside, and posed his own personal problem.

'Is it true,' he asked, 'that you forbid the satisfaction of certain natural desires?'

'Yes, outside the conditions imposed by God.'

'But then you are asking the impossible.'

'With the grace of God nothing is impossible,' replied Lourdel. 'Strengthened by grace, the Christian can lead a most chaste life.' He went on to describe the life of a true disciple of Jesus Christ.

'Quite true,' said Mwanga, interrupting the priest and addressing Kulugi, his favourite, 'Such a one was Mukasa.'

This was praise indeed for the man he had put to death. But, as if sorry for having made this admission, Mwanga exclaimed, 'But that Mukasa insulted me! He, a simple page, rebuked me! Why did he not ask *you* to come and make me see my fault? From you, Mapèra, I would have accepted a rebuke : but from a slave? Never!'

There is little doubt that Mwanga, in his better moments, sincerely regretted the execution of Joseph Mukasa Balikuddembe. It seemed also, for the moment, as if Père Lourdel was regaining the influence he had formerly possessed with the young Kabaka, and commanding once more the respect he had been accorded at the Court of Buganda. The ban on missionary activity was gradually sufficiently relaxed to allow the priests to resume their ordinary courses of instruction.

However, despite the appearances of renewed goodwill towards the missions, Mwanga was in fact drifting still further away from Christianity. This was largely due to the Baganda Muslims around him, whose impudence Joseph had kept in check. 'Before the death of Joseph,' says one witness, 'the practice of unnatural vice was the subject of secret conversation; the Kabaka spoke of those things only with his private servants and with the Muslims, and practised them like one that steals; but after Joseph's death, they were spoken of in public, and practised without restraint.'

The Muslims and pagans in Mwanga's entourage seem to have deliberately set themselves to break the resistance of the Christian pages, and chastity became the mark of Christianity at Court. Fortunately, Blessed Joseph Mukasa was watching over his former charges, and his mantle had fallen on the capable shoulders of Charles Lwanga. Encouraged by him, the Christian pages not only bravely resisted the tempters, but frowned on obscenity in any form, even in speech, putting to shame the Kabaka and his evil companions. These, chafing under their discomfiture at the hands of mere children, taunted Mwanga with his lack of authority and control over his slaves. 'Do you not see that they despise you?' complained the Muslim Mujasi. 'Does one refuse anything to a Kabaka? Are you still their king?' Another warned him : 'When the white men have taught all these children, *they* will be the masters of this country. These boys are among men what young shoots are among trees.'

Thus did his companions rub salt into the wound to Mwanga's pride and self-conceit, and thus, as one witness puts it, the virtue of the Christians began to be called vice, and the religion which taught them to resist temptation became a crime, an unprecedented revolt, an insult to the Kabaka.

In protecting and guarding his charges amidst these dangers and temptations, Charles Lwanga adopted the methods of his martyred friend. Resembling Joseph Mukasa in appearance, he resembled him still more closely in greatness of soul, chastity, obedience, self-control, kindness, prudence and courage. Even as a catechumen he had been an eager learner and teacher of others. Now he was untiring in his zeal to instruct his boys, and as many others as came to him. Without the advantage of the high standing at Court enjoyed by his predecessor, he managed to win the respect, admiration and affection of his charges, whom he instructed, advised and, as far as possible, shielded from bad company. On no account would he allow any boy of bad character to sleep in the audience hall, which served as a dormitory for himself and his helpers.

Like Joseph Mukasa also, whom Ashe himself acknowledges as a worthy opponent, Charles was no mean adversary in an argument on religion, as is shown by an encounter he had with one of the English missionaries about this time. One Sunday in Lent, Charles had gone to the Anglican mission with a present, to show his gratitude for some medical attention he had received. As on previous occasions, one of the missionaries, eager to win over this intelligent young man, entered into discussion with him. 'I have heard,' he said, 'that you people fast. Is that so?' 'Certainly, we fast,' replied Charles. The other laughed and told the young man that fasting was quite out-of-date and ridiculous. 'I have not come to enter into an argument,' said Charles, 'but tell me this. Is it true that Our Lord fasted?' Receiving an affirmative reply, he said, 'Well then, do not blame us for doing what Our Lord Himself did.' Reporting this interchange to Père Lourdel, the young man added, 'How illogical they are! In the books they themselves distribute it is said that Our Lord fasted and that fasting is good; and then they make fun of us for doing it.'

It was not only the Protestants that hoped to wean this outstanding young man from his allegiance to the Catholic Faith. Kabaka Mwanga, during this period, tried hard to persuade him to leave the white men and their religion alone, but Charles remained firm and, in spite of prohibitions and threats, managed from time to time to go to Mass and receive instruction at the mission. 'He experienced such great happiness on those days,' wrote Père Lourdel, a few months later. 'Not having been able to assist at Mass on Easter Sunday, because it was feared that the Christians would be arrested at the mission, Charles said to me afterwards : "We have failed at Easter, but we shall make up for it on Ascension Day. On that feast we shall not fail to be there ! How we shall celebrate it !" ' How truly he spoke ! He died, a martyr, on Ascension Day.

With the Kabaka listening more and more to the evil counsellors who surrounded him, and the Christians loyally persevering in the Faith they had embraced, and firmly rejecting their master's base solicitations, the atmosphere of the Court was explosive, and an outburst of fury against the Christians appeared likely to occur at any moment.

It was feared at first that the disasters of February 1886 would provide the spark to inflame the Kabaka's anger to the point which would drive him to act against his better judgement. On 22 February, at about eight in the evening, fire broke out in the royal enclosure, and spread rapidly from building to building. The powder store exploded, killing and injuring a number of the royal servants. In a moment, the riches amassed by Kabaka Mutesa were destroyed, and the young Muslim Chamberlain, Sempereza, fatally injured in his attempt to save them. Mwanga, alarmed by the explosions and the flames, and thinking that the country was in revolt, or that the Europeans, supposed to be looking for Hannington in Busoga, had stormed his palace, rushed from his house, a naked sword in hand, followed by about a dozen boys, and fled by the private road which led to the Catholic mission. Lourdel, hastening to the scene of the conflagration, met him and attempted to reassure him and calm his fears. Then some chiefs arrived on the scene and led Mwanga off to the residence of his Chancellor. Before the Kabaka had got over this fright, lightning struck the store in the Chancellor's enclosure, on the afternoon of the 24th, and Mwanga, now in a panic, took himself off to Munyonyo, some six miles from Mengo, where he had a small enclosure used mainly as a hunting lodge.

Other disasters followed, among them the failure of a great expedition against the Banyoro, in which the commander was killed, and Kyambalango seriously wounded. The Arabs did not fail to accuse the white men of being the authors of all these calamities. The native Muslims, annoyed that the Kabaka had appointed Peter Damulira, a Catholic of long standing, to succeed the Muslim Chamberlain who had perished in the fire, warned him that his new Chamberlain would make him eat snakes,[1] and seized the opportunity to revive all the old calumnies. Mwanga, pining over his lost treasures, was in a mood to listen to any tale against the Christians. 'I am tired of these Christians,' he said to some friends, 'and I will have them all put to death. They obtain from God anything they want. At one time, they considered me as their friend and prayed for me; and God shielded me against danger. Now, they are trying to prevail on Him to overthrow me. I must at all costs rid myself of these villains.' On several occasions, he said to his pages, 'If you do not give up religion, I will have you all put to death'.

At the end of February there was a rumour that persons who went to the English mission were to be arrested, and Mackay received a warning from no less a person than the Chancellor that the Kabaka had ordered Mukajanga, the chief executioner, to kill him when next he brought the mission-boat to the port the Kabaka had given him. The Chancellor had no love for the white men, but considered that the murder of another European at this time would be bad policy and, somehow, he endured Mackay better than any other white man. Mackay kept away from the danger spot, and for some weeks did not go to Court. When next he visited Mwanga, about the middle of April, a scene occurred that throws some light on Mukajanga's reply to Joseph Mukasa's last message to the Kabaka.

In the audience hall, Mackay reproached Mwanga for treating him as an enemy.

'What proof do you offer of that?' asked the Kabaka.

'What order did you give to Mukajanga?' countered Mackay.

'Who told you about that?'

'Is it not true?' replied the missionary.

'Well then,' suggested the Kabaka, 'let us plead our case.'

Lukoto, an assistant judge was present, and a sort of informal trial scene was enacted. Kulugi stated the case for the Kabaka and then Mackay stated his own. When he had finished, Kulugi said, 'The case goes against us.'

Joseph Mukasa and his executioner must have envisaged a similar sort of scene before the judgment seat of God, when the former said that, if the Kabaka did not repent, he would be his accuser, and the executioner offered to conduct the defence of his master.

Mwanga was, however, incorrigible. When, a few days later, a letter arrived from the British Consul at Zanzibar reproaching him for the murder of Bishop Hannington, he reacted to it by imprisoning on some trivial pretext Honorat Nyonyintono and Bruno Serunkuma; deposing his new Chamberlain, Peter Damulira; and threatening to burn down the village of Alexis Sebowa, a Catholic chief who was emulating the example of Andrew Kaggwa and Matthew Kisule in charity to his fellows and zeal for the spread of Christianity.

Easter Sunday, 25 April 1886, passed quietly although, because of a strong rumour that the Christians were to be seized on that day, there were poor attendances at both missions. Exactly one month later, on 25 May, the storm, which had been threatening for so long, finally broke.

During that month, other incidents had occurred to increase Mwanga's anger and exasperation with the Christians. One of these was the exploit of the Princess Nalumansi, an act that thoroughly shocked the pagan public opinion of Buganda.

The Princess, a daughter of the late Kabaka, had been baptized by the Protestants. Then, contrary to the old Kiganda tradition, which forbade princesses of the blood to marry, she became engaged to Joseph Kaddu, a Catholic baptized in 1880. She was married, with dispensation for a mixed marriage and, later, two days after Easter 1886, received into the Catholic Church, taking the name Clara. Some days later, she was appointed to succeed a namesake, who had died, as guardian of the tomb of Kabaka Jjunju.

When Clara and her husband arrived at Luwunga to take up the appointment, they found the predecessor's house littered with amulets and charms. Clara, unwilling to live in a house containing 'the things of Satan', made a bonfire of all of them and also drove away the witch-doctor in attendance on the shrine. Not content with these shocks to public opinion, she next, on 22 May, took her umbilical cord, which her mother had just brought from Kasubi and which she was supposed to preserve with superstitious reverence, cut it in pieces, and threw it into a hole.

In the eyes of the pagans these acts were crimes of the most serious nature, bound to provoke the vengeance of the gods in the form of some public calamity. They thought that the Princess and her husband should be burnt to death, to expiate the offence and to appease the outraged gods. However, although both Kabaka and chiefs were highly annoyed, laying the blame for the 'sacrilege' on the influence of the missionaries, their anger was soon diverted into other channels, and the Princess, for the moment, went unpunished.[1] In the eyes of Mwanga himself, the worst feature of the case was the courageous independence shown by a mere woman, an independence which not only put him, her brother, to shame, but led him to believe the oft repeated accusation that the Christians would, when powerful enough, follow the English example and place a woman on the throne of Buganda.

Another incident, in connection with the Protestant page Matthias Gayiya, took place on the same day, 22 May. One of Mwanga's Muslim friends, the new Domestic Chamberlain, Lutaya, asked for the loan of this young page for an evil purpose. Although Mwanga granted the request, the boy bravely stood out against the shameful treatment to which Lutaya wished to subject him. As a punishment, he was severely beaten and confined in the stocks for two days. Ashe suggests that 'this splendid act of disobedience, when reported to Mwanga, served to set the spark to the train which had already been prepared'. In fact, such refusals on the part of the Christian pages, many of them to the Kabaka's own face, were not uncommon at this period, and Mwanga had come to expect them. Gayiya's noble resistance undoubtedly added fuel to the fire of his anger, as did the actions of Clara Nalumansi. Either incident might well have set off the explosion that was imminent, but neither actually did so.

Ashe was probably led to conclude that it was Gayiya's refusal that 'set the spark', because the event that finally did so, the absence of the page Mwafu when Mwanga wanted him, appeared too trivial to have produced so violent a reaction. Indeed, for lack of one piece of evidence, later supplied by Daudi Nyondo, and because of a misquotation of Mwanga's words (involving one syllable only in the Luganda), hardly anyone hitherto seems to have realized the full significance of the events of 25 May 1886. That it was indeed this incident that finally threw Kabaka Mwanga into a paroxysm of rage, to which the adjectives 'mad' or 'beserk' may be applied without exaggeration, is confirmed by James Miti, who writes : 'The persecution period began with an incident which though trifling in itself and affording little provocation, later resulted in a wholesale slaughter of Christian converts.'

Before this 'trifling incident' is described, however, we must briefly review the personnel and dispositions of the little army of martyrs on the eve of its battle for Christ, so that there is no need to interrupt the story of events later.

15th November 1885

I   Protomartyr   JOSEPH MUKASA   Majordomo
                          BALIKUDDEMBE   of Kabaka
                                                       Mwanga

26th May to 3rd June 1886

II	Mityana Group	{ MATTHIAS KALEMBA the MULUMBA Luke Banabakintu Noe Mawaggali	} Officials of the county chief of Ssingo

III Pages under Kabaka Mutesa	{ ANDREW KAGGWA James Buzabaliawo Pontian Ngondwe Bruno Serunkuma	} Kabaka Mwanga's Bandsmen and Guards
	Anatole Kiriggwajjo Athanasius Bazzekuketta Adolphus Mukasa Ludigo Gonzaga Gonza	} Kabaka Mwanga's Pages, employed in the

IV Pages under Kabaka Mwanga	CHARLES LWANGA Achilles Kiwanuka Ambrose Kibuka Mukasa Kiriwawanvu† Mbaga Tuzinde* Gyavira Musoke*	} (a) Court of the audience hall
	Mugagga Lubowa* Kizito* Denis Ssebuggwawo	} (b) Private section of the Palace

27th January 1887

V   Last Martyr   Jean-Marie Muzeyi   Ex-Page of
                                                             Kabaka
                                                             Mutesa

---

Leaders in Capital Letters
*Baptized by Charles Lwanga
†Unbaptized.

Chapter Eleven

ACTION STATIONS

Of the twenty-two Uganda Martyrs declared 'Blessed' in 1920 by Pope Benedict XV, twenty died between 26 May and 3 June 1886. The other two were Joseph Mukasa Balikuddembe and Jean-Marie Muzeyi. The former was put to death in November of the previous year, and the latter in January of the year following, in 1887. Thirteen of the Catholics who died during the nine days of 1886 were royal pages; four were royal bandsmen or guards; and three belonged to the entourage of the county chief of Ssingo.

It was the pages who bore the brunt of Kabaka Mwanga's fury. Indeed it seems possible that, but for the intervention of Chancellor Mukasa, the pages and royal retainers alone might have suffered. Mwanga himself was not moved by any strong or enduring hatred for Christianity itself but by anger against those who, instead of being the abject slaves that both he and Kiganda tradition expected them to be, dared, under the influence of Christianity, to call their souls their own, and refused to comply with demands they considered sinful.

But Mukasa, the Chancellor, and the more die-hard pagan chiefs who surrounded him had a deep and enduring hatred of Christianity and all that it represented. They were simply awaiting the opportunity to translate that hatred into calculated and deliberate action. The Kabaka's outburst of fury against his Christian pages gave the Chancellor the opportunity for which he had been waiting and he used it to seek out and destroy most of the Christian leaders, both Catholic and Protestant.

When, on 25 May 1886, the storm finally broke, the Court was at Munyonyo, a royal enclosure near the Lake about six miles from Mengo. But for this circumstance, due to the destruction by fire of the Mengo buildings in February, the death-roll amongst the pages and royal retainers would certainly have been much higher. The enclosure at Munyonyo, little more than a hunting lodge, was so much smaller than that at Mengo that the usual small army of pages and servants could not be accommodated there, and so numbers of Christians, who otherwise, on the morning of the 26 May, would have had to make the choice between God and the Kabaka, were absent from Court and having missed the first flush of the royal anger remained fairly safe from molestation, unless they chanced to be on the Chancellor's list. Mwanga himself lacked the tenacity of purpose to seek them out and the Chancellor was not interested in the smaller fry.

The buildings and grounds at Munyonyo, although much smaller, were laid out on the same traditional plan as those at Mengo. One of the more important buildings was the audience hall, of which Charles Lwanga was in charge. Under his command were the four senior pages, who had formerly served Kabaka Mutesa and been pupils of Joseph Mukasa, and five more recently appointed pages. The four seniors were the two Banyoro pages, Adolphus Mukasa Ludigo and Anatole Kiriggwajjo; the Musoga Gonzaga Gonza and the Muganda, Athanasius Bazzekuketta. All these had been baptized by Père Lourdel the second night after Joseph Mukasa's death. The five junior pages, all Baganda, were Ambrose Kibuka and Achilles Kiwanuka, also baptized on 18 November, and three catechumens, Mbaga Tuzinde, Gyavira Musoke and Mukasa Kiriwawanvu.

Mukasa Kiriwawanvu was already in prison when his companions were called upon to make their momentous decision on 26 May. Shortly before, in the course of a quarrel with Gyavira, he had struck the younger boy on the abdomen with a piece of wood and drawn blood. Probably more frightened than hurt, Gyavira had run in tears to the Kabaka, who roundly abused the culprit for striking a boy smaller than himself, and sent him to the prison of Mukajanga, the chief executioner.

Anatole Kiriggwajjo also, though remaining at liberty, was in disfavour with the Kabaka because of his refusal to accept a promotion which would, he felt, have placed him in grave moral danger.

Also at the Palace, but employed in the private apartments and therefore not under Charles Lwanga's jurisdiction, were the two catechumens, Mugagga and Kizito and, in personal attendance upon the Kabaka, Denis Ssebuggwawo, a neophyte baptized on 16 November.

Mugagga and Kizito, and their fellow-page from the audience hall, Gyavira, all good-looking boys, were special objects of Kabaka Mwanga's unwelcome attentions but, encouraged by their fellow Christians, had managed to stand firm against both blandishments and threats. Like his companions, the little Kizito, aged about fourteen and youngest of the martyrs, had no illusions about the danger of resisting his Kabaka's evil desires. He was constantly beseeching Père Lourdel to baptize him because, he said, the Kabaka would not think twice about putting him to death. The priest put him off, telling him that he was too young to know his own mind and also insufficiently instructed; but, refusing to be discouraged, the lad persisted with his entreaties. On one occasion he stayed the whole night at the mission, declaring that he would not leave until the date for his baptizm was fixed. On another evening, Lourdel was only able to get rid of him by taking him in his arms and putting him out through the window. Finally, yielding to the boy's importunities and moved by his obvious sincerity, Père Lourdel promised to baptize him in a month's time. Before the month was over, Kizito was both baptized and a martyr.

Apart from the pages but closely associated with the Court, were the head bandsman, Andrew Kaggwa; his lieutenant, James Buzabaliawo; and the two guardsmen, Pontian Ngondwe and Bruno Serunkuma.

Andrew Kaggwa, a Munyoro, was still a great favourite of the Kabaka, and his constant companion on hunting and fishing trips. He generally lived at Kiwatule, close to Kigowa which, under his guidance, had become a flourishing Christian centre dear to the hearts of the Christians as the first place where they had practised their religion openly after the death of Mutesa. Andrew also had an estate at Ttaka Jjunge, not far from Munyonyo, where he had taken up residence while the Court was at Munyonyo. Living with him was his chief assistant, James Buzabaliawo. Andrew Kaggwa was a tower of strength to the Christian pages, who went to him for instruction and guidance when they needed it; for nursing when they were sick; and for encouragement and refuge when the Kabaka's importunities became too irksome. His was one of the first fully Christian families : he himself was baptized in April 1882, and his wife and infant daughter in November 1885. His popularity and the great influence he had with the Christians and even with the Kabaka himself made Andrew a particular object of the Chancellor's hatred.

Of the two Palace guards Bruno Serunkuma, by nature imperious and passionate, was not finding it easy to break with the past and school himself in Christian virtue. On one occasion at least, when tax collecting for the Kabaka, he used methods which, although common enough in his day, were definitely extortionate. He also accepted as a present from the Kabaka a Musoga slave girl, who was soon with child by him. Père Lourdel came to hear of these lapses and went in search of the stray sheep. He was successful; for not only did Bruno repent and fulfil wholeheartedly the penance imposed but, feeling that the company and example of his fellow Christians, especially of his great friend Charles Lwanga, would be a help and safeguard, left Kitebi, where he lived with his nephew Alexander Kadoko, and settled down in his guard's tent in the royal enclosure. Here he took up again, with renewed zeal, the work of spreading the faith and helping to instruct converts. On the morning of 26 May he voluntarily joined the group of Christian pages set aside by the Kabaka for slaughter.

The other guard, Pontian Ngondwe, like Mukasa Kiriwawanvu, was already in prison when the persecution broke out. Shortly before, the Kabaka had decided on a cattle levy, and had sent out collectors to seize one cow from each herd that they could find. The Muslim, Abdul Aziz Buliwadda, was appointed collector in chief and Pontian Ngondwe one of his assistants. Both men ran into trouble in carrying out their task, and both ended up in prison.

Abdul Aziz is mentioned in most accounts of the Uganda Martyrs as a 'cattle-thief'. He was in fact a royal servant who was unfortunate enough to offend the wrong people when fulfilling the delicate and hazardous task entrusted to him. Abdul, having sent Ngondwe to conduct the levy in Kyaddondo County, went off himself to Buddu. He seems to have made the mistake of not first presenting himself to the county chief and asking for the chief's legate. He had, nevertheless, managed to collect a number of cattle and cover part of the county when he came to the hamlet of Lusalire, where he proposed to corral his cattle overnight before proceeding on his way. Probably because there was no legate with the party, the local chief objected and blows were exchanged. In the course of the dispute, Abdul Aziz shot the sub-chief, wounding him in the leg. When the county chief, who was a protégé of the Chancellor, heard of this, he confiscated the cattle, arrested Abdul and sent him in custody to his patron the Chancellor. The unfortunate Abdul Aziz found himself committed to prison under sentence of death on two counts, failure to collect the cattle required by the Kabaka and wounding the sub-chief. He was actually taken to Namugongo with the martyrs, to be burnt to death with them, and only spared at the last minute as a result of their earnest entreaties on his behalf. As he was an eye-witness of the death of the martyrs, and actually saw Charles Lwanga suffering his slow martyrdom, his evidence is most valuable and helps to clear up a number of points that were formerly obscure.

Pontian Ngondwe's 'crime' was of a different character. He completed the levy in Kyaddondo County without incident, and returned to the Capital with his quota of cattle for the Kabaka, but was then accused of taking a cow belonging to Mukajanga, the executioner, instead of one belonging to the herdsman. It is easy to understand how this could happen, if one knows something of the custom of the country. The Bahima, the professional herdsmen of Buganda, used to herd their clients' cattle together with their own and, in the absence of any system of branding or marking the cattle, they naturally reported any loss by theft, death, or wild animals, or any barrenness in a cow, as occurring to the client's property and not to their own. It seems clear that Ngondwe carried out his instructions, which were to take one cow from each herdsman, and that this particular herdsman, in deciding upon which of his client's should bear the loss, picked on the executioner. When Mukajanga complained to the Kabaka, the latter committed Ngondwe to prison, saying, 'his Christian friends will join him there'.

The third group of 1886 martyrs was not attached to the royal court but to that of the chief of Ssingo County. Two of them, Matthias Kalemba and Luke Banabakintu, ranked as sub-chiefs and the third, Noe Mawaggali, was the county chief's potter. Under the guidance of these leaders, a flourishing Christian community some two hundred strong had grown at and around Mityana, the county headquarters. Most of these were still catechumens who received instruction from the three Christian leaders and also, second-hand, from the priests at the capital.

When the persecution broke out, Noe Mawaggali was at Mityana, and Matthias Kalemba was at Mengo with his chief, whose duty it was to rebuild the burnt-out Palace. Luke Banabakintu, who had come up to Mengo with the Mulumba and the county chief but been sent back to Mityana on some errand, was actually on the road back to Mengo when he heard the news of the arrest of the Christians. Scorning the opportunity to go into hiding, he continued his journey and gave himself up to his chief.

There were other groups of Christians in various parts of the country. Some of these escaped molestation altogether; some had their leaders arrested and imprisoned; but none, as far as is known, was called upon to give martyrs to the Faith. Around Matthew Kisule, the royal gunsmith, for instance, there was quite a numerous gathering of Christians and catechumens. No less than five of his retainers were baptized with him, on 17 November 1885, and many others were under instruction. Kisule, having missed the first frenzied outburst of the Kabaka's anger, during which no one was safe, was later protected by his specialized knowledge, so valuable to the Kabaka. Even when the persecution was at its height, Kisule practised his religion openly, moved about freely, and gave refuge and shelter to fugitives, both Catholic and Protestant. James Miti, himself a Protestant, pays tribute to Kisule's charity in this respect and, incidentally, contradicts the theory that the later dissensions between Catholics and Protestants were due to the efforts of the early missionaries. Miti writes :

Of all the hiding places, the most frequently used was Matthew Kisule the blacksmith's estate at Natete, where even before the persecution days catechumens would turn in at noon, or late in the

136

evening, on their way from the Natete (Protestant) Catechumenate and put up there for the night. In the early days, especially during the persecution, there was no distinction of religion or denomination; we were all Christians, whether one went to Mackay or Père Lourdel for religious instruction. All Christian converts were one family, with two internal arbitrary divisions as it were; we loved one another, and wished one another well. It was only at Kabula, during our exile, that trouble began, that religious differences sprang up and culminated in the well-known religious civil wars of the early days.

Another Christian centre had grown up around Alexis Ssebowa, chief of Kitabazi, who actually gave himself up as a Christian to the Mujasi. However, he was saved from harm and set at liberty through the intervention of the Chancellor himself, who had a personal liking for him.

Joseph Nsingisira, on the other hand, though saved from death through the good offices of Kulugi and other chiefs, was imprisoned and kept in chains for over two years, as were Isaac Kajane, twin brother of Denis Ssebuggwawo, and another convert named Lwanga.

The persecution, then, was by no means systematic or comprehensive. Of those who died, or suffered in other ways, some were victims of Mwanga's outburst of anger, some were deliberately sought out by the calculating and cold-blooded Chancellor, and some were just caught up in the flood of anti-Christian feeling unleashed by the Kabaka's violence.

The occasion for Mwanga's outburst was the absence, when he wanted them, of two of his pages, and especially the absence of the Chancellor's young son, Mwafu. To understand how so apparently trivial a cause could have produced so violent a reaction, one must know of the relations existing between the Kabaka and this page. The clue is provided by Daudi Nyondo, one-time chief of Mukono (Busiro), who says, 'When Mwafu, the son of Chancellor Mukasa, came to Court, he was a very pretty boy. Soon, the Kabaka took a fancy to him and committed sodomy with him'. This piece of evidence, read in conjunction with Mwanga's fulsome praise of the youth, quoted in the next chapter, explains why Mwanga's smouldering anger against his Christian pages burst suddenly into an all-consuming flame. Their attempt to convert Mwafu was, in his eyes, the crowning infamy. Not content with humiliating him themselves by refusing to comply with the wishes of their Kabaka and thus offering him an affront unprecedented in the history of Buganda, they were now, deliberately he thought, attempting to rob him of his favourite and so far always compliant toy by teaching him the religion which made them prefer death to submission to his shameful demands.

This, for Mwanga, was the last straw which broke the always slender rein he had upon his temper and turned him, for the time being, into a raging fury.

James Miti, who makes no mention of the Kabaka's homosexuality, confirms that it was indeed the instruction of Mwafu which caused Mwanga's mad rage. He writes :

> Meanwhile, both Denis Ssebuggwawo and Mwafu were brought before the Kabaka, who fumed with rage against the former for daring to give religious instruction to the latter, who was otherwise a most obedient and dutiful servant of the Kabaka.

Chapter Twelve

THE DAY OF WRATH

On the afternoon of Tuesday, 25 May 1886, Mwanga suddenly decided to go hippopotamus hunting and, sending the young Kizito ahead to order the canoes, left his palace at Munyonyo at about two o'clock with some twenty attendants. No hippo was sighted; so after shooting at a few birds the royal party returned to the lake-shore at about five o'clock.

On disembarking, the Kabaka, already disgruntled at the failure of his hunt, walked a few paces, looked around and said :

'I do not see any of my attendants here. Where are they all?'

'They did not know that you were out hunting,' replied one of his companions, probably Andrew Kaggwa.[1] 'If they had known they would have been here to a man.' Mwanga refused to be placated.

'Rubbish!' he said. 'I know very well where they are; they have gone off to the white men to study religion. Now I know that the country is no longer mine, but the white men's. Even Mwafu, the son of my Chancellor, the only one of my pages who is completely loyal and devoted to me, always ready to obey my slightest wish, even he is absent; and here am I, alone and foresaken. It's a disgrace!'[2]

A boy called Kayiggwa, who was watching the return of the hunting party, said :

'I met Ssebuggwawo and Mwafu on the road, near Ttaka Jjunge. They were on their way towards Mengo.'

'There!' exclaimed Mwanga. 'They have gone to Kisule's place to learn religion. Am I your Kabaka? Or does Buganda belong to the white men? Don't I provide enough meat for you at the Palace, or are the snakes you eat at the white men's place more palatable than the meat I provide?'

All the way back to the Palace, Mwanga continued to grumble in the same vein.

Arrived at the Palace, he entered the enclosure by the rear gate and made his way to his own apartments where, finding no pages in attendance, he began to shout angrily for them. The cry was taken up by others, and, before long, both Ssebuggwawo and Mwafu came running. Meanwhile, Mwanga demanded his spears from Apolo Kagwa, his armourer and, too impatient to wait for the store to be opened, seized Apolo's sword and hacked open the door himself. When the boys arrived, he shouted angrily at Mwafu :

'Where have you come from? Tell me exactly where you have been, and no lying!'

'I have been with Ssebuggwawo,' replied the youth.

'What have you been doing?'

'He has been teaching me religion.'

'So!' shouted the Kabaka, striking the boy with his hand. 'It is Ssebuggwawo who sets you against me, and takes you constantly to Kisule's to study religion! Did your father send you here to serve me or to learn the religion of the white men?'

Mwanga then turned on Ssebuggwawo.

'Has Mwafu been with you?'

'Yes,' replied Sebuggwawo.

'What business had you with him?'

'I have been teaching him religion.' Turning back to Mwafu, the Kabaka said angrily :

'So, it's true! You're learning religion too now, are you?'

'Yes, I am studying religion.' Beside himself with fury, Mwanga again shouted at Ssebuggwawo :

'And you constantly take the son of my vassal along to Kisule's place to instruct him in religion! Haven't you heard me forbid the teaching of religion here?'

'Yes, I have been instructing him in the Christian religion,' replied Ssebuggwawo.

'So, it is you that are responsible for trying to convert him?'

'Yes, I am the one that instructs him.' Kabaka Mwanga, by now in a raging temper, picked up the spear *Muwa butwa* (which gives poison), a small spear which had belonged to his father Mutesa, and savagely belaboured the boy, beating him about the head, neck and chest, until the spear broke in his hand.[1] Then, seizing the stunned and prostrate boy by the arm, he dragged him out of his own court-yard, through the ivory court, into that of the audience hall, shouting wildly all the while for men to take Ssebuggwawo and kill him.

The official executioners were not at hand, so the two Muslims, Kyayambadde and Mberenge, Mwanga's constant companions, ran to relieve their master of his victim and dragged the martyr out of the royal enclosure.

Still holding the broken spear, Mwanga strode off to the court of the stores where he found the assistant Treasurer, the Protestant Apolo Kagwa, whom he promptly assaulted. Apolo himself describes the incident :

And me, Apolo Kagwa, the Kabaka gave many strokes of the stick and three gashes on the top of my head; and he kicked me and kicked me; and when he had finished kicking me he threw my books into the fire and said, 'Don't pray any more!'

Mwanga is also reported to have said to Apolo : 'If Kulugi had not told me that you are very obedient, I would have killed you.'

Still seeking for further victims to vent his rage on, Mwanga set off for the house of Andrew Kaggwa, outside the palace grounds. On the way, he encountered his majordomo, Honorat Nyonyintono, a prominent Catholic.

'Who is that fellow?' asked the Kabaka.

'It is Nyonyintono,' replied those who were with him.

'Isn't he also a Christian?' Nyonyintono, coming up to his master, answered for himself.

'Master, don't you recognize me? I am Nyonyintono, your servant. Don't you know that I am a Christian?' Mwanga's answer was to order one of his followers to take the 'snake-eater' to Sebatta, the executioner usually entrusted with this horrible task, to be castrated.

At the hut of Andrew Kaggwa, Mwanga found only James Buzabaliawo the bandsman, Andrew's second-in-command. There was no need to ask whether James was a Christian. He had often, while Mwanga was still a Prince, attempted to put him through his catechism. James knelt before the royal visitor who merely pushed him over with his foot and ordered his arrest. The young man was promptly stripped of his clothing and taken off to prison.

It seems probable that in the course of his rampage through the palace and to Andrew Kaggwa's the Kabaka also encountered the Protestants Muddu-aguma and Musa Mukasa. The latter was butchered that night near the royal well, and Muddu-aguma, having suffered the same barbarous mutilation as Nyonyintono, died as a result of it on the following day, 26 May. Hardly anything else is known of this victim. Miti mentions him, his religion and the manner of his death, but does not give his tribe or clan.

The first object of Mwanga's violence on this memorable evening, the young page Denis Ssebuggwawo, was not, as the Kabaka had ordered, killed at once, but was lying in custody at the house of Mpinga Kaloke, one of the official executioners.

Kyayambadde and Mberenge, after relieving their master and boon companion of his stunned and bleeding victim, dragged Ssebuggwawo towards the main gate where they were seen by Simeon Nsubuga, himself to suffer mutilation for his faith. In the square outside the gate, they stripped the martyr of his clothing and then took him along the road to the left, past the residence of the Guardian of the Cord. As neither of the Muslims was armed, Kyayambadde ran into the house where Mberenge lodged and seized a knife that was used for cutting up the Kabaka's meat. The occupants of the house objected, saying, 'What! Are you proposing to use a butcher's knife on a man?' But the Muslim insisted on taking the knife and, together with his companion, went off with the intention of trying to behead the martyr with the knife.

Before they could carry out their horrible plan, one of the professional executioners, Mpinga Kaloke, seems to have arrived on the scene and relieved them of their prisoner. The rest of the story was told to Desiré Wamala by a boy named Louis Musoke, at that time a pagan in the service of Mpinga Kaloke.

> When Kyayambadde had taken Ssebuggwawo from the Kabaka's presence, he handed him over to the executioner, Mpinga Kaloke. This man took Ssebuggwawo to his house; he did not kill him at once, but let him spend the night there. Next morning, Mpinga ordered his men, Mattembe and Mulyowa, to put Ssebuggwawo to death, and they killed him in a wood adjoining the enclosure of the executioners. They took knives, not spears, with them; which fact led people to believe that the victim was hacked to pieces.
>
> At that time I was still a pagan and a servant of Mpinga Kaloke. When Ssebuggwawo was brought in, he was made to spend the night in the hut in which I slept. I saw him there with my own eyes. He had been given a small piece of bark-cloth about his loins. He spent the night without speaking a word, and the executioners did not attempt to make him apostatize.
>
> The reason why they let him live the night was, as they said amongst themselves, 'This fellow is a nephew[1] of the Chancellor. Perhaps his uncle will want to intercede for him and save him.' But, in the morning, when they heard that it had been decided to put the Christians to death, they took him away, at about eight o'clock, to kill him.[2]

In Buganda, as in Ninive of old, victims of the royal anger were not buried. Their corpses were left lying where they had been slain, to be devoured by hyenas, jackals, vultures or ants. Nor was there for the martyr Ssebuggwawo any Muganda Tobias to brave the anger of the Kabaka and give his body decent burial. It was left lying in the wood where, six days later, one witness saw vultures feeding on the remains.

When the Kabaka had stormed into the court of the audience hall, dragging Ssebuggwawo by the arm, shouting for someone to kill him, and uttering threats of death to all Christians, there was a momentary panic amongst the younger pages, who were gathered there taking counsel with their leaders.

Reports of Mwanga's behaviour on the way back from the lake-shore had made it clear to the leaders that the pattern, already set in Mwanga's attack upon Joseph Mukasa, was repeating itself; that the Kabaka was deliberately working himself up into a passion, and that some violent action could be expected. Nyonyintono, Charles Lwanga, Andrew Kaggwa, Nasibu and other leading Christians advised the younger pages to flee from the Court for the time being. These, however protested that to do so would be equivalent to denying their religion. Charles Lwanga argued that it was not right for all, both big and small, to perish, and urged the boys to leave the enclosure before the gates were closed for the night.

The question was still being debated when the Kabaka burst in on their deliberations, dragging Ssebuggwawo with him, and yelling like one possessed. As might be expected, the younger boys were stricken with panic at this violent eruption and fled from the presence of the madman. Most of them, however, did not go far. They halted their flight and gathered again near the main gate to the Palace where, after a short discussion, they decided that the only charge that could be brought against them was their religion and bravely returned to their posts.

Two of them, Denis Kamyuka and a friend, went a little further afield. They decided to go to Matthew Kisule at Ttaka Jjunge, to tell him what had happened to Ssebuggwawo, what the Kabaka had threatened in his rage, and to ask for Matthew's advice.

'My young friends,' said Kisule, after he had listened to their tale and asked a number of questions, 'none would deny that you have every right to take to flight and escape; but, if I judge rightly, I believe that your dearest wish is to lay down your lives for the King of Heaven?'

'We assured him that this was indeed so,' says Kamyuka, to whom we owe the report of this conversation.

'In that case,' said Matthew, 'I am sure that Père Lourdel himself would be the first to advise you to return quickly to the Court, where Charles and the other pages are waiting for you. They will not fail to set you an example in courage; and if the Kabaka has you beheaded, Kamyuka, like your friend Ssebuggwawo, it will be a glorious death.'

Denis and his companion, boys of about fourteen, quoting the words of Christ that they had heard so often from the priests in these days of peril, 'Whosoever shall confess Me before men, him shall the Son of Man confess before the angels of God,' made up their minds to go back to the Kabaka.

'We pressed the hard calloused hands of the noble blacksmith,' says Kamyuka, 'and sped away quickly. Soon, however, my friend Kato,[1] without any fear of the two hours' journey in the dark, parted from me, saying, "I must go first to Nalukolongo to warn Mapèra (Père Lourdel)". As for myself, I found the gate to the palace shut and guarded, so I decided to seek shelter with the gallant captain, Andrew Kaggwa.'

Kamyuka was unable to enter the palace that night because the Kabaka, on returning from his excursion to Andrew Kaggwa's house, had given orders to the executioner, Mukajanga, to post his men on guard around the enclosure, so that no pages might escape during the night. Fires were lighted near each of the gates and the executioners gathered round them, beating their drums, drinking beer, singing, dancing and jesting about the work in store for them on the morrow.

Mwanga himself, the edge of his fury blunted by the orgy of violence, slaughter and mutilation in which he had indulged, began to reflect upon the need for moral support in the further action he planned against the Christians. He therefore summoned a meeting for the next morning of the chiefs likely to back him, and retired to his own quarters.

Did the young tyrant, barely out of his teens, manage to sleep? It seems unlikely. Apart from the hideous din created by the executioners around their camp-fires, the violent paroxysm of rage in which he had indulged himself would hardly be conducive to repose. He would also have found it necessary to bolster up his naturally vacillating resolution by reviewing his grievances against the pages. One 'insult' that he seems to have brooded over during the night was the refusal of the Munyoro page, Anatole Kiriggwajjo, to accept a promotion offered to him. He certainly singled out this youth for punishment first thing in the morning, before the other pages could be assembled. Mwanga must also have prepared himself to justify his actions of the evening to the chiefs who had been summoned for an early morning meeting.

Amongst those who expected to die on the morrow, the greatest calm prevailed. They were by no means insensible of the fate that awaited them and the monotonous drumming, the songs and howls of the executioners were a constant reminder of their peril. But they had long been expecting this trial and had prepared themselves to face it. After the first moment of panic, the pages who had fled returned to the audience hall, where Charles Lwanga was delighted to welcome them and offer them words of encouragement. The hours of darkness were passed in prayer, instruction and exhortation, and when dawn approached, Charles Lwanga baptized five of the most promising catechumens.

Elsewhere in the palace, the Protestant pages, most of whom belonged to the outer courts, seem to have been similarly engaged. At least one of them, named Mukasa,[1] visited the audience hall to consult with the Catholic leader and, on his return, told his fellow pages that Charles had just baptized his companions. 'We also are going to be killed,' he added, 'but do not renounce your religion. Let us pray!'

By early morning the young page Denis Kamyuka, who had found himself locked out the previous evening, was back in the palace, having been smuggled in, almost certainly through one of the private gateways, by his patroness the Princess Nassiwa. He rejoined his companions in the audience hall in time to hear the conclusion of Charles Lwanga's words of encouragement to the pages. He reports :

> Far from thinking about escape or concealment, the Christian pages, gathered round their leader Charles Lwanga, listened with close attention to his words. 'Several times,' he reminded them, 'the Kabaka has commanded you to apostatize. It seems likely that very shortly he will again order you to forsake your religion. Then, you have only to follow me in a body, and boldly affirm that you are Christians. Not one of you need feel indebted to me: I count it a privilege to be your leader. If, however, it happens that on this occasion also you are not called upon to suffer for your faith, never weaken in your resolution.'
>
> All, and I was one of them, swore wholeheartedly that we would remain faithful.
>
> Then Charles Lwanga's glance rested on Mugagga, Kizito, Mbaga, Gyavira and Werabe, who had all long sighed for baptism. He had instructed them, watched over them and protected them. Now that martyrdom was about to interrupt their catechumenate, how could he deny them baptism? He did, however, refuse this favour to Mwafu and four others of whom he was less sure. As for myself, I had already been baptized by Père Lourdel on 26 April, with eight others.
>
> I congratulated especially my friend Mugagga, who was overjoyed. As for Kizito, he had been somewhat unnerved by the barbarous treatment of Honorat Nyonyintono, Denis Ssebuggwawo and James Buzabaliawo. From time to time, an involuntary shudder shook his small frame. Charles tried to re-assure him, his voice sweet and persuasive, 'When the decisive moment arrives, I shall take your hand like this. If we have to die for Jesus, we shall die together hand in hand.'

Thus did the young leader, with words of encouragement for one and all, strive to prepare his young charges for the fearsome ordeal that awaited them.

A few miles away, at Nalukolongo on the slopes of Rubaga Hill, the two priests, Lourdel and Giraud, were consumed with anxiety for their flock. At about midnight a Christian, probably the youth

Kato, who had left his friend Kamyuka for this very purpose, had come to the mission to inform them of the events of the evening, and of the perils threatening the Christian pages. Unable to take any action before daylight, the priests prayed for their Christians and waited with heavy hearts for the dawn when, they had agreed, Père Lourdel should set out for Munyonyo, attempt to see the Kabaka, and intercede with him for the pages and other Christians.

Chapter Thirteen

DAY OF JUDGEMENT

When Wednesday 26 May dawned, the sun was obscured, and heavy rain was turning the roads and paths into seas of mud. The weight of sticky red mud that clung to Père Lourdel's shoes, making every step of his six mile walk one of discomfort and misery, was as nothing compared to the weight of anxiety in his heart. As he drew nearer to Munyonyo, his fears mounted. First he met some fugitives, among them the page James Miti, who gave him further particulars of the events of the previous evening and told him of the arrest and mutilation of Honorat Nyonyintono; then he encountered bands of armed men, hurrying off to raid and pillage the property of Christians and seize their leaders. Fearful of arriving too late to do any good, he tried to hasten his steps, and continued on his way, slithering and slipping at each step, in acute distress of mind and body.

At Munyonyo, meanwhile, Kabaka Mwanga had obtained the backing of his chiefs for further measures against the Christians.

First thing in the morning, about six o'clock, he had summoned the principal chiefs to his private apartments. As no Christians were present, the account of what happened at the meeting was not received first-hand, but would seem to be substantially accurate.

After telling the chiefs that he had found it necessary to order the execution of the 'rebellious' page, Ssebuggwawo, Mwanga took the offensive and began to upbraid and blame his hearers for the disobedience of his pages. He said:

'It is your duty to find me loyal servants, but you have given me only traitors, the dregs of your clans. See how they have rebelled against me! Time and time again, I have forbidden them to practise religion, but they do not listen to me. They are disobedient, and learn rebellion from the white men. What am I to do with them?'

Some of his hearers, who like the Chancellor were pagan diehards, delighted to vote for the massacre of the Christians whom they hated. Others, who may have been more sympathetic, were dismayed by the suggestion that they themselves might be held responsible for the actions of those they had presented at Court, and hastened to divert the royal anger from themselves.

'Master,' said one of them, 'when we gave you our children they

147

were good. If now they have become bad, that is not our fault, but the effect of the spell which has been cast upon them. Kill them! We shall provide you with better ones.' Others also expressed their approval of this suggestion, which was clearly what Mwanga wanted from them. Before withdrawing, the servile counsellors went down on their knees and thanked the Kabaka for not making them accountable for the crimes of their children.

Satisfied with the subservience of his chiefs, Mwanga gave orders for all the pages to be assembled and brought before him; commanded the attendance of Mukajanga and his assistant executioners; and appointed Mbugano as royal legate, with powers to seize and plunder Christians in the villages away from Munyonyo.

While waiting for the pages to assemble, Mwanga seems to have found it necessary to find a whetstone for his anger, and picked upon Anatole Kiriggwajjo for the purpose. This Munyoro page, it will be remembered, had refused promotion to a position of importance in the private part of the Palace because of the moral danger associated with it, and by his refusal had offended the young Kabaka. Although Mwanga had not made much of it at the time, the offence rankled. Now he sent for the young man to upbraid him and abuse him and, when he had finally worked himself up to a satisfactory pitch of fury, to commit him to prison, where he would shortly be joined by his fellow Christians.

It seems to have been during this scene of recrimination and abuse that Père Lourdel arrived at the Palace, at about eight o'clock. Because of the rain, very few people were about, but those who were stared in wonder at the bedraggled priest, astonished that he should risk his life by appearing at Court at a time like this.

Commending himself to God, and offering the sacrifice of his own life, the priest first presented himself at the court-house, to pay the customary respects to the Chancellor, and then hurried on to the inner courts. To his surprise, he had no difficulty in penetrating as far as the court of the audience hall, where he was still more astonished to see his Christians at liberty, going about their duties as if nothing untoward had happened. However, he had not been there long before the heads of the various sections began to assemble their charges near the gate leading to the Kabaka's private quarters.

Several neophytes, five of whom had been baptized that morning, seemed unconcerned about what was to come, and joked together as if they had not a care in the world. Others, mainly the older ones, looked grave but calm. Though fully conscious of the ordeal by fire and sword that awaited them, they had schooled themselves to face it bravely without flinching. Some of their pagan companions told

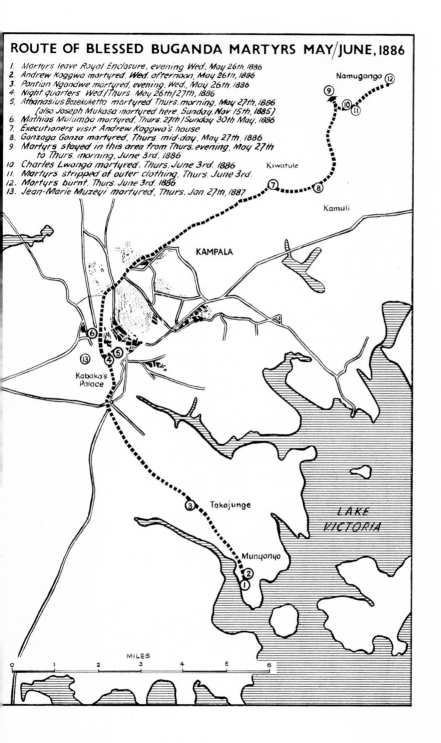

ROUTE OF BLESSED BUGANDA MARTYRS MAY/JUNE, 1886

1. *Martyrs leave Royal Enclosure, evening Wed. May 26th. 1886*
2. *Andrew Kaggwa martyred, Wed. afternoon, May 26th, 1886*
3. *Pontian Ngondwe martyred, evening, Wed. May 26th, 1886*
4. *Night quarters Wed/Thurs May 26th/27th, 1886*
5. *Athanasius Bozekuketta martyred Thurs. morning. May 27th. 1886
   (also Joseph Mukasa martyred here, Sunday, Nov 15th, 1885)*
6. *Mathias Mulumba martyred, Thurs. 27th/Sunday 30th May, 1886*
7. *Executioners visit Andrew Kaggwa's house*
8. *Gonzaga Gonza martyred, Thurs. mid-day. May 27th, 1886*
9. *Martyrs stayed in this area from Thurs. evening, May 27th
   to Thurs. morning, June 3rd, 1886*
10. *Charles Lwanga martyred. Thurs. June 3rd. 1886*
11. *Martyrs stripped of outer clothing, Thurs. June 3rd.*
12. *Martyrs burnt, Thurs. June 3rd. 1886*
13. *Jean-Marie Muzeyi martyred, Thurs. Jan 27th, 1887*

Namugongo ⑫
⑨
⑩ ⑪

Kiwatule

⑦ ⑧

Kamuli

KAMPALA

⑥
⑬ ④⑤
Kabaka's Palace

③ Takajunge

Munyonyo
②
①

LAKE VICTORIA

MILES

0   1   2   3   4   5   6

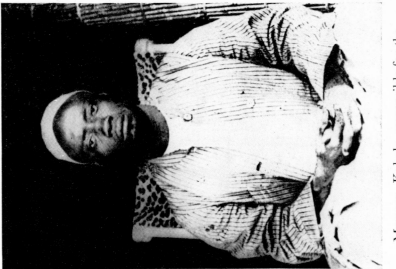

Mwanga, Kabaka responsible for the martyrdoms.

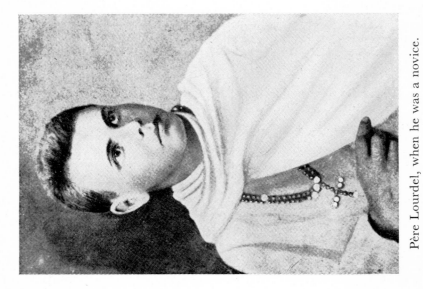

Père Lourdel, when he was a novice.

them that they were fools to sacrifice themselves, and urged them to flee before it was too late. To these they replied : 'Flee? Why should we? So that the Kabaka can treat us as deserters, rebels and cowards? Never! We know that the sole reason for our death is our Faith, and we are ready to sacrifice to our Heavenly King even life itself.'

Père Lourdel, waiting patiently for a chance to intercede with the Kabaka, watched the pages arrive from the different parts of the enclosure and join the groups to which they belonged. Charles Lwanga marshalled his own group and also, because he was next in rank to the imprisoned Majordomo, supervised the gathering of the pages from the private courts. When all had assembled, Charles said in a firm voice, 'Let us go in'.

Followed by the pages, Lwanga went through the gateway to the ivory court, the one adjoining the Kabaka's private courtyard. Their passage through this court was accompanied by taunts and cries of derision from the hundred or so executioners already gathered there. These ferocious-looking men, with cords or nets looped about their shoulders, clad in skins and wearing grotesque wigs and head-dress, were a fearsome sight at any time, but never more than now to the eyes of the young pages; yet, mastering any feelings of dismay they may have experienced, the pages bravely followed their leader through the yelling mob to the Kabaka's private apartments.

Père Lourdel could no longer see his flock, but he heard the yelling mob of executioners, and, rising above the din, the raised voice of the Kabaka still screaming abuse at Anatole Kiriggwajjo.

According to Denis Kamyuka, a member of Charles Lwanga's party, as they reached the threshold of the royal courtyard, they heard Mwanga shouting angrily, 'Take him away and kill him!'

When the pages entered the Kabaka's own courtyard, they found him seated just inside his house, which had a wide open doorway, and with him the Princess Nassiwa, his eldest sister, and two young pages of the Cane-Rat clan.

Charles led the way to the threshold of the house, where he prostrated himself before the Kabaka and gave the usual greeting, to which the Kabaka replied. The other pages, following his example, greeted the Kabaka in turn, singly or in groups of two or three, and then ranged themselves alongside their leader, who had now seated himself on the border of beaten earth, built up to protect the house from flood-water. As the greetings continued, Mwanga began to lose patience and started taunting his pages. 'This dog of mine,' he said, 'behaves better than any of you. When I call him, he comes; when I throw him a bone, he eats it; but you fellows don't obey me at all.'

149

When the last of the pages had greeted him, Mwanga asked, 'Are they all here?' Being assured that none was missing, he ordered the gates to be closed and then, pointing towards the reed fence to his left, said, 'Now, let everyone who follows the religion of the white men go over there. If anyone of that religion tries to hide himself amongst those that remain, he will be beheaded immediately. Those who are not Christians must remain near me.'

At once, Charles Lwanga stood up, saying as he did so, 'That of which a man is fully conscious he cannot disavow.' Then addressing himself to the Kabaka, he said, 'You, Sire, are always telling us that we must do our duty, and you know that we have never shirked it despite the threats of your enemies. To-day then, once again, we take up the position you command.' Then, taking Kizito by the hand, and closely followed by the other Christian pages, he walked calmly to the spot indicated by the Kabaka. His face and the faces of his companions reflected the joy they felt at being called upon to confess their faith in this way.

The group by the fence consisted of Charles Lwanga, Athanasius Bazzekuketta, Adolphus Mukasa Ludigo, Achilles Kiwanuka, Ambrose Kibuka, Gonzaga Gonza, Mbaga Tuzinde, Gyavira Musoke, Mugagga Lubowa, Kizito, Bwewussa, Denis Kamyuka, Werabe, Simeon Sebuta, Mwafu, Ngapi, and the two Protestants, Nasibu, the Kabaka's tailor, and Byakutunga, in charge of the royal hearth. All were pages, either from the court of the audience hall or from the private courts beyond it. Almost at once, however, they were joined by the palace guard, Bruno Serunkuma. Bruno had not been summoned to the Kabaka's presence, but was probably on duty at one of the gates to the courtyard, when he decided to join his fellow Christians in their public profession of faith, thus re-enacting a scene, so common in the days of the early Roman persecutions, when guards or jailors would publicly proclaim themselves Christians and range themselves alongside their prisoners, to share their fate.

When the pages had sorted themselves into the two groups, the Kabaka asked :

'Have all the Christians gone over there? Are there none amongst those who have remained in their places?'

'None,' replied the latter group.

Not satisfied, Mwanga turned to the Muslim Kyayambadde and said, 'Have a look to make sure that there is not a single Christian amongst those who have remained seated.'

While Kyayambadde was going about his task, the Chancellor, who seems to have entered the royal courtyard about this time, probably to ensure that the Kabaka did not proceed to extreme measures against his son Mwafu, was looking over the group by the fence. Noticing Mugagga Lubowa amongst the Christians, he exclaimed :

'You there, Mugagga! What are you doing amongst the Christians? Don't be a fool! When have you learnt to pray? Don't try to make us believe that you are one of them!'

Mugagga, not to be turned from his purpose, rejected the chance of escape thus offered to him. Stepping forward a pace, he said :

'Most certainly I am. Only I have been receiving instruction by night, so as to avoid vexing the Kabaka, and being troubled by you. Charles has been my instructor, model and protector, and I wish to die with him for Jesus. I have spoken.'

Kyayambadde, meanwhile, had found a youth named Wasswa in the other group, and asked him whether he was not a Christian.

'I was receiving instruction,' replied the boy, 'but I am not doing so now.'

The Muslim called out to the Kabaka, who was still seated in the doorway of his house :

'I have discovered this Wasswa here; he used to learn religion, but has since given it up.'

'He lies, the coward!' shouted Mwanga. 'His elder brother Kajane wanted to teach religion to me personally; do you believe that he would not teach his own brother? Go and kill him at once. Don't let him live the night!'[1]

The luckless youth was handed over to the waiting executioners and while being led away by them, professed his belief in Jesus Christ. He was not killed immediately, but put in prison to be burnt to death at Namugongo with the others.

Kyayambadde then reported finding another catechumen named Ntutumo, later baptized Anselm, but Mwanga said, 'Leave that Munyoro slave of mine alone.' Then, satisfied that there were no more Christians in the group near him, he turned to the others.

'Are you all Christians?' he asked.

'Yes. We are Christians,' came the reply.

'Are you unshaken in your resolve to remain Christians?'

'Yes, quite definitely! If you choose not to regard that as a crime, we shall be grateful to you, but we shall never cease to be Christians, whatever the outcome.'

The pagans who heard this answer were astonished and muttered amongst themselves, 'They are simply delivering themselves into the hands of the executioners.'

Mwanga then called in the executioners and shouted, 'Tie up all the Christians!' Then turning to his victims, 'I am going to burn you all!' Then he gave the order to Mukajanga, 'Take them to Namugongo and burn them!'

The executioners threw themselves on the young men and began to tie their wrists and necks with cords. In the confusion, their chief, the old man Mukajanga, pretended to busy himself with his own 'son and father', Mbaga Tuzinde, pleading desperately with the boy to renounce his religion. 'Give up this foolishness which will send you to the stake! Only say that you have abandoned religion, and I will hide you.'

The seventeen year old boy, baptized that morning by Charles Lwanga, firmly rejected the offer. 'Hide me?' he said, 'Father, what are you thinking of? I am a Christian, and I shall remain one to the last.' In despair, the old man begged his fellow executioner, Sebatta, to try whether he could break the boy's resolution. 'Go across to Tuzinde,' he said, 'and say, "What! Since when have you been a Christian? Run away, quickly!"' Sebatta did as he was asked, but Mbaga Tuzinde replied, 'Do you really believe that the Kabaka is my father, as you say? My true father, whom I must obey before all, is in Heaven. I am truly a Christian, so leave me alone.' The executioner had no choice but to let the boy be tied up along with his Christian friends.

When all had been bound, the Kabaka reprieved Mwafu, Ngapi, Bwewussa, Nasibu and Byakutunga. Mwafu, whose absence the previous evening had opened the flood-gates of Mwanga's wrath, was the son of Mukasa, the Chancellor, and protected by the blood-pact which the latter had made with Mwanga's father. He was confined in the stocks for four days before being set at liberty. Ngapi, it is said, was spared because he was an accomplished fly-swatter and, therefore, a contributor to Mwanga's comfort. However, according to Miti, he was castrated. No definite information is available as to why the other three were spared, but one witness suggests that the last two had, on occasion, yielded to Mwanga's solicitations. 'Among the young men who were put to death for their religion,' he says in this connection, 'I have not known a single one who consented to commit sin with the Kabaka. Had they ever consented, he would have spared them, as he spared others, and would not have had them killed.'

Those not reprieved were roped together in two groups, one consisting of the older and taller pages, the other of the smaller boys. One of these at first gave way to tears, but after being comforted by Charles Lwanga with the words, 'Don't cry! Have you not confessed your faith?', dried his tears and assumed the same cheerful expression that distinguished the faces of his companions.

The executioners were astonished. They were accustomed to

wailing and loud lamentations on the part of those being led to execution. The silence, calm resolution and even eagerness for death displayed by these young victims was an entirely new experience.

'Go then! Hurry off to your heavenly King. He has the fatted calf ready for you,' was Mwanga's final taunt to the young Confessors of the Faith. As they were being led out of the royal courtyard, the Princess Nassiwa was heard to ask Mwanga, 'Are you going to kill little Kamyuka too?' Those who overheard the words said to Kamyuka, 'Nassiwa has ransomed you.'

The two bands of prisoners made their way across the ivory court to the court of the audience hall, walking as steadily as their bonds would allow. Mbaga Tuzinde, in his anxiety to get away from the further entreaties of Mukajanga, was even seen to urge his companions to greater haste. On their way, the captives met the group of pages from the outer courts, who were being marched in for their ordeal before the Kabaka, and were able to exchange a few words with them. Gonza called out cheerily to one of his friends in the other group, 'Good-bye! We're off!' and Kizito, noticing his fellow-clansman, Simeon Nsubuga, amongst the others, cried out to him, 'What! Are you going in now? I am sure that you are going to deny your faith.' Happily, he was mistaken.

Their way through the court of the audience hall led the prisoners past Père Lourdel, still waiting patiently in the hope of an audience. Although unable to speak to their Mapèra, the martyrs greeted him with their eyes and then marched on to the prison of Mukajanga, where they were to be kept for the present. As they passed the court-house, the chiefs assembled there hurled insults at them, calling them snake-eaters and shouting, 'Let the Kabaka kill you! We shall give him other pages.'

Overcome with grief, Père Lourdel leaned wearily against the palisade after gazing at the faces of his beloved children, faces which reflected resignation, courage and holy joy. Despite his sorrow, he thanked God for the honour which he was bestowing upon the mission of Buganda by deigning to choose from among its children the first witnesses to the Faith amongst the negroes of Central Africa.

'They were bound so tightly,' he wrote later, describing the encounter, 'that they could scarcely walk and kept knocking against one another. I saw little Kizito laughing at the odd situation. He looked as happy as if he were at play with his friends. ... I saw Charles Lwanga come out, laden with cords that bound him to his companions. The cords which held them together so tightly were but an image of the charity which united them at that solemn moment, when they suffered together and were going to die for the same cause. Strength of purpose showed on the face of Charles. His eyes were slightly misted with tears, not because he feared death, but on account of the emotion which the bitter reproaches of Mwanga had aroused in him.'

About the ordeal of the servants from the outer courts, there is little information available. Lourdel says that there were few Catholics among them; but their chief, the Muslim Sabakaki Wamala, on being asked by the Kabaka how many were Christians, replied that as far as he knew Nabugo was the only one who was not. It should be remembered that the name Christian was applied to anyone who had received some instruction, however meagre. It would appear then that the majority were either Protestants, or had at one time or other attended instruction or reading classes at the Anglican mission.

Wamala's reply, that practically all of his pages were Christians, apparently led the Kabaka to alter his procedure with this group. To separate all the Christians and condemn them en bloc would mean denuding a large part of his palace of servants; so, instead, he began to pick upon individuals.

One of the first to be dealt with was the Catholic, Simeon Nsubuga, said to be a brother of Kizito, although there is actually no evidence of any closer relationship than membership of the same, Lungfish, clan.

'Aren't you also a Christian?' asked the Kabaka.

'Yes. I am a Christian,' was the reply.

'Why have you adopted that religion?'

'Well,' replied Nsubuga, 'I thought that you yourself were going to become a Christian.'

'Did you, indeed? And I suppose you imagined that you were going to teach me?' replied Mwanga with a sneer, and ordered the young man to be taken to the executioner, Sebatta, for castration.

Other victims from this group of pages, who were condemned to death by fire, were Kifamunyanja and Wasswa's companion at the royal prayer-house, Mubi, otherwise known as Mubi-azalwa or Nzalambi. Both were adherents of the Anglican mission, but not baptized, and probably but partly instructed. Both, like Wasswa, at first denied that they were Christians, but later professed their belief in Christ.

It is quite likely that some of the other Protestant martyrs were condemned at this session, but which of them is not known.

The ordeal came to an end suddenly, through the intervention of Kulugi, the pagan treasurer. Kulugi was quite well disposed towards the missionaries. He had been the only chief to counsel moderation when Bishop Hannington was first known to have entered Busoga and, on this terrible morning, he had generously acted as Père Lourdel's messenger to the Kabaka. Now, entering the royal courtyard, probably still on the same errand, he must have noticed that Mwanga, who could never concentrate for long, was beginning to tire of his sport and, seizing the opportunity, asked the Kabaka : 'Do you propose to kill off all your servants to-day, right down to the very last?'

Mwanga, who was just then interrogating the Catholic catechumen, Nganda-za-Kamwa, whom he knew to be a Christian, contented himself with striking the boy, and then dismissed him and all the others.

Lutaya, the Muslim Chamberlain, who had been present and who had given the lie to Kifamunyanja when he denied being a Christian, now asked for the favour he had come to obtain, namely, for Bruno Serunkuma to be handed over to him so that he could satisfy an old grudge. His request was granted, and he had Bruno taken to his own quarters and flogged.

The old score which Lutaya attempted to settle in this way seems to have been in connection with Bruno's sister. Bruno, while yet a pagan, had given his sister in marriage to Lutaya. The woman had since left her husband. This may have been the sole reason for Lutaya's resentment or, possibly, Bruno had also refused to return the dowry.

If the Muslim hoped to make his victim cry out for mercy, he obtained little satisfaction. The soldier bore his flogging stoically and, poking fun at the Kiganda belief in Walumbe, the god of death, said to his tormentor, 'Why not take us away and kill us? Why the delay? We are going to die as proxy for you. Who knows? Perchance, when we have paid for you your tribute to Walumbe, you might escape death altogether.'

After his flogging, Bruno Serunkuma was returned into the custody of the chief executioner, Mukajanga, where he was soon joined by the soldier-bandsman, James Buzabaliawo.

It may have been Lutaya's request for the person of Bruno Serunkuma that reminded Mwanga of the man he had commited to prison the previous evening. He now sent for the prisoner. Buzabaliawo, who seems to have been something of a wag, arrived at the Kabaka's house at the double, as if he were expecting to receive some great favour, although he well knew what was in store for him. The story of this interview was recounted by Sabali, one of the executioners who was present.

'Are you the chief of the Christians of Kigowa?' asked the Kabaka. Mwanga knew very well that Andrew Kaggwa and none other was the leader of the Kigowa Christians but, having got over the first flush of his rage, he was hoping to spare that stalwart friend and companion and ignore his religion, as he did that of Matthew Kisule.

'I am a Christian,' replied Buzabaliawo, 'but the title of chief, which you graciously bestow, does not belong to me.'

Struck by his boldness and assurance, Mwanga turned to those about him. 'This young man gives himself airs,' he said. 'To look at him, one would take him for the Mukwenda!' Mukwenda was the title of the county chief of Ssingo, and a recent holder of that post had been a notorious popinjay.

Buzabaliawo deliberately affected to misunderstand the Kabaka's remark. He prostrated himself before the Kabaka and, placing his hands palm to palm, raised them and brought them down again with a sort of chopping action, diagonally, first from left to right and then from right to left—the traditional Kiganda way of showing gratitude,—exclaiming at the same time :

'Thank you, Sire! Thank you so much for the great chieftainship that you are bestowing upon me.'

Mwanga pretended not to notice this piece of cheerful impertinence, and said :

'This is the fellow that actually attempted to make a Christian of me. Take him away and kill him at once. I want to commence with him.'

'Good-bye, then,' said James, not a whit dismayed. 'I'm off to Paradise to intercede with God for you.'

His words were greeted with laughter by the pagans present, who remarked, 'These Christians must be mad, to talk like that.' The martyr was tied up by the executioners, and led away through the court of the audience hall, where Lourdel was still waiting.

'James passed close to me,' wrote the priest. 'His hands were tied together, and he had a rope round his neck. I lifted my hand to give him a last absolution and he answered by lifting his, bound as they were, to Heaven. He smiled and seemed to say to me, "Mapèra, why be sad? What I suffer now is little compared with the eternal happiness which you have taught me to look forward to".'

James Buzabaliawo was not executed at once, but taken to join the other Christians awaiting execution. To these were added, on Mwanga's orders, the two Christians already in prison, Pontian Ngondwe, the guard, and the page Mukasa Miriwawanvu.

Chapter Fourteen

ANDREW KAGGWA, PONTIAN NGONDWE AND ATHANASIUS BAZZEKUKETTA

Ever since his arrival at Munyonyo at about eight in the morning, Père Lourdel had been making determined efforts to see the Kabaka. He had repeatedly attempted to enter the court adjoining the Kabaka's private residence, but the guards would not let him pass. Most of the courtiers shunned him. Only Kulugi, the Treasurer, had greeted him in a friendly manner and had agreed to bear a message on his behalf to the effect that he was prepared to make any sacrifice the Kabaka demanded, if only he would spare his servants.

Although Mwanga refused to see him, the priest waited on for several hours in the hope that Mwanga might relent and grant him an audience. At last his fears for the safety of the mission itself, and of the orphans in its care, prevailed over his reluctance to leave without fulfilling his mission, and he turned his steps homewards.

Leaving the royal enclosure, he attached himself to the Chancellor, who was also on his way home from the palace. The latter treated the priest with exaggerated politeness as they walked down the hill together, but when Lourdel raised the question uppermost in his mind, and begged him not to put the young Christians to death but rather, if that was thought necessary, to banish the missionaries, the Chancellor replied :

'It is our own children that we are killing, not yours. As for you people, you are our guests; we will not drive you away. Teach as much as you like, but as many as you teach, we shall kill.' As they reached the entrance to his own enclosure, where their ways parted, Mukasa added a final taunt :

'You men of God know many things, but you did not know what was going to happen to-day.'

Weary and discouraged, Lourdel continued on his way alone. His grief would have been even greater had he known that the man from whom he had just parted was returning to his residence for the express purpose of adding to the martyrs the leader of the Christians outside the Palace precincts, Andrew Kaggwa.

After the discomfort of rain and mud in the morning, and the long, weary and fruitless wait in the Palace grounds, Père Lourdel was now tormented by the heat. He writes :

I was parched with thirst after the sad scene I had witnessed. Thirst is said to be one of the most terrible sufferings of the tortured: their last words are nearly always the 'I thirst!' of Our Blessed Lord on the cross. The executioners of Buganda, merciless though they are, generally show themselves responsive to this request by offering their victims some water or plantain wine, but, for fear of compromising himself, no one would have dared to offer me any refreshment. I passed the house of Matthew Kisule the gunsmith, where I used to rest a few minutes on my way back from the royal enclosure and accept gratefully the cooling drink which they hastened to offer me. But to-day the place was deserted and silent with the silence of death.

Farther on, I was about to quench my thirst at a small stream, when I heard a voice saying, 'The corpse of one of the night's victims was thrown into that water.' Horror-stricken, I turned away. At last I came to another stream of limpid water and was able to drink. I would gladly have rested a while in the shadow of the great trees that surrounded it, but I was anxious to know how things were at the mission, so I went on.

Père Lourdel was not, as it turned out, able to allay his anxiety at once, or obtain the rest he so much needed. Before he reached the mission, he met Adolphus Nantinda, the commander of the fleet of canoes which had been sent to the South of the Lake a few months earlier to fetch Bishop Livinhac.

Adolphus was on his way to Munyonyo to report the arrival of the Bishop at Entebbe. He also carried a letter to Père Lourdel from His Lordship, who had already heard of the trouble. The priest was worried about the possible effect upon the Kabaka of the arrival of further Europeans at this critical moment. Weary as he was, he felt it necessary to go back to Munyonyo with Nantinda to report their arrival to Mwanga and, as far as possible, allay the Kabaka's suspicions and fears.

On approaching the palace, Nantinda fired the customary salute, the report of which so frightened Mwanga that he sent out at once to enquire what was afoot and promptly admitted the visitors to his presence.

The Kabaka appeared somewhat shamefaced when he saw Lourdel, but soon recovered his composure and enquired of Nantinda, 'Has the Bishop brought many goods?' He then issued instructions for the Bishop and his companion, Père Denoit, to be brought to Mutungo, the royal port, eight miles from the mission, and for porters to be sent for the luggage. Lourdel then seized the opportunity of raising the subject which was nearest to his heart. He writes :

When Adolphus had gone, I spoke to Mwanga of the harm he was doing to himself by putting to death the most faithful of his servants. Whatever I said seemed to make no impression on him. He simply laughed at it. 'I will no longer allow my servants to pray,' he said. 'I am master here. I am Kabaka. That is not given to everyone. I do not want anyone to resist me.'

Refusing to be silenced, I began to plead for our poor Christians, assuring him that all he had been told of them was simply false. 'They shall not all be killed,' he said at last, with a burst of laughter, 'I shall spare a few.' That was all that I could get from him.

On my way home, I met Lusaka, an old gate-keeper who, though himself a pagan, was the father of three of our neophytes, and a good friend of ours. He was in tears. 'My three sons have been arrested,' he said. 'What harm have they done to the Kabaka? He says they pray; but is that a crime?' The old man wrung my hands in sorrow, but with such friendliness that I was greatly moved. Most of the relatives of our Christians had looked at me that day as if they thought that I was the cause of their trouble. One woman had exclaimed that if she were a man she would pierce my heart for causing the death of her children. . . .

I met several bands of raiders, laden with spoils from the Christian villages that they had sacked. At last, tired out, I arrived at our Lady's mission.

Kabaka Mwanga had to all appearances been quite happy about the arrival of Bishop Livinhac and his companion, but Lourdel had been right in thinking that he might view it with suspicion. Mwanga, after consulting with his Chancellor, made plans to keep the two parties of Catholic missionaries from meeting. Fearing, apparently, that five white men in one house would constitute a threat to his kingdom, he decided to keep the new arrivals virtually prisoners in a couple of miserable mud huts, two hours' walking distance from the mission.

The priests at the mission learnt of this plan from a Christian at Court and decided to steal a march on the Kabaka. Knowing that the canoes would arrive at Mutongo on the evening of 27 May, Lourdel went there to meet them and first thing in the morning, set the Bishop and Père Denoit on their road to the mission, while he stayed behind to arrange the transport of the luggage. Heavy rain, which lasted throughout the three hours' journey, did not contribute to the Bishop's comfort, but it kept within doors all except some of the Christians eager to welcome him, and ensured for him an un-hindered passage. Under such circumstances did the first Vicar Apostolic to set foot on the soil of Buganda reach the mission on the slopes of Rubaga Hill, on the morning of 28 May 1886.

In returning to the story of the martyrs, it is necessary to go back to the afternoon of Wednesday, 26 May, to the moment when Lourdel parted from the Chancellor at the entrance to his enclosure. As soon as the Chancellor entered his house, he sent an urgent message to the Kabaka, his third that day, on the subject of Andrew Kaggwa.

The first message, sent from the court-house where he was hearing cases, had been a polite reminder to the effect that 'that Munyoro', a prominent Christian, was still at liberty. To this Mwanga replied that he could not afford to lose the chief drummer of his European-type drums.

The second message had been couched in stronger terms. The Chancellor had pointed out that it was not right to kill the children of the chiefs and allow the leader of the Christians to go on teaching religion. 'Religion will continue to be taught,' he added, 'as long as that man is alive. He has even instructed my own children.' To this, Mwanga seems to have made no reply.

The third message, which Mukasa sent from his own residence, took the form of a peremptory demand : 'Give me the chief of the Kigowa! I will dispose of him myself.' To forstall any further attempts at temporizing by his royal master, he added that he was quite determined not to sit down to a meal until Kaggwa had been arrested.

Reluctantly, Mwanga acceded to the demand of his imperious Chancellor but, ashamed to face Andrew himself, told Sabakaki Wamala, chief of the Palace staff, to apprehend Andrew Kaggwa and hand him over directly to the Chancellor's own servants. Wamala, accompanied by the executioner Gongobavu and by his fellow Muslims, Lutaya the Chamberlain and Muvwewo, at once set off for the house of the Christian leader.

Andrew Kaggwa was ready for them. He had been waiting patiently all morning for the call to bear witness to his faith. The suddenness with which the crisis had arisen had prevented the other martyrs from fortifying themselves by a reception of the sacraments but Andrew, living outside the royal enclosure and left at liberty until the afternoon had, according to Archbishop Streicher, seized the opportunity, like his great friend Joseph Mukasa, of receiving Holy Communion on the day of his death. If this is correct, he must have gone to the mission during the early hours of the morning, because at dawn he was back at his post at Munyonyo. He could easily have fled, but he had been a loyal servant of the Kabaka and flight would have given the appearance of disloyalty and desertion of his post. He does, however, seem to have sent the other members of his household into hiding, while he himself waited calmly for whatever might befall.

Some time after two in the afternoon, the summons came. Wamala and his companions arrived at his house and demanded of him : 'Deliver to us the Christians in your house.'

'If you are looking for Christians,' replied Andrew, 'there is but one here. I am myself a Christian.'

He offered no resistance or objection while they bound him and then led him along the road, which skirted the Kabaka's enclosure, to the Chancellor's residence.

'I followed him for a few moments,' says Aleni Nganda-za-kamwa, a witness of the arrest, 'together with a friend of mine, Gwotamwa Lutagajjo; then, halting near the main entrance, we watched him being taken into the enclosure of the Chancellor.'

Andrew was at once ushered into the presence of his mortal enemy. According to Nikodemo Sebwato, a Protestant sub-chief, and to other reports, the Chancellor pretended not to recognize Andrew, and asked :

'Are you the Mugowa?'

'Have you forgotten me?' replied Andrew, 'We have met often enough, in particular when I came to thank you, with my men, after my promotion to the Kigowa.'

'Was it you that taught my children religion?'

'Yes, it was I. What of it, have I taught them the plague?'

'Yes, you have given them the plague. Are they not dead, or as good as dead?'

'Why, then, did you have to put them to death? Why not let them die a natural death, or wait to see whether my teaching would prove fatal to them?'

'Tell me : Why have you learned religion, and why do you teach all Buganda?'

'If I choose to practise religion,' replied Andrew, 'surely that is my own business.'

Baffled, the Chancellor tried a new line of attack.

'Why did you, at the time of Joseph Mukasa's death, conceal his gun? To shoot the Kabaka, I suppose?'

Andrew made short work of this ridiculous charge. He replied :

'At his death, Kabaka Mutesa left you a number of guns; in doing so, did he mean you to shoot his successor? If I had wanted to shoot Kabaka Mwanga, would not the gun he himself gave me have done the job equally well?'

The Chancellor was obtaining no satisfaction from this interrogation of the prisoner, so he cut it short and turned to the executioner in attendance, a man named Bidandi, and said :

'Take this man away and put him to death.' Then, knowing full well that the Kabaka was liable to change his mind at any moment and deprive him of his victim, he added, 'Be quick about it, and bring me his arm to prove that you have done your work. I will not touch food until I have seen it.'

Bidandi and his helpers led Andrew Kaggwa out of the Chancellor's enclosure and then hesitated. The executioner was in a quandary. He dare not offend the Chancellor, but he knew just as well as the latter that the Kabaka had given up the prisoner with great reluctance, and was likely to send a pardon at any moment. His victim was an important man, a favourite of the Kabaka, a man of considerable means. If he could delay the execution until the expected pardon arrived, he might expect to be richly rewarded, and he remembered how the executioners of Joseph Mukasa had lost their chance of a reward by a matter of moments only. He did not know what to do for the best.

His prisoner came to his assistance in making a decision. Andrew left the Chancellor's residence with a radiant face and brisk step. He knew why the executioner was hesitating, and, with the same impatience shown by the martyr Ignatius on hearing the roar of the lions that were to devour him, he said :

'Why don't you carry out your orders? I'm afraid delay will get you into serious trouble. If your master had asked you to serve him a kid, would you keep him waiting? You would go and kill it at once. Well, he wants my arm, and he cannot eat until he gets it. Take it to him without delay!'

Eight executioners, clad in skins, surrounded the martyr. They took him to a thicket at the back of the Chancellor's residence, and at a spot near the palisade, facing the property of the Chamberlain, they despatched their victim.

'I had not long to wait,' says Aleni, who still stood watching from the gateway to the royal enclosure, 'for in a few minutes the Chancellor's gate-keeper re-appeared, carrying, suspended from a length of fibre, Kaggwa's bleeding arm, severed at the shoulder.'

The actual martyrdom was seen by four young girls, one of whom was Rakeri (Rakeli or Rachael) Binimumaso, then a child of fourteen. Her testimony, obtained by Père Joire in 1927, is to the effect that she and her companions attempted to conceal themselves nearby in order to see who was being killed. Her description of the scene is as follows :

Andrew was dressed in reddish-brown bark-cloth and a white loincloth. He was holding a small book in his hand. He begged the executioners not to strip him naked, and they agreed. Then they threw him down and, after laying him flat on the ground, cut off his arm with a knife, so that the white tendons could be seen hanging out. The only sound that came from Andrew's lips was the invocation, Katonda (My God!). After this they cut off his head and finally chopped his body into pieces, which they scattered over the ground.

The four witnesses of the martyrdom were most barbarously punished for their curiosity. Their presence was detected by one of the executioners and reported to the Chancellor who at first had them imprisoned in a hut, near the scene of the martyrdom, from which they could watch the vultures descending from a big tree to feed on the martyr's remains. Later they were brought before the Chancellor and sentenced with inhuman savagery. Rakeri and one of her companions were committed to the Kabaka's harem, while the other two girls had their hands cut off and their eyes gouged out.

Andrew Kaggwa died at about three o'clock in the afternoon of Wednesday 26 May. Later, as is mentioned in *Black Martyrs,* some of his friends searched for the body but failed to find it. Their failure, it appears, may have been due to the fact that others had already reverently buried his remains.[1]

While Andrew Kaggwa was dying, a victim of the Chancellor's hatred, the Kabaka's own victims were still awaiting their fate in the huts of the executioners at Munyonyo.

In the march of a considerable body of condemned persons to their place of execution, a traditional ritual had to be observed. This included the slaughter of one victim at the point of departure, and one at each execution-site or main cross-roads along the route. The reason for this practice, which seems to have had something to do with diverting the revengeful activities of the ghosts of the victims, is somewhat obscure but, as the dismembered bodies of those killed in this way were left lying where they met their death, it served to provide passers-by with evidence that an execution party had passed that way and, if they so wished, with a gruesome sort of paper-chase —human remains being substituted for paper—to the place of execution.

The Kabaka had not yet given the order for the death march to begin, possibly because the tale of victims was not yet complete. According to Abdul Aziz, the order did not come through until about five in the evening. In the meantime, the condemned were divided out amongst the various executioners for safe-keeping. '... We were separated from each other,' says Denis Kamyuka, 'and quartered, two here, one there, three somewhere else, until none remained outside. We were kept there for an hour or two while the executioners ate their mid-day meal.' Abdul Aziz tells that the prisoners were also given food, including meat, which he himself was unable to eat because of his fear.

Abdul Aziz Buliwadda and his fellow prisoner, Pontian Ngondwe, who had both got into trouble over the cattle-levy, were added to the group of condemned on the orders of the Kabaka. Unlike the others, who were tied with ropes, these two were fastened together in the same pair of stocks, and remained in these when the death march began. These stocks were not the fixtures known in Europe but consisted of a log of wood with a hole through it, large enough for a hand or foot to pass through. A peg was then run through the log, at right-angles to the hole, narrowing it so that the limb could not be withdrawn. Stocks for the feet had one hole only, for a person seldom had more than one foot in the stocks at a time. Even so, as the hole was at one end of the log, he could move about only by lifting the other end of it by means of a length of fibre tied to it for the purpose. The stocks for the arms had two holes through the log, about twenty inches apart. It was with one of these that Ngondwe and Abdul were fastened together.

Another Catholic martyr already in prison was the catechumen page Mukasa Kiriwawanvu. He was lodged in the house of Muka-janga, the chief executioner, who, as Lwanga and his companions were leaving the Palace, was heard to say that the Kabaka had ordered him to kill Kiriwawanvu as well, because he was one of those who had adopted the white men's religion. When he arrived at his encampment with his prisoners, the old executioner formally announced to Kiriwawanvu the sentence of death passed upon him, saying :

'Are you not the Mukasa who practises the religion of God ? The Kabaka has condemned you to death. I must take you away at once.'

'I am grateful to the Kabaka for condemning me thus,' replied the young man. 'I am anxious to die for my religion.' Little Gyavira, the boy with whom Kiriwawanvu had quarrelled but a few days before, exclaimed :

'Well done, my friend ! I thought they might forget you; but thanks be to God for bringing you too ! Let us stand together and support each other.'

'Thank you for praying for me,' replied the older boy. 'Now we shall run our course together. No longer shall we quarrel about our little affairs, but fight together for God.'

It seems probable that during the course of the afternoon a number of the Protestant victims also joined the waiting group of condemned, although only one, Dani Nakabandwa, is mentioned by name (by Abdul Aziz) as taking part in the march to Mengo that night.

The prisoners travelled in two groups, and dusk was approaching when the first finally left Munyonyo. This party included Pontian Ngondwe, Bruno Serunkuma, James Buzabaliawo, Dani Naka-bandwa, Simeon Sebuta, Abdul Aziz Buliwadda and several others. The story of the march and of the martyrdom of Pontian Ngondwe is gathered from the accounts given by Abdul Aziz and Sebuta, accounts which corroborate each other in almost every detail.

The prisoners, who were fastened together in pairs to prevent any attempt to escape in the darkness, were guarded by Mukajanga's assistants, their chief himself having gone on ahead to make pre-parations for the ceremonial opening of the death-march, which was scheduled to take place at Tabataba, now known as Ttaka Jjunge, about a mile from Munyonyo on the road to Mengo. When the party reached this place, a halt was called near the entrance to Kulugi's residence, where a fire had been kindled and was burning fiercely.

Mukajanga, hearing that his victims had arrived, staggered out, according to Sebuta, completely drunk. He was, however, not too drunk to observe the formalities which the occasion required. These began with the posing to each captive individually a formal query about the crime for which he had been condemned.

'We were asked, one by one,' says Sebuta, 'what was the charge brought against us, and we all replied that it was the religion of God.' Abdul Aziz confirms this and adds information about the man to whom he was fastened, Pontain Ngondwe :

> Then when he asked which of us was a Christian, I told him that I was not, but those that were, all admitted it. When Ngondwe was asked what charge was levelled against him, he replied that it was 'following Christ'. 'I happen to know,' said Mukajanga, 'that you were charged with something else.' (Actually with taking one of the old man's own cows in the course of the cattle-levy). Ngondwe replied that the original reason for his arrest was unimportant, he was about to die for God's name, for the sake of his Creator.

Twice more did the old executioner ask Ngondwe if he was a Christian, and twice more the martyr affirmed that he was, adding that he had no wish to deny it, and expressing his readiness to die for his faith.

Then Mukajanga called upon his assistants to swear that they would guard their prisoners faithfully and defend them against any attempt at rescue. After the oath had been taken, he ordered a drum-call to be sounded which, taken up by all the drummers, produced a thrill of excitement and terror in the hearts of the hearers. One of these interpreted the meaning of the call as 'Kasana jjangu! Mpewo genda e Ttanda!' (Heat arise! Wind depart to Ttanda!) and says that it signalled the beginning of the execution.

As the echoes of this awe-inspiring sound died away, Mukajanga staggered up to Pontian Ngondwe and drove his spear, aptly named the 'drunken man', into the breast of the gallant soldier, who bravely stood to meet it. The first thrust did not kill him, so the old man stabbed again, shouting, 'Now it goes in without effort, like a knife into butter.' He continued to pierce the body of the martyr long after life was extinct, stabbing and stabbing again with his spear until he tired. While this was going on, the other Christians, believing that their turn would follow, went down on their knees where they stood and recited aloud the Lord's Prayer. Abdul Aziz, who seems to have been the only non-Christian amongst the captives, was stricken with horror and terror. He says :

> As my hand was fastened with Ngondwe's in the same stocks, I could not leave him when he was killed. I was thus tied to the dead body. I was helpless, unable to escape and expecting death at any moment. I called upon Sebwira to release me, and Mukajanga replied in a terrible voice. 'You call upon Sebwira! Do you think I cannot set you free?' Then he ordered his assistant Sitankya to free me from the dead body.

Mukajanga then told his men to hack the martyr's corpse to pieces, which they did, scattering the remains in all directions. The Protestant, Nakabandwa, asked, 'Why kill us here?' and Bruno Serunkuma at once interjected, 'Why not? Let them kill us here! These ropes are very painful!' Mukajanga's reply to this was to order his men to roll the prisoners in the muddy pools left by the morning's rain, thus contracting the ropes and adding to their sufferings.

It would appear that Ngondwe was selected as the first victim, not because of any personal grudge that Mukajanga may have harboured, but because he had proved himself difficult. According to one report, he had objected, at first, to going any further than the square in front of the royal enclosure, saying, 'I have told you that I am a Christian. Kill me here on the spot! Is death any more in evidence in the place to which you are taking me, than here?'

Similar tactics were employed by the page, Athanasius Bazzeku-ketta, a member of the second party of prisoners, which included Denis Kamyuka, Werabe and others.

Immediately after his condemnation by the Kabaka, while being led to the executioners' quarters for detention, he had remarked,

'So you want us to bite through the stocks (i.e. keep us in prison)? Are you not going to kill us? We are the Kabaka's meat. Take us away and kill us at once!'

'This fellow talks as if he longs for death,' said one of the executioners, hitting him with a stick.

When taken out of prison at Munyonyo, Bazzekuketta again objected to the delay : 'The Kabaka ordered you to put us to death. Where are you taking us? Why don't you kill us here?'

Perhaps the sight of Ngondwe's blood, which Denis Kamyuka says they saw on the road, encouraged the youth to hope that he could at last goad the executioners into granting him the martyr's crown, for at Ttaka Jjunge, near the residence of Kulekana, he stopped and sat himself down on the road, exclaiming, 'I am not going to walk after death all the way to Namugongo. Kill me here !'

The guards laid about him with sticks until he said, 'Very well! You can stop beating me. I will march. I was only thinking that you would kill me here.'

The prisoners reached Mengo late in the evening, and were lodged for the night in the executioners' encampment. 'When we got to Mengo,' relates Kamyuka, 'we were taken to a place close to Mukajanga's prison. There, fetters were brought. Some of us had our arms put in the stocks, others their legs. Some had chains on their feet, or had their necks fastened in slave-yokes.' The slave-yoke, of which Kamyuka speaks, was introduced into Buganda by the Arabs. It was a forked branch of a tree, locked round the neck.

There was little sleep for any of them that night, because of the excitement of the day and the discomfort of their bonds. In the morning, the executioners informed them that they intended putting one of them to death at the near-by execution-site, where Joseph Mukasa had met his death some six months earlier. Immediately, Athanasius Bazzekuketta, still thirsting for martyrdom, volunteered. 'Take me!' he exclaimed. Mukajanga, who had been informed of the youth's behaviour on the previous evening, gave his assent. 'Since he has given you trouble,' he said to his assistants, 'go and kill him at once. Later on the Kabaka might remember (i.e. pardon) him.'

Athanasius was promptly taken to the spot at the foot of Mengo Hill, just at the back of the present Nakivubo Stadium, and there hacked to pieces, his executioners chanting, as they went about their task, 'The gods of Kampala will rejoice'.

Thus died the fifth of the Blessed Martyrs of Uganda, on the morning of 27 May 1886, aged about twenty.

Having butchered the gallant Bazzekuketta, and granted him the martyr's crown which he had craved with such holy impatience, the group of executioners returned to their other victims and glee-fully told them what they had done. 'The Christians,' they said, 'are getting what they deserve; they are simply asking for death.' Far from being dismayed by the gruesome recital, their prisoners said to one another, 'Our friend Athanasius has proved his courage; he did not shrink from laying down his life in God's cause. Let us be brave like him!' The cortège was then assembled and, shortly after, set out on what was to be for most of the prisoners their last journey on earth, the journey to Namugongo.

The choice of Namugongo as the scene for their martyrdom seems to have been due to the fact that most of the victims were royal liege-men or pages. This site had been set aside for the execution of princes during the reign of Kabaka Kyabagu, some hundred years before, and ever since then had been reserved mainly for the execu-tion of persons of royal blood, chiefs, and others of importance. It was to the Baganda what Tower Hill used to be to the people of England.

The Baganda had thirteen such execution-sites, each with its own custodian, peculiar usages, and methods of execution. At five of them, including Namugongo, the victims were burned to death, this form of capital punishment being considered least degrading to the condemned person. Roscoe, seeing a religious element in all the executions at these 'Matambiro', renders the word as 'sacrificial places' instead of 'execution sites'. Certain it is that many of the deaths at them were indeed ritual murders, the number of victims in such cases being invariably nine, or multiples of nine, and the reason for their death being given as the will of one of the gods, most frequently Kibuka. Whether, in the execution of the ordinary criminals, which was carried out at the same thirteen places, there was also a religious significance, is a question in dispute, but the chant of Bazzekuketta's executioners, 'The gods of Kampala will rejoice', and the words of Senkole at the death of Charles Lwanga, 'We have not killed you, but Nende and Kibuka and all the gods whom you have despised, they are the cause of your death', would seem to imply that in the eyes of the common people at least, there was a sacrificial element in every execution.

However, the Kabakas themselves probably attached no religious significance to any of the executions, whether ritual or otherwise. As Gale points out, the Kabakas did not regard the tribal gods as their masters but as tools and convenient instruments of government. The gods were useful scapegoats upon whom could be laid the responsibility for any excesses of cruelty or any wholesale butchery in which the Kabaka cared to indulge. They provided the Kabaka with a means of keeping his people in a state of terror and abject subjection, without detracting from his pose as a benevolent despot.

Namugongo, as the crow flies, is a little over eight miles from Mengo. The route followed by the martyrs was rather more than ten, which proved too much for one of them, Gonzaga Gonza. The account of their journey is provided mainly by Denis Kamyuka, supplemented here and there from other sources.

As many of the roads they followed were little more than narrow tracks through the bush, the prisoners marched in single file, tied neck to neck. As they went along, words of encouragement were passed backwards and forwards along the line. 'Then we talked of God,' says Kamyuka, 'and said to one another, "First to offer one-self to do a good act and then to omit it, is playing the fool and the coward. The day has come for us to make good our promise. Let us die bravely for the cause of God".'

One cannot help being struck by the resemblance of these words to the pledge of fidelity which Baganda warriors used to give when passing in review before their commander prior to a battle. 'When I meet the enemy,' each warrior cried, 'I shall not be afraid, but will fight with all my might.' On re-passing their leader, they all shouted, 'We will not look backward.'

Another subject discussed by the martyrs as they trudged along the dusty road was the constancy of the newly baptized. 'Friends,' said some of those who had been baptized by the priests to those bap-tized by Charles Lwanga, 'we were afraid that you people would deny your religion.' 'Deny our religion!' exclaimed the young pages, 'Have not we given ourselves to Jesus Christ as well as you?' Mis-givings about Mukasa Kiriwawanvu may however have remained in the minds of some of his companions, because he had but recently become a regular catechumen and had been absent in prison when Charles Lwanga baptized the other catechumen pages. One witness suggests that a practical difficulty prevented him from being bap-tized during the journey to Namugongo, or during the week's imprisonment there; namely, that even if he was fortunate enough to have had a Catholic companion in his prison, the latter would have been unable to give the sacrament with his hands confined in the stocks. There is certainly no record of this catechumen having received the sacrament.

Typical of the sentiments of the martyrs during their journey to Namugongo are those expressed by the seventeen-year-old Achilles Kiwanuka to his companion Werabe : 'As for me, they may kill me, but I will not renounce my religion!'

Mukajanga, the chief executioner, marched at the head of the file, to the sound of the little drum which proclaimed his chieftainship and which was recognized as his by the whole country. The prisoners, whose necks and feet were chafed by the cords and slave-yokes or by the stocks, could not keep up with him, but they struggled along, reciting prayers and the lessons of the catechism as they went. Denis Kamyuka reports :

> We took the road which skirts the front of the enclosure of the Chief of Kyaddondo County. Having crossed Kampala Hill, we reached Kagugube market, and from there went down into the valley until we came to the main road separating Makerere Hill from Mulago Hill, where we caught up with Mukajanga who was waiting for us. He made us halt a few minutes during which he gave the executioners a scolding. 'Why have you not come more quickly?' he said. 'Don't you know that the Kabaka is coming to Mengo to-day, to inspect the new enclosure which is being built? Did you want him to find us still there?'
>
> Then we started off again. We crossed Mulago Hill and took the road to Kiwatule, the hill on which Andrew Kaggwa had built his residence. Mukajanga kept ahead of us all the time.
>
> On Kiwatule Hill we rested for about an hour under the trees, and were joined by James Buzabaliawo and Bruno Serunkuma who had been sent after us. They told us that they had been arrested after us on the previous day and had also spent the night at Mengo. I for one had not seen them there, for on arriving at Mengo we were not lodged in the prison itself, but each executioner took with him the prisoners under his charge and made them sleep in his own hut. For that reason I did not see those friends until their arrival in the square of the Kigowa. 'Here we are too,' they said, 'let us encourage one another to die for our Lord Jesus Christ.'

The two soldiers indeed proved an asset to the group of martyrs. They, together with Charles Lwanga and Anatole Kiriggwajjo, were to be God's instruments in supporting to the end the courage of their younger brethren.

Already, on the march from Munyonyo to Mengo, Bruno Serunkuma had given proof that he was of the material of which martyrs are made. He had been cruelly beaten, had spent the heat of the afternoon shut up in the hut of one of the executioners, had witnessed the butchering of Ngondwe and, in considerable agony from the tightness of the cords that bound him, had walked for two hours on the road from Munyonyo to Mengo. When the party of which he formed part came abreast of the house of a relative of his, named Bosa, Bruno paused and called out loudly, 'Bosa, Bosa! Bring me some plantain-wine.' Bosa poured some wine into a bowl and brought it to the spot where Bruno was waiting, guarded by an executioner. Bruno then said to him, 'You see, Bosa, that they are taking us off to execution; but we are going (to Heaven) to keep places for you. A well which has many sources never runs dry. When we are gone, others will come after us.' Bosa said, 'Here is the plantain-wine for which you asked'. Then Bruno looked his relative in the face, fixed his eyes on him for a moment, and then refused the wine. Turning to the executioner, he said, 'Let us go on.'

Denis Kamyuka's account of the party of martyrs at Kiwatule continues :

> We asked the executioners to let us visit the residence of Andrew Kaggwa, the Mugowa. They consented, and we saw that the houses had already been raided. There was nothing left, neither men nor goods, except some old rubbish scattered about in the courtyard. When Bruno and James told us that our friend, Andrew Kaggwa, had been arrested just before they left Munyonyo, and had been taken to the Chancellor to be put to death, we understood why.
>
> Although we had spent over an hour at Kiwatule, our friend Gonzaga Gonza had not yet caught up with us. We left Kigowa before he arrived, and covered a good distance to Lubawo Hill, but we marched on until we reached the square in front of Mukajanga's residence at Namugongo.[1]
>
> We were made to wait for a full hour in the square at Namugongo. In fact we were still there when the executioners, who had stayed behind with Gonzaga Gonza, arrived and told us that they had killed our friend on Lubawo Hill by order of Mukajanga.
>
> At Namugongo there was a prison, but we were not confined in it. Mukajanga ordered the executioners to lodge us in their enclosures throughout the village. As we separated to be taken to our lodgings, those who had been the first to become Christians said to us, 'You have heard that our friends have been put to death. They are now with Jesus Christ. Let us remain firm like them, and we too shall go where they have gone, to Jesus Christ.' Those who inspired us with courage were Charles Lwanga, Bruno Serunkuma, James Buzabaliawo and Anatole Kiriggwajjo.
>
> Then the executioners took us away. I shared a hut with my friends Gyavira and Mugagga. They put our necks in rings which were then fastened to the posts of the hut.

Just before the prisoners were dispersed and billeted in the various huts they were joined by a new arrival from Mengo, Luke Banabakintu, the Ssingo Christian, who told them that his companion, Matthias Kalemba the Mulumba, had been separated from him on Kampala Hill and put to death there.

Kamyuka has described how he and his companions were secured in the hut to which they were assigned. Others of the captives were put in the stocks, or had their necks fastened in forked tree branches. Charles Lwanga was one of those put in the stocks for having said to Mukajanga, 'We know very well that you are going to kill us. Why do you make us wait?'

One of the prisoners, Mbaga Tuzinde, was separated from the rest and handed over to his own relatives. Mukajanga had not yet abandoned the hope of saving his son by getting him to apostatize. Having failed himself, he now called upon the other members of his family to add their entreaties to his. As the youth was led away, the others heard some of the executioners voicing their opinion of this. 'Mukajanga will not put him to death,' they said. 'He will take him back to the Kabaka and say, "This boy has given up his religion".' When they heard this, his fellow Christians were sad at heart, and said to one another, 'Poor Mbaga! If only his people do not prevail upon him to renounce his religion!' Charles Lwanga exhorted them all to pray earnestly that their friend might remain firm in his resolve, and not yield to the temptation to which he was about to be subjected.

For a full week, the prisoners were kept in confinement at Namugongo, and for a full week the seventeen to eighteen year old youth, Mbaga Tuzinde, stood firm against the ceaseless prayers, entreaties and tears of his many relatives.

During the week, Mukajanga and his assistants set about the task of preparing for the holocaust. Vast quantities of firewood had to be cut and brought in to build the pyre, some thirty-three feet by twenty-two, and sufficient firewood placed in reserve to ensure that the bodies of the victims were entirely consumed. Time was also needed for cutting the elephant-grass reeds, which were then laced together to make the rush-mats, in which the victims were to be wrapped before being placed on the pyre. The preparations were not completed until the eve of the Ascension, 2 June 1886.

Chapter Fifteen

GONZAGA GONZA, MATTHIAS KALEMBA AND NOE MAWAGGALI

Mention was made in the last chapter of two more martyrs, the two Basoga, Gonzaga Gonza and Matthias Kalemba, both of whom suffered on 27 May 1886.

The Musoga page, Gonzaga Gonza, formed part of the cortège which left Mengo for Namugongo on the morning of Thursday, 27 May but, in spite of his efforts to keep up with his companions, he soon fell behind the rest of the party. Like some of his fellow victims, he had spent the night in chains; but in his case the chains around his legs had been fixed so tightly that, during the night, the flesh had swollen around them, and it was found impossible to unhook them in the morning. He had to set out on the ten mile journey with the chains biting into his flesh, and could only drag himself along slowly, every step an agony. Before long, raw wounds encircled his legs and blood trickled to the ground. Although the fierce sun and the flies, attracted by the scent of blood, contributed to his sufferings, Gonza displayed an almost unbelievable heroism in struggling along after his fellows for over seven miles. Finally, in sight of Lubawo hamlet, at a spot where three roads met, he collapsed.

The custom of butchering one prisoner at each road junction has already been mentioned, and was probably not unknown to the martyr. It may well have been this knowledge, as much as sheer physical exhaustion, that made the gallant youth fall to the ground at this spot and wait for the stroke that would release him from his agony. It came from the spears of the executioners or, according to one report, from that of Mukajanga who had waited there for the laggard. One of the executioners later paid tribute to the courage displayed by this young man of twenty-four. 'That boy,' he said, 'was very brave, he did not show any signs of fear.'

It seems that the martyr's body was not hacked to pieces, like those of Ngondwe and Bazzekuketta. Sotieri Zibalaba of Gayaza claimed to have seen Gonza's body lying on the road, two or three days after his death. The head had been severed from the trunk and decomposition had set in. Kamyuka, on the way back from Namugongo a week after Gonzaga's death, saw only the martyr's hair on the road. Gonzaga Gonza died about noon on Thursday, 27 May.

The second of the Basoga martyrs, Matthias Kalemba, the Mulumba, who was to suffer the most brutal death and most lingering agony of all the martyrs, was the leader of the Ssingo Christians, amongst whom were found two other martyrs, Luke Banabakintu and Noe Mawaggali.

When the storm of persecution broke, Matthias was at Mengo with his chief, who had the task of rebuilding the royal palace, destroyed by fire in February. Kalemba's friend and helper, Luke Banabakintu, had also been present at Mengo but had been sent back to Mityana on an errand. He was actually on the way back to Mengo when the persecution began and stayed the night of 25 May with a Christian friend, Cyprien Kamya, who had been baptized together with him and Matthias almost four years earlier, on 28 May 1882. The two friends had much to say to each other and spent a considerable part of the night discussing their religion. Early next morning, Luke took leave of his host and continued his journey back to the capital. Before he reached it, he heard the news about the Kabaka's attack upon Ssebuggwawo and about the threat to arrest all Christians. The thought of going into hiding until the storm had blown over must have occurred to him, only to be firmly rejected. He hastened on to the capital, reported his arrival to his chief, and said, 'There is no need to place us under restraint. We shall not run away, because we would not wish to get you into trouble'. Matthias Kalemba had already given a similar assurance that morning. When he heard of the arrests at the palace, he went to the county chief and said :

'I have come to inform you that the Kabaka intends to put us to death because of our religion. Do not be uneasy however. We will never inform against the children whom we have taught religion in your household. We do not wish you to get into trouble through us.'

This attitude was typical of that adopted by practically all the Christians, both Catholic and Protestant, holding office either at court or under the greater chiefs. Their sense of loyalty forbade them deserting their posts and taking to flight. If the Kabaka wished to put them to death for their religion, they were ready to offer the sacrifice with resignation and even joy; but they were not prepared, by flight, to give any grounds for an accusation of disloyalty. Quite prepared to suffer themselves, they were not prepared to sacrifice their dependants; so, knowing that the womenfolk, children and servants of condemned men were considered the legitimate spoils of their captors, all who had sufficient warning sent the members of their households into hiding and then calmly awaited whatever might befall. The same precaution was taken by Mackay; so that when an armed band did actually arrive to search the Protestant mission, it found no one there but the missionaries themselves.

The county chief of Ssingo knew he could rely upon the word of his two Catholic followers and left them at liberty for the time being. Later in the day, on receiving a message to the effect that Mbugano, the royal legate, expected to collect from him the Christians in his retinue, he thought it wiser to place them under arrest. In order to make a show of his loyalty to the Kabaka, the chief had his two faithful servants confined in the stocks. An account of their imprisonment is given by Joseph Bwagu, at that time a pagan, and a servant of the chief.

> When we, the servants of the county chief who were still pagans, saw them in the stocks, we said to one another, 'What fools these Christians are! They knew that they were going to be arrested: Why then did they not take to flight?'
>
> Mpimbwa, the chief's cup-bearer, was a great friend of theirs. He called me and told me to cook food for them. This I did and brought it to them. I expected to find them in sorrow and in tears, but on the contrary, they seemed quite happy and even merry. 'So,' they said, 'You are bringing us provisions for our journey? ' 'Yes,' I replied. 'Very well then. Will you unwrap the plantain mash (from the leaves in which it is steamed), then roll it into little balls to cool it, and put them into our mouths; for, as you see, we have no arms left.' (The prisoners were unable to feed themselves because their hands were in the stocks.)
>
> I did as they asked, and gave them food in the way that small children are fed. All the time they laughed heartily. When they had finished their meal, they said to me, 'Well, the chief has provided us with food. Will you please thank him for us?'

Matthias and Luke passed the night of 26 May imprisoned at the county chief's town residence. It must have been a night of acute discomfort and suffering for not only were their hands and feet fastened in the stocks but their necks were also encumbered with the forked tree-branches, introduced into Buganda by the Arab slave-raiders. Less than two miles away, Charles Lwanga and the others arrested at Munyonyo were also spending the night in bonds, although less rigorously confined than the two Ssingo Christians.

Whatever their sufferings during the night, morning found both prisoners undaunted. Matthias Kalemba, in particular, on the day that was now breaking was to display a courage and endurance unparalleled in the history of the martyrs of Uganda.

Early on the morning of the 27 May Mbugano, the legate, relieved the county chief of his two prisoners and took them to Mengo, there to await the arrival of the Kabaka and his party, who were coming to inspect the rebuilding operations. When the royal party arrived, Mbugano ordered his two assistants, Tabawo-muyombi and Lukowe, to lead Matthias and Luke before the Chancellor, not for trial, because they stood self-condemned as Christians, but to show his catch to his employer. The two martyrs knew that they could expect no mercy from the cruel Chancellor of Buganda. The story of this interview comes from Nikodemo Sebwato, the Protestant sub-chief who had also been present at the condemnation of Andrew Kaggwa.

The Chancellor began by asking: 'Are you the Mulumba?'

Matthias replied, 'Yes I am.'

'Why do you pray? What has induced a man of your standing to adopt the white men's religion, at your age too?'

'I follow that religion because I wish to.'

'You have sent away all your wives, I am told. So you cook your own food, I suppose?'

'Is it because I am thin, or because of my religion that I have been brought before you?' asked Matthias.

Addressing both prisoners, the Chancellor said with a sneer, 'So you are the people who are content to marry only one woman? And you are trying to persuade other people to agree to such a monstrosity!'

Custom required that Luke should be asked separately whether he pleaded guilty to the charge of being a Christian. When he had admitted this, the Chancellor pronounced sentence: 'Take them and burn them with the others at Namugongo.' He added further instructions to the executioners with regard to Matthias. 'Cut off his hands and feet, tear strips of flesh from his back and roast them before his eyes; let Katonda (God) deliver him!'

Cut to the quick by this insult to the majesty of God, Matthias retorted, 'Indeed, Katonda will deliver me, but you will not see how He does it. He will take my soul and leave you my body.'

This particularly savage sentence seems to have been meted out by the Chancellor to those he considered the most influential of the Christian leaders. Andrew Kaggwa had been treated in a somewhat similar manner and the same treatment to which Matthias was condemned is said to have been inflicted upon the Protestant martyr, Robert Munyagabyanjo, before his mutilated body was laid upon the pyre at Namugongo. By such refinement of cruelty in the slaughter of their principal leaders, this bitter enemy of Christianity probably hoped to strike terror into the hearts of the Christians, and so stamp out their religion once and for all.

Matthias and Luke were led from the Chancellor's presence and lodged for a time in a small hut not far from the crossing of the Kabaka's road and the road to Kampala. Here they found a fellow Catholic, Andrew Kiwanuka, who had been arrested the previous day and was waiting to be taken before the Kabaka. 'In that hut,' Andrew relates, 'I met Matthias Kalemba the Mulumba and Luke Banabakintu, who were being taken to execution. They wore pieces of bark-cloth, and their arms were fastened in stocks. I was left with them for about half an hour; after which we said good-bye to one another because a messenger came to take me before the Kabaka.[1] As I left them, I said, "Friends, the moment of separation has come." "Very well," they replied. "Let us go and die for Our Lord".'

It cannot have been much after ten o'clock when Matthias and Luke, guarded by the two executioners, Tabawo-muyombi and Lukowe, and possibly others, set out on the road for Namugongo. Matthias, his hands tied behind his back, and a rope round his neck, followed his guards with a brisk step and joyous countenance. On their way, the party encountered a man whom the executioners suspected of being a Christian. They seized him and were already tying him up when Matthias intervened, saying, 'I know all those that practise religion. That man is not a Christian. Let him go on his way!' Evidently impressed by the Mulumba, and by his air of authority, the guards obeyed and released their victim.

When, after a short walk, they reached the estate of Sebalijja, Matthias Kalemba turned to his fellow prisoner and said, 'We are only servants of a county chief. The Kabaka may decide to pardon his personal attendants who have been arrested, but do you think he will concern himself about us, who are not his own men? I am not going any further!' Seating himself on the ground, he said to the executioners. 'I am not going to walk after death all the way to Namugongo, as if there were no land here to bury people in. What is the use of taking me to Namugongo? Kill me here!' Then he said to Luke Banabakintu, 'Au revoir, my friend. We shall meet again in Heaven.' 'Yes, with God,' answered Luke.

The two executioners, Tabawo-muyombi and Lukowe, either on their own initiative or, as some suggest, after consultation with Senkole, took Matthias at his word, and proceeded to butcher him on the spot,[2] employing every refinement of cruelty of which they were capable. Their own account, as told to their relative, Ignatius Lumu, is as follows :

The Chancellor had ordered us not to kill the Mulumba quickly, but to make him suffer a long time. Therefore we began by cutting off his arms at the wrists, and later at the elbows, and then his legs at the knees. After that, we cut pieces of flesh from his body, and left him there.

When the hatchets of his torturers cut into the martyr's flesh and severed his bones, only one word came repeatedly to his lips, the invocation, 'Katonda! Katonda! (My God! My God!)' His courage and endurance only served to spur the bloodthirsty executioners to greater efforts to break his indomitable spirit. Using slivers of cane, sharp as razors, they cut strips of flesh from all over his body, and roasted them before his eyes; finally, in order to prolong his agony to the utmost, they carefully tied up the severed arteries and veins. 'After that . . . we left him there . . .'

The Mulumba's passion began about noon on Thursday, 27 May. On Saturday, it had not yet ended. On that day, some men from the village of Kitulungunya, unaware of the martyr's presence, went to cut reeds near where he lay, and heard a voice calling out, 'Water! Water!' One of the men went over to see where the voice was coming from, but horrified at the sight that met his eyes and dreading to interfere with the Kabaka's victim, he fled from the spot. The following tribute to this noble martyr comes from the pen of the Protestant historian of Buganda, James Miti.

> Left alone, in untold agony and without the consolation of any-one save his Lord and Master, Matthias suffered in silence both the excruciating thirst caused by the loss of so much blood, and the smarting pains of the wounds which had been inflicted over his whole body. Deprived of his limbs and attacked by swarms of flies and other biting insects, and exposed to the scorching heat, Mulumba lay suffering at his place of sacrifice for two full days, and on the second day, hearing human voices near, Matthias called out to them, and when they approached, asked them for a drop of water. But the men, instead of taking pity on the poor sufferer, ran away instead, fearing to come near such a spectacle any more. And thus Matthias, deserted by all, passed away in agony and went to his reward.
>
> Mulumba's pains can better be imagined than described. And the heroism with which he bore his sufferings for two long days is beyond comprehension. God alone can know to the full the extent of the agonies of his martyrs; we poor mortals can only feebly imagine and less accurately describe them.

Matthias Kalemba, the Mulumba, died, presumably on Sunday 30 May on Kampala Hill, now generally known as Old Kampala. His companion, Luke Banabakintu, was taken on to Namugongo where he joined Charles Lwanga and his companions sometime in the afternoon of Thursday, 27 May.

The royal legate, Mbugano, had, after handing over the two captives to the merciless Chancellor, set out for Mityana with his men for the purpose of looting the property of the two Christians and, if possible, of capturing more Christians from the flourishing community there. The move had been foreseen by Matthias who, anxious for the safety of his wife and children and of the other Ssingo Christians, had sent a messenger, before his own arrest, to warn Cyprian Kamya, the friend with whom Luke Banabakintu had stayed the previous night. The messenger was ordered to hasten on from there to Mityana to warn the Christians of their danger.

Unfortunately, the messenger was held up, a few miles West of Mengo, by the River Mayanja which was in spate because of the rains. The youth lost valuable time in searching for a place where he could cross the river and arrived at Mityana too late for the warning to be of use.

The raiding party also seems to have been delayed somewhat by the river, because the journey took more than three days, instead of the usual two. Mbugano arrived at Mityana only on Sunday evening 30 May, or early on Monday morning. He first called upon the deputy of the county chief to ask for a legate to accompany him on his errand. The deputy gave him the chief's drummer and the raiders set about their task as quietly as possible, hoping to secure a number of prisoners before the Christians became generally aware of their presence in the district. The following story was told by Munaku, later baptized Maria Mathilda, the sister of the martyr Noe Mawaggali :

> For some time before the persecution, the leading Christians of Ssingo had realized that, because of their religion, their lives would some day be forfeit for they knew that the Kabaka was coming to hate Christians, and had already put to death their leader, Joseph Balikuddembe. The priests also had warned them: 'Be firm in your faith, for the Kabaka may have you put to death as well.' Local pagans too, although admiring the behaviour of the Christians, shook their heads, saying, 'these Christians no longer believe in the tribal gods. They will bring calamity on the country.'
>
> When Matthias the Mulumba left for the Capital, three weeks before his martyrdom, he left Noe in charge of his household. Noe also undertook to give catechism classes in his stead. On Sunday 30 May, when rumours of the outbreak of persecution were circulating in Mityana, Noe took me aside after the instruction. When we were alone, he said, 'Munaku, I see that you are a good girl; you keep the commandments of God; you are industrious and neat at your work and you pray well; but you have yet to learn what the priests made very clear to us on the eve of our baptism. To be a Christian

implies a readiness to follow Our Lord to Calvary and even, if need be, to a painful death. As for myself, I am convinced that there is a life after death, and I am not afraid of losing this one; but what about you? Are you determined to remain loyal to the Faith?' 'Certainly, I am,' I replied. 'Very well then,' he continued, 'when we have been killed, never cease to be a good Christian and to love the Christians who will come after us.' He said this to strengthen me in the faith, because I was not yet baptized.

When Noe left me, he said that he was going to Kiwanga, Luke Banabakintu's place, to appoint a man to go to the capital. The Christians of Ssingo were accustomed to send one of their number every week to the mission at the capital to attend the priest's explanation of the catechism, so that he could repeat what he had learnt to his fellow-Christians at home. On this occasion, the man was also to bring back tidings of Matthias and Luke.

Next morning, Monday 31 May, after saying our morning prayers, my mother and I went to cultivate our plot, and Noe went across the swamp to Kiwanga, about a mile away, to see the man who was to leave that morning for the capital.

We were working in the bananary when we heard the approach of the raiders who had come from the capital to arrest us and loot our property. They entered the house of Matthias not far from that of Noe, and seized his wife, Kikuvwa, his two children, Arsenius[1] aged ten and Julia aged two or three, and a boy who only slept there. When my mother and I heard them coming, we ran into the elephant-grass that surrounded the bananary and tried to hide. However, they overtook my mother and arrested her. Then they went on to the house of Luke Banabakintu.

I did not see with my own eyes the manner of my brother's death, but, from my place of concealment in the elephant-grass, I overheard some of the villagers, who had accompanied the raiders, discussing the details as they walked along the nearby path.

The story of how Noe Mawaggali met his death was told by a number of the villagers who witnessed it.

It was still early in the morning and Noe Mawaggali was inside Banabakintu's house, giving final instruction to the two catechumens who were going to the capital and discussing with them the news of the arrest of Matthias and Luke. Suddenly, the raiding party under Mbugano closed in on the house, shouting as they did so that they were looking for Christians. Noe, walking-stick in hand, came out from the house to meet the raiders, saying, 'Here we are!' and, incidentally, giving his companions an opportunity, of which they availed themselves, to escape through the back of the house.

'Is that you, Mawaggali?' called out one of the raiders.

'Yes, it is I,' replied the potter, at the same time drawing over his head the bark-cloth he was wearing, so that he might not see the death-stroke that he was expecting. It came from the spear of Kamanyi, the chief's drummer, acting as legate, who well knew Mawaggali to be one of the leading Christians. Levelling his spear, Kamanyi plunged it into the martyr's back, and Noe fell to the ground grievously wounded. At this, one of Mbugano's followers, attempting to outvie his companions in cruelty, proposed : 'Now that this Christian can no longer defend himself, let us feed him to the dogs.'

This horrible suggestion was adopted. The wounded martyr was lashed to a tree, and the dogs of the village set upon him, further wounds being first inflicted upon his defenceless body so that the animals might become maddened by the scent of blood.

Archbishop Streicher mentions reports to the effect that Mawaggali's agony lasted until evening. Throughout the day, until consciousness mercifully left him, he could feel the savage dogs leaping at him and tearing at his flesh, which they devoured before his eyes. At nightfall, his mangled remains were untied from the tree and thrown on to the main road, to serve as a warning to other Christians, and to those with leanings towards that religion.

The brutal treatment of Noe Mawaggali seems to have shocked one at least of his executioners, men hardened to cruelty. Noe's sister Munaku, from her place of concealment, overheard one of them addressing his companions : 'What men these Christians are!' he exclaimed. 'How obstinate in their religion and how hardened to pain! This Mawaggali now, we gave him what he deserved, but, all the same, it was cruel to feed him to the dogs.'

Then Munaku, with her mother a captive and her brother dead, decided to give herself up. She emerged hastily from her place of concealment and ran after the murderers of her brother, crying out, 'I am Mawaggali's sister. You have killed my brother : Kill me too!' The men, taken aback, looked at her in astonishment. 'My brother has died for his religion,' insisted the girl, 'I wish to die also. Plunge your spears into me !' 'You are mad!' answered the men, ignoring the girl's plea and continuing on their way.

Munaku refused to be put off. She followed the men to the square before the county headquarters, where she found some thirty Christians in bonds, including her own mother, Meme, the widow and daughter of Matthias Kalemba, the boy, Arsenius or Anselm and a boy who lodged with this family. Mbugano, the legate, seeing in this comely young girl of eighteen an unexpected windfall, decided to take her as part of his share of the spoils and had her tied up with the others.

AH 7

During the evening, the boy who had been captured in the Mulumba's house, and also Meme, the mother of Noe and Munaku, managed to free themselves from their bonds and escape. Meme found asylum with some pagan friends who hid her and befriended her. To prevent further escapes, Mbugano had the other prisoners put in the stocks. In spite of this discomfort, Munaku was able to say later, 'I had never been so happy, or passed a better night.'

According to one account, the party of raiders and captives left Mityana for the capital on the following morning, 1 June. Archbishop Streicher, however, mentions that the prisoners remained for another day at Mityana, subjected to the jeers and insults of their captors and of the few pagan villagers who were hostile to their religion. If the latter account is correct, it would appear that Mbugano delayed his departure in the hope of rounding up more Christians. In this he seems to have been generally unsuccessful. The majority of Christians and catechumens were by then fully aware of their danger and easily able to keep out of the way of the raiding party, which received little help from the local inhabitants who were generally well-disposed towards their Christian fellows and unwilling to betray them to the 'foreigners' from the capital. Many of the Christians took refuge in the hamlet of Kiteregga, which had a Catholic chief named Mjanwe, in the belief which events proved correct, that Mbugano with his small force would not dare molest them if they were together in sufficient numbers.

Although he does not appear to consider it conclusive, James Miti mentions some evidence, uncovered by himself, which suggests that the Protestants, Kayizzi Kibuka, Mayanja Kitogo and a chief named Muwanga were also done to death in Ssingo County.

When Mbugano and his captives finally left Mityana, their route led them past the spot where Noe Mawaggali's body had been thrown, but hyenas had completed the work begun by the dogs, and very few traces of the body remained on the road.

Munaku had confided to the Mulumba's widow Kikuvwa, her intention of forcing the soldiers to kill her when they reached this spot, by refusing to go any further. The older woman managed to dissuade her young companion from this course of action and offered her some wise and timely advice. She explained that although martyrdom was a noble and glorious death, God did not desire his followers to seek it for themselves. She also warned the girl that the greatest danger to which her captors were likely to expose her was not to her life, but to her chastity and to her soul. Munaku pondered over this warning. She had already promised her brother that she would not, after his death, endanger her new-found faith by going to live with their pagan relatives. She therefore decided that she would renounce these entirely and begged the older woman not to reveal to anyone who they were.

What Kikuvwa had foretold soon came to pass. Mbugano declared his intention of taking Munaku as one of his wives and began to question her about her male relatives, so that he might learn which was entitled to receive the bride-price. The girl asserted that, since her father was dead and he had killed her brother, she had no male relatives. She also refused to reveal the name of her clan, declaring that her status was now that of a slave. As for becoming his wife, she would rather die. Greatly offended by this rejection, Mbugano determined to break the spirit of this courageous girl.

On reaching the capital, Mbugano went to report to the Chancellor the success of his mission. It was then that the Chancellor learnt that Matthias Kalemba, whom he had so cruelly done to death a few days before, had been adopted and brought up by his own uncle, Magatto. On hearing this, he said, 'If I had known that, I would not have put him to death, but I would have installed him in my household, and given him charge over all my goods, for I know that those who practise religion do not steal!' Because of the newly discovered relationship the Chancellor ordered his brother to establish Matthias's widow on their own family estate.

The names and fates of most of the other captives brought from Mityana do not seem to be known. The boy Arsenius escaped and took refuge at the Catholic mission, and Mawaggali's sister, Munaku, was taken by Mbugano to his home in Kyaggwe County, where heavy stocks were fastened to both her feet. For a full month he tried every means to bend her to his will. After a few days in the stocks, all the skin had gone from the girl's ankles and raw wounds encircled her legs. Mbugano's other women, moved with pity, wished to pack the apertures of the stocks with soft fibres to lessen the friction, but their master would not allow it. 'Her feet will be cared for,' he said, 'and even freed entirely, when she has come to her senses.' He resorted also to daily beatings and threats to sell her to the Arab slave-traders but nothing he could do was able to break down her resistance.

Finally, baffled by Munaku's constancy, Mbugano decided to cut his losses. Professing pity and admiration for his victim, he offered Père Lourdel the chance to redeem her. The priest was delighted and a bargain was struck. That same night, July 1886, in exchange for a gun and some ammunition, Mbugano handed the girl over to the care of the mission.

Père Lourdel decided that the heroic profession of faith made by this young catechumen merited her exemption from the customary four years' period of probation before baptism. She was therefore given an intensive course of instruction and some weeks later, on 22 August, baptized and given the name Maria-Mathilda.

Chapter Sixteen

SEVEN DAYS TO MARTYRDOM

While Mbugano was raiding and looting in Ssingo county, time was running out for the captives at Namugongo. The prisoners were not only resigned to their fate but awaited it calmly in a spirit of confidence and even joy. Denis Kamyuka, who shared a hut with Gyavira Musoke and Mugagga Lubowa, tells how each day they exchanged greetings with James Buzabaliawo and Anatole Kiriggwajjo, who were confined in a nearby hut. ' "Friends over there," we called out to them, "take courage! The time draws near for us to return to Jesus the life which he has bestowed upon us." '

Some of the prisoners were in the stocks and others had slave-yokes or metal rings fastened to their necks, but the discomfort particularly mentioned by Kamyuka was the biting cold of the early morning. They were not provided with the customary bark-cloth blankets, and most of the pages wore only the toga of thin cotton-cloth which they had been wearing when they were arrested. Of the pages, only Adolphus Mukasa Ludigo was better provided. He is said to have been wearing bark-cloth and an antelope skin. The three soldiers or guards would also have been more warmly clad. The others, although able to sleep peacefully in spite of their predicament, were usually woken up in the early hours of the morning by the biting chill of the dew and the damp rising from the bare ground upon which they lay.

Their guards offered them no molestation, although some loaded them with insults and abuse for having deserted the gods of their fathers. Others of the guards were puzzled by the determination of these young boys to die for a mere belief. To these the martyrs attempted to explain their position : 'We have accepted the religion of God because we have learnt to understand it. When you learn to know it, you will follow our example.'

During their week of waiting, the martyrs always said their morning prayers, grace before and after meals, Angelus and rosary. For the rest, their conversation was, 'Let us remain firm and die for Jesus Christ! Death comes only once, after but a short time of suffering, whereas the joys of Heaven will never cease.' At other times, their thoughts and prayers must have been devoted to their companion, Mbaga Tuzinde, fighting his lone battle against the supplications and entreaties of his many relatives.

At their mission stations near the capital, where they were virtually prisoners, the European missionaries, Catholic and Protestant, were consumed with anxiety for their young flocks. Reports of the deaths of some of the martyrs had been brought to them secretly under cover of darkness and they knew that many still remained under sentence of death. Mackay was in hopes that the sudden arrival of Bishop Livinhac might help to move Mwanga to clemency and proposed that the Catholic and Protestant missionaries should take joint action. His account of this proposal is to be found in the *C.M. Intelligencer and Record* of 1886 :

> Thinking that the arrest and murder of many of their pupils, along with ours, would bring them to see the value of unity of action, Mr Ashe and myself agreed to write to them, offering to join with them in any plan they thought best to prevent the massacre of some forty Christians, who had been condemned to death, but were not yet executed. We suggested one or other of two plans. First, to combine and give the king and Katikiro a large quantity of goods, so as to redeem the prisoners; or, secondly, to go together to the court and insist on our all leaving the country, unless the sentence were cancelled.
>
> The reply I received was as follows. I give the translation as the note was written in Kiswahili.
>
> 'Roubaga, 27th May 1886 (This should be 28th).
>
> Mon bien cher Monsieur,
>
> I have arrived to-day. M. Lourdel is absent, having gone to Mutongo to forward our goods. Probably he will return to-morrow. The other day he saw the king, and entreated him. He pleaded hard but in vain. I think that interference on our part will greatly increase this evil, and perhaps for us to be seen (acting) along with you will increase the evil just the same. Compliments to yourself and Mr Ashe.
>
> Dignetur Omnipotens adjuvare credentes et sperantes in Eum!
>
> > Votre tout dévoué,
> >
> > Léon Livinhac.'

> On finding that the Romanists refused to act with us, we resolved to try what we could do alone. Accordingly, on the 29th, I went to the capital at Munyonyo, and found M. Lourdel in the store-house. By-and-by we were called into the king's presence. I told the Père that I meant to speak for the prisoners; would he help me? He said that he had done his best the other day, and would not say anything more. I said it was always well to try again, when not successful at

first. After being ushered in ... I reminded the king that he had a short time ago promised me anything I liked if I would show his gunsmith how to make cartridge cases, and now I asked for my reward; would he give it? 'Yes.'

I said I begged the lives of those condemned but not yet executed. This took him aback. He said they were all already killed. I knew that this was not the case, and pleaded again. He then said that if any remained alive, 'there may be five or six, or even ten, I shall not kill them'. I begged that the executioner be brought and given orders accordingly. This was not done, nor would he give me a messenger to go and tell the executioner, but insisted that he had already given orders to spare several, while all the others were dead.

I pressed my request as far as I thought it advisable to go without irritating him, and thus causing the immediate execution of all in bonds and probably the arrest of more. So I desisted.

Mackay had obtained no more than a repetition of the vague promise made to Lourdel on 26 May, 'I will spare a few.' Mwanga was clearly quite obdurate, and Lourdel made no further effort to move him when he saw him on 29 May. He merely informed the Kabaka that Bishop Livinhac and his companion had arrived at the Catholic Mission. Mwanga seemed surprised, but made no reference to the failure of his plan to keep the new arrivals away from their confrères at the mission.

The Protestant missionaries made further efforts to intercede for the captives on the succeeding two days. Ashe went to Munyonyo on the 30th, but failed to obtain an audience. He did see, however, what must have been the remains of the martyr Pontian Ngondwe. 'On the side of the road,' he writes, 'there was a human head, which looked as if it had been carefully placed there after being severed from the trunk. It had a sort of fascination for me. I tried to discern the features, but it was the face of no one I knew. A little further, on the other side of the road, were the limbs, hacked in pieces at the joints. I went on, sick at heart. . . .'

Mackay, who went to Munyonyo the following day, was equally unsuccessful in his efforts to obtain an audience.

On 1 June, Bishop Livinhac, accompanied by Pères Lourdel and Denoit, went to pay his respects to the Kabaka and to pay him, in the form of presents, the fare for crossing the Lake in his canoes.

Mwanga at first showed some embarrassment at meeting the Bishop but soon recovered his composure and even grumbled at the smallness of the present. The Bishop was much struck by the deterioration in Mwanga's appearance and behaviour since he had last seen him, nearly four years earlier. He writes :

How different was King Mwanga from the young Prince who came to bid me farewell when I left Buganda three years ago. Then he was naïve, affable and full of confidence in the missionaries. Now his face was drawn, his look undecided, his smile forced and false, his speech incoherent. Although never fervent in the practice of religion, he at one time respected it, and seemed happy to see his subjects becoming Christians; now he looked on them as enemies to be persecuted.

As long as he allowed himself to be guided by the maxims of religion, and consulted good and enlightened Christians, his rule was wise; but since he has chosen to follow only caprice and the perfidious counsels of witch-doctors and hypocritical and ambitious pagans, and to allow himself to be enslaved by his passions, he is like a pilot without a compass, and all the measures he takes are against his own interests. If only he would open his eyes and understand that no king can have a truly glorious reign unless he endeavours, before anything else, to give glory to the true God and to favour His religion!

Without any reproaches, which would only have irritated him and made matters worse, we pointed out that the line of conduct which he had been following for some time was depriving him of his best subjects, and was keeping strangers away from his kingdom. We added that, under the circumstances, we could not remain at Our Lady's mission in any large numbers, and I asked him to give me canoes to return to the South of the Lake.

This request seemed to astonish him; he declared that he could not allow me to leave Buganda so soon. 'To see a friend like you depart,' he said, 'is like taking leave of ten.' Nevertheless, he took care not to give us any indication that the persecutions would stop. We insisted, and he ended by allowing me to leave and ordering Adolphus Nantinda, who was present at the audience, to go and collect the canoes.

Elsewhere, Bishop Livinhac wrote that he left this audience with the impression that Mwanga had become thoughtful, and somewhat sorry for having gone to such extremes. 'Subsequent events,' he added, 'showed me to be right; for the time being, he did not pronounce any further death sentences.'

On their return from this audience, the Catholic missionaries learnt that the Russian explorer, Dr Junker, had arrived from Bunyoro. Lourdel sent him a note which brought him to the mission on the following day. He then went on to visit the Protestant mission where he eventually decided to stay, as it was the older and more comfortable establishment.

While he was there, Bishop Livinhac and Père Lourdel paid a return visit to the English missionaries who had come to see the Bishop soon after his arrival. Dr Junker offered to join with the missionaries in a protest against the massacres and a demand for permission for the eight Europeans, Livinhac, Lourdel, Giraud, Denoit, Amans, Mackay, Ashe and himself, to leave the country. The Catholics did not think this wise and made it clear that they were not in favour of joint action, not, they assured the others, because of religious differences, but because they feared that the Kabaka would resort to violence against the Christians still at liberty and against the Europeans in his power.

Dr Junker sides with Mackay in condemning the Bishop's refusal to act in concert with the Protestants. He deplores the fact that 'so little cordiality prevailed between the two missions, and that no joint action was possible even on the vital question of Mwanga's atrocious persecution, in which both parties were involved'. Ashe, however, is prepared to concede that the Catholic missionaries may have acted wisely in this. Referring to Bishop Livinhac's reply to Mackay's first proposal, Ashe says, '. . . possibly he was right . . . the chiefs were in an angry and irritated state of mind . . .'. Again, in talking of Dr Junker's proposal, Ashe writes, 'the Frenchmen settled the difficulty by declining to act with us in the matter and, as I said, referring to the former occasion, possibly wisely'.

Bishop Livinhac explains his own reasons for deciding against joint action in a letter to the Editor of *Missions Catholiques*. He wrote:

> Shortly after my arrival in Buganda, the English missionaries proposed that we should go and see the King together with them, in order to ask him either to cease persecuting the Christians, or to allow us to leave his dominions. I arrived at the conclusion that I ought not to accept their proposal. In the opinion of all my confrères and of the neophytes whom I consulted, its effect would have been to make the Christians more odious and the missionaries more suspect. Very likely Mwanga would have kept us all prisoners, or, if we had been allowed to leave, he would have had us all massacred on the Lake. Even had we succeeded in getting away without danger, it would have been cowardice to abandon our neophytes at a moment when they had the greatest need of our advice, encouragement and example. I therefore replied to these gentlemen that they were free to do what they judged best, but that we on our part would meet the trouble in the way that appealed to us.
>
> It is possible that in their letters they will blame me for having refused to act with them, and will accuse me of fanaticism. I must say, however, that in Buganda they have been very civil to me, visiting me first, and even going the length of assuring me that they were pleased to see me arrive, in the hope that my presence would contribute to the good of religion.

Reviewing the episode after the lapse of years, one is inclined to judge that the Bishop acted for the best. In the event, the persecution lost its impetus, and only one further victim died after the Namugongo holocaust. This is only what might have been expected from Mwanga's wayward and fickle character, which made him unlikely to persevere for long with any one line of conduct. Strong opposition, however, might well have rendered him stubborn and driven him into the arms of those who desired the extermination of Christianity in Buganda. It seems most unlikely that any intervention could have saved the Namugongo prisoners. Withdrawal from a position one has taken up, implying as it does an admission or error, is only possible to a strong character : it would have been impossible to Kabaka Mwanga. The best that could be hoped for from him was that, once having demonstrated to his own satisfaction that he was still the all-powerful ruler and master of Buganda, he would desist from further violence. This, in fact, was what actually happened.

Fortunately, the prisoners at Namugongo were building no hopes upon what their pastors might achieve with the Kabaka. They were expecting no reprieve, and were quite resigned to die for Jesus Christ. In fact, had a reprieve come, it is certain that many of them would have received it with very mixed feelings.

On the evening of their seventh day at Namugongo, the pulse of Mukajanga's drum sounded through the village and penetrated to the huts in which the captives were chained. Gradually, the clamour grew in intensity as other drums and cymbals took up the call, and the chief executioner's assistants, answering the summons, gathered around his quarters, shouting, yelling and howling in a frenzy of anticipation.

Within their prison quarters, Charles Lwanga and his companions quickly realized that their time of waiting was over, and that ordeal by fire awaited them in the morning. 'Nevertheless,' says Denis Kamyuka, 'we slept as during the preceding nights. But if one of us happened to wake up, he whispered to his neighbour, "I say, are you awake too? To-morrow we are going to fight our battle; let us be firm in our resolve to die for Jesus Christ." Each time we woke up, we recited our prayers. The Our Father and the Hail Mary were continually on our lips.'

That the captives awoke from time to time is not surprising. The wonder is that they managed to sleep at all. The executioners, about a hundred strong, rendered the night hideous with their clamour, as they danced, sang and drank around the fire which they had built in Mukajanga's compound, working themselves into a frenzy of excitement for the horrible task they were to perform on the morrow.

Chapter Seventeen

THE HOLOCAUST

Early on the morning of Ascension Thursday, 3 June 1886, the executioners, their faces smeared with red-ochre and streaked with soot, swooped upon the huts in which their victims were confined. On their heads were fantastic wigs, fashioned from the tails of small animals and bird's feathers and, to complete their attire, they wore the skins of leopards or other animals around their waists, strings of amulets round their necks and bangles of bells on their ankles.

Pandemonium reigned as the executioners danced around their prisoners, brandishing spears or knives, beating drums and uttering their chants. These chants followed the usual Kiganda pattern, sounding something like the travesty of a litany : the leader, in a raucous voice, would intone a phrase to which all the others would reply with the refrain, then the leader would go on, either repeating the same phrase, or improvising variations of it, the chorus answering each time with the same refrain. The theme of one of the chants used on this occasion was, 'The women who have borne children shall weep to-day,' answered by the refrain, 'Yes, they shall weep to-day'.

Having removed the stocks, slave-yokes and rings from their prisoners' limbs and necks, the guards tied their hands behind their backs and led them out into the open space before the chief executioner's house. Here an astonishing scene was enacted, unique in the history of the Namugongo execution site, a scene which for all the world resembled the gathering of children for a Sunday-school outing. As each fresh batch of prisoners was led out from its quarters, they were hailed with cries of joy and congratulation from those already assembled. This joyous enthusiasm reached its peak when Mbaga Tuzinde was seen approaching, between two guards. 'Here comes Mbaga,' cried one. 'Look, they are bringing him too!' 'Well done, brave lad !' they called out as he drew nearer. When he joined the waiting group, all his companions gathered round him, offering their congratulations and expressing their joy at this reunion. 'Well done !' they said. 'You have overcome the devil ! Our Lord is pleased with you ! You are a credit to our religion.'

The executioners were lost in wonder and amazement at this scene, and said to one another, 'These people must be quite mad! From their behaviour, you would imagine that we were taking them on a picnic. Have they no fear of the furnace? Or do they think to pass through it unscathed?'

When all the prisoners were assembled, Mukajanga gave the order to proceed. Denis Kamyuka describes their progress :

> We set out with unconcealed joy, walking in single file; Gyavira, Mugagga, Kizito, Werabe and myself; each of us with a silent prayer on his lips. After ten minutes' march, we encountered Senkole and his following, their faces streaked with soot. He held in his hand the Sacred Fuse with which, as we filed past him, he tapped on the head each of those singled out for death. Me, he allowed to pass untouched, as if to say, 'Not fit for martyrdom! Too small, my boy!' 'My poor Kamyuka,' whispered Mugagga to me, 'you are going to miss the rendezvous in Heaven.'
>
> Already, Senkole had singled out Charles Lwanga, our gallant leader, declaring, 'You, I am keeping for myself, to sacrifice to Kibuka, Mukasa and Nende. You will make a prime offering.'
>
> In taking leave of the rest of us, Charles said, 'My friends, we shall before long meet again in Heaven. I stay here and go on ahead of you. Keep up your courage, and persevere to the end.'

In choosing his own personal victim, Senkole was following the traditional procedure of a ritual execution, which prohibited the presence of the Guardian of the Sacred Fuse at the actual scene of a large execution. He was, instead, expected to select one victim and burn him apart from the others. The rite of tapping each of the condemned with the Sacred Fuse was designed to render the ghosts of the victims powerless to take their revenge upon the spirit of the Kabaka. According to Miti, the words uttered by Senkole, when tapping each victim, were, 'Your own disobedience is responsible for your death, and not the Kabaka'.

Before proceeding on their way with the main body of prisoners, the executioners probably lit, from the Sacred Fuse, the torches with which they were to ignite the main pyre.

After they and their victims had passed on, Senkole took Charles Lwanga to a spot about fifty yards from the road, not far from the tree known as *Ndazabazadde,* where a smaller pyre had been prepared. Senkole's assistants, among whom was Sebabi, to whom we are indebted for the details of this martyrdom, then tied up their victim so that his legs were held firmly together in the extended position and his arms fastened tightly to his sides. Abdul Aziz, who saw the martyr in his agony, says that he was wrapped, like the other martyrs, in a section of reed-fencing, constructed very much like a picket fence but with the pales closer together. He also says that Charles had a slave-yoke attached to his neck.

When the executioners began to strap him down, Charles Lwanga said to them, 'Will you please untie me and allow me to arrange the pyre myself?' His request was granted, and the martyr arranged his own death-bed of firewood. Then lying down, he was tied and strapped as before. Senkole lit a torch of grass from the Sacred Fuse and set fire to the wood under the martyr's feet. Slowly the flames burnt his feet and legs to charred bones, leaving the rest of his body unharmed. Senkole, as he went about his task of controlling the fire so that it should not spread too quickly, said to Charles, 'Ah, let me punish you properly, and let us see whether your God will come and deliver you from the fire.' Charles, bearing his agony without a murmur, replied, 'You poor foolish man! You do not understand what you are saying. You are burning me, but it is as if you were pouring water over my body. I am dying for God's religion. But be warned in time, or God whom you insult will one day plunge you into real fire.'

After this exchange, Charles lay quietly, praying and waiting for the moment when his soul should be set free from his tortured body. The fire spread slowly. Just before it finally stopped the beating of his heart, Charles Lwanga cried out in a loud voice, 'Katonda! (My God)', and so died.

The Muslim, Abdul Aziz Buliwadda, who saw Charles in his agony, has left us a brief but vivid description. Abdul must have been somewhat behind the rest of the captives, and only arrived at the spot where Senkole had met the others after the latter had started torturing Charles Lwanga. The Guardian of the Fuse called the Muslim aside from the road to show him his handiwork. Abdul says:

> This is what I saw when Lwanga Lugajju was killed. He had a slave-yoke on his neck and a mat of reeds, tied round him with ropes, up to the armpits. They had started the fire at his feet. When I saw him, the sweat was just pouring from him, but he was uttering no sound. He was breathing heavily, as if taking too much air into his lungs, and expelling it in gasps, as if to blow away the smoke. I did not see his eyes properly, because he just opened them for an instant and immediately closed them again. When he had shown me this sight, Senkole sent me on to join the others at the main funeral pyre.

When Senkole and his assistants had finished their work, they took handfulls of young reeds, still in bud, and scattered them on all sides, chanting, 'We have not killed you, but Nende and Kibuka and all the gods whom you have despised, they are the cause of your death'.

Charles Lwanga died on the morning of Ascension Thursday, the feast to which he had been looking forward with joyous anticipation ever since his failure to celebrate Easter in a fitting manner. 'How we shall celebrate that feast!' he had said to Père Lourdel.

While Lwanga was suffering alone, his friends and fellow-pages were still, as they loved to call it, 'fighting the battle for Jesus Christ'. Kamyuka's account continues from their parting with Charles:

Then we started off again on our march. As we ascended the hill, we came to a bark-cloth tree. There the executioners stripped us of all the old and torn bark-cloths with which they had covered us in the square, when taking away our cotton cloths from us, and hung the rags on its branches. The local people call the tree *Sezibugo*, master of bark-cloths, because of the custom of hanging on it the *embugo*, the bark-cloths, of the people executed there. When they had taken our clothing, leaving us only a small strip of cloth about the loins, one of the party said aloud, 'In but a short time we shall be clothed in the nuptial garment which will admit us to the heavenly banquet.'

Then Bruno Serunkuma, addressing the three of us that Senkole had not tapped with his fuse, said, 'Children, I am very sorry for you. I am very much afraid that the Kabaka and his creatures will try again to make you renounce Jesus. It would have been better for us all to die, and so reach Heaven together.'

We arrived at the place of execution, a mile and a quarter from the residence of Mukajanga, and sat down in a group. We kept saying to one another, 'Here we are, at Heaven's gates. In the twinkling of an eye, we shall see Jesus.' The poor pagans laughed at us, saying, 'Hark at their ravings! Don't they fear the flames? Do they think we are preparing a treat for them?'

Then Mukajanga gave each of us a small gourdful of plantain-wine (Mwenge), it being the custom of the Baganda to give plantain wine to everyone who is about to be put to death. James Buzabaliawo, (probably in memory of his Master's refusal on Calvary) refused to drink.

This final rite completed, Mukajanga dedicated us to his pagan deities and addressed us with a number of mock-farewells. Then he gave the order to tie us up.

We were stretched on reeds held together with fibre thongs, our hands tied firmly behind our backs, and our legs strapped together. The edges of the reed covers were folded over our bodies, and we were rolled in them so as to make movement impossible. Whilst one group of executioners was busy tying us up in this way, others built the pyre from the piles of firewood which had been collected. Then lifting the human faggots they had prepared, they laid them on the pyre. When they came to Sebuta, Werabe and myself, they tied us up perfunctorily, but instead of throwing us on to the heap of firewood, like Mugagga, Gyavira, Kizito and the others, they placed us to one side. We began to protest, with tears in our eyes, 'We are Christians too, and we shall never abandon our religion! We wish to be burnt with our brothers!' To keep us quiet, Mukajanga said, 'Don't worry! I shall burn you too, but only when I need more fuel to revive the flames over the ashes of your friends!' As he said it, he winked and leered at us in a wicked manner.

James Buzabaliawo seemed to be especially concerned about Simeon Sebuta. 'I know well,' he said, 'that the Kabaka is not going to have you burnt. You are to remain alone amidst the temptations and evils of the Court. I beseech you, Sebuta, never to think of denying your faith. See how happy we are to die for it. We are going to Heaven, my lad.'

Did James have a presentiment about the fate of Sebuta, or had he already detected a weakness in his character? His anxiety about the youth was, in the event, well justified.

Mukajanga, in his count and inspection of the living faggots, which his assistants had thrown on to the funeral pyre, recognized amongst them his son, Mbaga Tuzinde, who, like his companions in glory, was calmly reciting his prayers, a serene and tranquil expression on his face. At the thought of the torment in store, his father's heart revolted. He had the boy untied, and took him aside. Mbaga, his hands still tied behind his back, knelt before his father, who pleaded with him once again. 'Give up this folly! Leave this European nonsense in the furnace and come with me to the Kabaka. He will pardon you at my pleading.' 'Pardon me, Father,' replied the boy, 'but praying is no crime. I have no desire to give up the service of Jesus, and I am happy to have the chance of dying for Him, my King.'

'But I,' protested Mukajanga, 'do not want you to die. Let me hide you. And, to please me, give up this religion.'

'Father, the Kabaka has ordered me to be burnt. He is your master, and you cannot shield me.'

'What kind of madness is this,' exclaimed Mukajanga, 'that drives you on to break my heart?'

In spite of himself, the old man could not but admire the determination of all these Christian pages and soldiers. He was heartbroken and distraught at having to commit to the flames his obstinate but lovable son. Out of pity, to spare him suffering, he ordered his assistants to club the boy on the nape of the neck, and throw his lifeless body into the flames. They took him some little distance apart and did so, killing him instantly. I saw all these things with my own eyes.

Denis Kamyuka's account contains hardly any reference to the Protestant victims who were burnt in the same holocaust, because his questioners were almost exclusively concerned with learning the details of the Catholic Martyrs, in connection with the Cause for their Beatification. Abdul Aziz Buliwadda, however, also an eyewitness, makes it clear that three others were clubbed to death together with Mbaga Tuzinde. He says :

> They first executed Sekabandwa (Nakabandwa) then Kidza of Kijasi and Tuzinde, and then the Chamberlain to the Princess Royal (Katikiro wa Nalinya). All of them lay down and were struck on the back of the head, once or twice.

Simeon Sebuta adds to this that, 'Mukajanga, after having killed the martyrs, took out his handkerchief, covered his face and wept, because he had killed his son, Mbaga Tuzinde, and his brother, Nakabandwa.'

The story of the consummation is given in the words of Denis Kamyuka :

> When all the victims had been laid on the pyre, the executioners brought more wood, which they piled on top of them. While this was being done, I heard the Christians, each reciting the prayers which came to his mind at that supreme moment. When the men began to spread wood over Mugagga, he cried out, 'Wait a bit! I must have something to drink first: I am suffocating in this jacket of reeds.' Mukajanga, informed of the request, agreed, saying, 'It is a last request which cannot be refused.'
>
> Our joyous friend was carried down from the pyre, untied and given two small portions of plantain-wine, for which he gave thanks. Some of the pagans thought within themselves, 'Here is one, at least, who flinches.'
>
> After the executioners had allowed him time to get rid of his stiffness and recover his breath, they came to Mugagga saying, 'Now you must be tied up again.' 'Wait just a little longer!' he exclaimed. Then Mukajanga said to him, 'I think that the others will be leaving without you.' 'In that case,' he replied, 'a truce to fooling! Wrap me up quickly in my reeds. I am at your service.' Then noticing Sebuta, Werabe and myself, below and to one side, he called out, 'Poor Kamyuka! I am going up to Heaven. We shall be separated for a time. Good-bye to you all, until we meet again.'
>
> I was stupified and speechless, unable to utter a word in reply.

My eyes filled with tears and my throat was dry and constricted with emotion. Gyavira, Kizito and Kiriwawanvu, who had heard Mugagga's farewell, hastened to add their voices to his. 'Good-bye, friends,' they called, 'we are on our way.'

When Mukajanga saw that all was ready, he signalled to his men to station themselves all round the pyre, and then gave the order, 'Light it at every point.' The flames blazed up like a burning house and, as they rose, I heard coming from the pyre the murmur of the Christians' voices as they died invoking God.

From the moment of our arrest, I never saw one of them show any lack of courage. The pyre was lit towards noon.

The executioners themselves admitted later that they had never seen the like. 'We have put many people to death,' they said, 'but never such as these. On other occasions the victims did nothing but moan and weep, but the Christians were wonderful. There was not a sigh, not even an angry word. All we heard was the soft murmur on their lips. They prayed until they died.'

Mukajanga himself reported to the Kabaka that he had never executed people who showed such fortitude and endurance and that they had prayed aloud to God even in the fire.

Although impressed by the courage of their victims, the executioners carried out to the full their wild ritual. Brandishing spears, knives and clubs, they danced round the flaming pyre chanting, 'It is not we who are killing you. Nende is killing you; Mukasa is killing you; Kibuka is killing you. All the gods whom you have despised and called demons, it is they who are killing you'. From the midst of the flames came voices in answer, most distinct that of Bruno Serunkuma, 'If the demons are killing us, it is you that are their slaves'. Another voice said clearly, 'We shall plead about that'.

When the fire was dying down, the executioners took forked branches and, lifting up the charred corpses, spread them afresh and piled more wood on them. The fire flared up again. A third time they added wood so as to reduce the bodies of their victims to ashes in order to thwart the revengeful activities of their ghosts.

Whilst the executioners were throwing the second lot of wood on the pyre, (says Kamyuka) Mukajanga came and unfastened our reed covers, and we stayed there with our hands tied behind our backs. We were there when wood was piled on for the third time, and it was still burning fiercely when they took us away to Mukajanga's house in the village.

Next morning, they took us back to the capital. ... On Lubawo Hill, they pointed to locks of hair lying about on the road, saying, 'That hair belonged to your friend Gonza.' We saw nothing but his hair, for the vultures had already eaten all the flesh from the corpse. Gonza had let his hair grow because we were not allowed to have our hair cut while we were at Munyonyo. We were considered to be in exile there, and had to let our hair grow as a sign of grief.

Back at the capital, they put us in prison, where we were kept for a full year and then released. Five of us were brought back from the place of execution; three Catholics, Sebuta, Werabe and myself; one Muslim, Abdul Aziz Buliwadda; and one pagan, Aliwali. We remained seven days at Namugongo.

Thirty-one, excluding Charles Lwanga, were burnt in the great holocaust at Namugongo on Ascension Thursday, 3 June 1886. Of these, twelve are officially recognized as Catholic martyrs, and nine are officially recognized by the Protestants, their names being inscribed on the Memorial Tablet in Namirembe Cathedral. It has generally been assumed that the remaining ten were pagans, who had been in prison and under sentence of death for offences other than religion. However, at least five, and possibly more, of these were definitely Protestant readers or catechumens, and Simeon Sebuta mentions one unknown Catholic. In two of his earlier lists of Catholic martyrs, James Miti mentions an Ambrozio Kizito of the Scaly Ant-Eater Clan. One is at first tempted to identify this name with the unknown mentioned by Sebuta, but, as Miti omits from these two lists the names of Ambrose Kibuka and Kizito, one is forced to assume that he has, in fact, run these two names together and produced Ambrose Kizito. Kibuka did in fact belong to the Scaly Ant-Eater Clan. Miti's final list of Catholic martyrs, in his *History*, tallies with the official Catholic list.

Miti also says that 'among the prisoners were six pagans and one Muslim, Abdullah Aziz Bulwadda, all of whom had also been sentenced to death on various charges other than religious conversion'. From Kamyuka, one knows that the Muslim and one pagan, Aliwali, were brought back from Namugongo; which would leave five pagan victims of the holocaust. This would agree with the conclusions reached in the Appendix.

It would appear that these pagans were, to say the least, not out of sympathy with the Christians with whom they died. Firstly, no protest against their presence seems to have been lodged by the Christians, although they did so in the case of Abdul Aziz, who in fact owed his life to the pleas of the martyrs and to their firm assurances that he was not a Christian. Secondly there is the fact, firmly established from a number of sources, that no outcry marred the serenity of the final consummation, which suggests that all the victims were resigned and united in one purpose, to die bravely for God. There can be no doubt that if these pagan victims spent the week of imprisonment at Namugongo in the company of these zealous neophytes, whether Catholic or Protestant, they, who even attempted to convert their executioners, would have spared no efforts to instruct their fellow victims and encourage them to dedicate their lives to Katonda (God), the Creator of all things.

News of the Namugongo martyrdoms reached the two Christian missions slowly and sporadically. As had happened after the martyrdom of Joseph Mukasa the previous November, numbers of catechumens made their way to the Catholic Mission under cover of darkness, begging for immediate baptism and confirmation, on the plea that they were liable to be arrested at any moment. Fifty-two neophytes were confirmed by Bishop Livinhac between 31 May and 6 June, among them Jean-Marie Muzeyi, who was to be the last martyr. The Bishop was astonished at the effects of grace on these recent converts : at any moment they expected to be handed over to the executioners, yet faced the prospect of dying painfully for their religion with calm courage and unwavering faith. Several even asked whether to remain in concealment was not a form of apostasy, and whether they should not give themselves up as Christians.

For the rest of the year, Kabaka Mwanga's behaviour remained as unpredictable as ever. Still uttering threats against the Christians, he yet restored to favour and reinstated as Majordomo, the confessor of the faith, Honorat Nyonyintono. Matthew Kisule also remained completely unmolested and was even able to attend Mass openly on Sundays in spite of Mwanga's threat, 'I know that you pray. I will have you killed one of these days, or at least have your ears cut off.' 'Look at these ears,' said Kisule to Bishop Livinhac, with a smile. 'They no longer belong to me. The Kabaka has promised to relieve me of them one of these days.' Undeterred, Matthew Kisule continued to visit the mission, give shelter to fugitive Christians, both Catholic and Protestant, send food to those in prison, ease their hardships, and ransom the wives of Christians.

In September the Kabaka imprisoned Joseph Nsingisira, a prominent Catholic who had been absent on a royal mission at the time of the persecution, but, yielding to pressure from Kulugi and other chiefs, released him again. He then attempted to have Joseph murdered but the plot was foiled by some of the chiefs who sent warning to the intended victim. Finally, Nsingisira was again arrested,[1] imprisoned and loaded with chains. 'In those chains,' said Joseph, 'I spent twenty-eight months, that is until the insurrection drove Mwanga from his throne.' Isaac Kajane (Kato), the twin brother of Denis Ssebuggwawo, and another convert named Lwanga were also kept in chains until Mwanga's deposition.

It soon became apparent to the Kabaka that, far from extinguishing the torch of faith in his dominions, he had spread the flame more widely. His evil counsellors did not hesitate to point this out to him and his resentment flared up afresh. However, the attitude of his chiefs had changed since they themselves had become the victims of his ill-humour and, as he could no longer count upon their support for a large scale persecution, Mwanga decided to wreak his vengeance upon selected individuals and, if possible, do away with them secretly.

The Kabaka, or his Chancellor, particularly desired to eliminate several key individuals, namely Jean-Marie Muzeyi, Joseph Kaddu —husband of the Princess Nalumansi—and two other former pages of Mutesa. Mwanga knew that the men he wanted were somewhere in the neighbourhood of the capital, but all his enquiries had failed to reveal their whereabouts. He decided to resort to guile and announced that he wished to reward with gifts of land, or positions of importance, all who had served Mutesa, his father, so faithfully, and appealed to them to present themselves at Court.

The wanted men were not deceived and continued in hiding. Then Mwanga, knowing that Kulugi, the Treasurer, had always been on friendly terms with Muzeyi, asked him to have a message delivered to Jean-Marie. Kulugi does seem to have been taken in by Mwanga's dissimulation, because he sent a man out to look for Muzeyi, who was then staying with Stanislaus Mugwanya. On receiving this personal invitation to come to Court, Muzeyi said to his friends, 'I think I will go. How long shall I have to go on hiding myself?' His friends tried to dissuade him, telling him that they were sure the Kabaka was playing the hypocrite, but Muzeyi said, 'I wish to go all the same. If he gives me an estate, then you may come too, and I shall present you to him. If, on the contrary, he wants to put me to death, let him do so; then you can remain on your guard, and I shall at least die for my religion, because there is no other charge against me.'

So Jean-Marie went, and Kulugi presented him to the Kabaka. Mwanga spoke kindly to him and told Kulugi to take him to the Chancellor, with orders to give him two women slaves to till his land. Kulugi, his suspicions probably aroused by this excessive cordiality, advised his protégé to take to flight; but Muzeyi refused, saying

'Where can I be safe, now that I am a marked man? Does not the whole country belong to the Kabaka? I cannot keep on indefinitely running about Buganda.'

The Chancellor also received his visitor graciously, told him that there were several unoccupied plantain groves, and invited him to return with his friends, so that all four of them could be given plots of land. Jean-Marie reported on his audience to his friends, who were not impressed.

The following morning, he went again to see the Chancellor, who showed himself as affable as before, appointed Segulira to act as his patron on future visits, and renewed the offer of land if he would bring his three friends with him the next day. Muzeyi promised to do so, although he had serious misgivings about the sincerity of the Kabaka and his Chancellor.

Before his first visit to Court, he had heard Mass and received Holy Communion, and spoken to Père Lourdel about his intention, at the same time mentioning his doubts. 'If Mwanga has really had a change of heart,' he said, 'why does he not release the Christians who are still in prison?' After his second visit, and the Chancellor's importunity about the other three Christians, Muzeyi can have had few illusions about the danger of returning, especially as the others flatly refused to accompany him. However, he was eager for martyrdom, and therefore quite ready to give Mwanga's protestations of friendliness a fair trial.

According to Lourdel, Jean-Marie Muzeyi again attended Mass and received Holy Communion on the morning of the 27 January. It was on that day that he paid his final visit to the Chancellor and disappeared.

There is no first-hand information as to how Jean-Marie Muzeyi met his death; but a woman, at that time living in the Chancellor's enclosure, said to Louis Masimbi, 'They have beheaded your friend, and have thrown his body into the swamp. At the place where he was beheaded they scraped up the earth which was soaked with blood and threw that also into the swamp'. The woman, formerly one of Kabaka Mutesa's women, had known Muzeyi when he was a page and was considered by Masimbi to be a trustworthy witness.

Her story was partly corroborated by the servants of Simeon Nsubuga, who two days later went to draw water from the swamp and noticed the smell of a dead body. On asking some women who were working in the fields nearby, what caused the smell, they were told; 'Why ask? There, where you notice the smell, a man was killed. Have you not noticed that the leaves have been cut from those wild plantains in order to wrap the body in them?' 'When my servants told me this story,' says Nsubuga, himself a confessor of the faith,

'I was sure that the man who had been killed there was our friend Jean-Marie Muzeyi, who had disappeared, and about whose fate all the Christians were concerned.'

Muzeyi was the last of the Christians to die for his faith, but there would no doubt have been other victims had it not been for the growing opposition of the chiefs, and even of the Chancellor himself, to further persecution.

In March 1887 Mwanga, who had been showing particular aversion to one of his Christian pages spared in the earlier arrests, ordered that he and a number of others should be arrested. This time however the Chancellor intervened. He protested to the Kabaka : 'In neighbouring countries they will get to know that we are killing all our young men, and that Buganda has only old men left; and then they will come and attack us.' It is not likely that Mukasa had experienced any change of heart towards the new religion but unlike Mwanga he was clever enough to gauge the temper of the chiefs and people, who were growing more and more exasperated with the whims and fancies of the fickle young tyrant. The Queen Mother also, who seems to have pleaded in vain for the pages during the May-June persecution, again urged her son to put to death only persons who were guilty of acts of direct disobedience and to leave his pages alone. These, she asserted, were his most loyal subjects, whereas the chiefs were in a state of discontent. Mwanga yielded, and the executioners, who had gathered in great numbers, left without being called into action.

As the year wore on, Mwanga showed himself increasingly friendly towards Père Lourdel and apparently more tolerant of Christianity. By the end of the year he had released all those imprisoned for their faith except Nsingisira, Kajane and Lwanga, but he had lost none of his capriciousness and arrogance and began to intensify his campaign of general and indiscriminate oppression of his subjects, irrespective of religion.[1] The latter part of 1887 may be said to mark the end of religious persecution, but the beginning of new and worse troubles for Mwanga's unfortunate subjects.

In Buganda, the Kabaka had always had a right to the property of his subjects, and even to that of the Lubale, the tribal gods. Under former rulers requisitioning of property had been carried out in an orderly manner, usually by levies organized through the chiefs, which ensured that even if the burden was not fairly distributed it was at least distributed over a large number of persons. Mwanga, disregarding tradition, began to use his personal bodyguard, the *Abapere*, to loot and plunder wherever he pleased.

Apart from this abuse, the Kabaka made the most exacting demands upon his chiefs and people for forced labour, over which the hated *Abapere* were placed as foremen. This kind of thing could not go on indefinitely, especially when it came from a tyrant who had lost the respect of his people and the support of his chiefs. The Chancellor warned the young Kabaka that he was riding for a fall and offered his resignation, which Mwanga refused to accept, although he made no effort to reform. Dissatisfaction was widespread, although the main resistance centred around the two more closely-knit and more enlightened communities, the Muslims and the Christians, who were forced by the Kabaka's atrocious behaviour to organize themselves for defence.

The rest of the story of Mwanga's reign should be regarded as a political struggle in which, most unfortunately, but quite naturally and inevitably in view of the history of the country, the division into parties took place on the basis of religion.

The story of the subsequent troubles and disorders that beset the Kingdom of Buganda—the deposition, on 10 September 1888, of Mwanga who, deserted by all except the Domestic Chamberlain and about a hundred of his pages, fled to Munyonyo and thence by canoe to the South of the Lake; the proclamation of Kiwewa, the eldest son of Mutesa, as Kabaka in his place; the Arab and Muslim coup which deposed Kiwewa and placed Kimera on the throne; the overthrow of the intolerant Muslim regime by the Christians and pagans; the restoration of Mwanga; the subsequent defeat, with Lugard's assistance, of the 'French' or Catholic party by the weaker 'English' or Protestant party; all of this is outside the scope of this work and may be read elsewhere.[1]

This account of the glorious martyrs of Uganda ends on a note of real tragedy. Fr Thoonen considers the story 'almost too sad to print', but it is given as a reminder and as a warning; a reminder that martyrdom is not just an easy way into Heaven, but a grace granted by Almighty God and then only to those who have rendered themselves worthy to receive the gift by fidelity to His service; and a warning that constant rejection of the graces offered by God can lead to such hardness of heart as almost nothing can soften. The story concerns Simeon Sebuta, the third of those spared at Namugongo, who unhappily justified the forebodings expressed by the martyr Buzabaliawo. In 1891, in a fit of pique at not receiving a coveted appointment, Sebuta abandoned his religion and joined the Protestants. He also took a number of concubines and later joined the breakaway sect of the Malachites.[2] His death took place in December

1926. The following translation of part of a letter from Fr
Verpoorter describes his last hours :

Naluggi
18.12.1943

... You ask for details about Sebuta. I have forgotten his clan but I remember perfectly his last hours.

He lived near the home of the catechist of Bwetamiza, at Luwunga. Because of the bad state of the roads, it took all of four hours to make the return journey from Gayaza to his place. In the course of three weeks, I made the trip seventeen times.

On my first visit he received me coldly. Sebuta was suffering from double-pneumonia and his condition was serious but not desperate. I offered to bring him some medicine, an offer which he accepted although he was a Malachite. The following day I took it to him.

On this second visit he was much more cordial: I did not, however, broach the question of his spiritual state. Thanks to the medicine I gave him, he passed a fairly good night.

When, two days later, I saw him again, he gave me a friendly smile. We spoke of Charles Lwanga and the martyrs. His memory of them was clear and accurate. I attempted to raise the question of the state of his own soul, but he cut me short brusquely with, 'No! Father, I am going to Hell,' and then he closed up like an oyster.

On the succeeding days I had no greater success. At the eleventh visit, six days before his death, I noticed that his sickness was getting worse. I began to speak to him about the Blessed Virgin. He shed a few tears and said, 'Holy Mary. Indeed, Father, at one time I had a great love for her, but ...' The rest of his words were quite indistinguishable.

When I got back to Gayaza, I sent a special messenger to Entebbe to ask the Reverend Mother for special prayers for the conversion of my dying apostate. She promised three nights of nocturnal adoration of the Blessed Sacrament. My catechumen children also took up the cause of the sheep that had strayed. They undertook three days of rosaries and penance.

On the seventeenth visit I hardly expected to find Sebuta still alive. He had been delirious the previous evening. I took a bottle of smelling-salts with me. When I entered the hut to which they had carried him, I found all his concubines wailing. Sebuta was in his last agony. I drove everyone out of the room and made the dying man sniff at the smelling-salts. For about twenty seconds, he completely regained consciousness. I spoke to him of Jesus and Mary. His last words were, 'Jesus, I don't love him! I am going to Hell!'

He lapsed again into a coma, and in a few minutes breathed his last.

APPENDIX I

THE PROTESTANT MARTYRS AND
THE NUMBER OF VICTIMS

This book would be incomplete without some details of those Protestant victims of the persecution who also died for their belief in Jesus Christ, side by side with their Catholic brethren. Mention of them has already been made in the preceding pages, and if they do not appear more prominently in the story it is because the account is drawn mostly from the evidence of witnesses at the judicial inquiry which preceded the Beatification, an inquiry which was concerned exclusively with the twenty-two Catholic martyrs. The Catholic Church has no mandate to judge and bestow honours upon those who have not died doing battle within her own ranks, and therefore the official inquiry did not concern itself with the Protestant victims. This, however, does not mean that Catholics should not give honour,[1] where honour is due, to persons outside the Church's fold.

In fact, there has been no comparable inquiry by any authority into the lives and deaths of the Protestant victims of Kabaka Mwanga's persecution, and of some of them nothing is known but their names. Nevertheless, at least with regard to those about whom information is available, there can be little doubt that they believed in good faith that they had embraced the true religion of Jesus Christ. They laid down their lives out of loyalty to the one true God, who had revealed himself to man in the person of Jesus Christ; they accepted him as the Way, the Truth and the Life. They were, in fact, under exactly the same condemnation as the Catholic martyrs and died side by side with them in the same holocaust. Although, owing to the tragic and unhappy divisions of Christendom, which were none of their making, the Protestant victims served God in a different way, there is no reason to suggest that the promise of our Redeemer, 'He that shall lose his life for my sake shall find it,' does not apply equally to them, or to deny them the honour accorded to Christian martyrs.

'The Protestants have never written authoritatively regarding their martyrs ...' and 'the absence of explicit Protestant record has led to confusion and obscurity ...', wrote H. B. Thomas, in an article in the *Uganda Journal,* March 1951. This is indeed true. Earlier Protestant missionary literature generally assumed that all the victims of the persecution were Protestant, and even the Catholic Bishop Livinhac seems to have thought, at first, that the martyrs were all Catholics. The standard work on Uganda, *Uganda,* by Thomas and Scott refers to two holocausts, one of thirty-two Protestants and one of thirteen Catholics. This error is unfortunately perpetuated in a recent work, *The White Nile* by Alan Moorehead (p. 297) where it is said that 'the pages were assembled at the palace, and those who had become 'readers' at Mackay's mission were asked to step forward. Some thirty or more acknowledged that they were Christians, and were asked to renounce the faith. They refused and were burnt alive in one great funeral pyre outside the capital.' Two other errors appear on the same page. One, a quotation from T. B. Fletcher, suggests that the Muslims were equally involved in Mwanga's persecution. A large number of Muslims were put to death by Mutesa, but there was no religious persecution of Muslims by Mwanga. The other error, possibly a misprint, gives early 1884 as the date of martyrdom of the first three Protestants. This was before Mwanga's accession: it should be January 1885.

Even the Memorial Tablet, erected in 1927 in Namirembe Cathedral, 'To the memory of the martyrs who laid down their lives for the sake of Christ: Uganda 1885', contains a number of errors, apart from the incompleteness of its list. The date should, of course, be 1885—1886. Munyagabyanjo's Christian name is given as Albert instead of Robert. Lwanga's name is placed amongst the unbaptized whereas Ashe, who certainly should have known, says that he was baptized; and lastly, there seems to be no sound reason for the feminine form of Kidza's Christian name, 'Ferederika'.

Mr H. B. Thomas made a valiant attempt to clear up some of this obscurity about the Protestant martyrs, and published his findings in the *Uganda Journal,* March 1951. The article, *'The Baganda[1] Martyrs, 1885-1887, with special reference to the Protestant victims,'* pays a generous tribute to *Black Martyrs* and shows a careful and painstaking collation of various lists of martyrs, concluding with a list which is, Mr Thomas says, 'what I venture to submit as the most probable roll of Protestant martyrs which can now be compiled.' Unfortunately, Mr Thomas was not then aware of the existence of what is probably the most important and complete document on the subject, an unpublished *Short History of Buganda* by James Miti, who was a Protestant page at the palace at the time of the persecution, later played an important part in public life and finally became Head of the Genet (Kasimba) Clan.

From a study of Miti's note-books, which are also in Makerere Library, one is led to suggest that it was he who drew up the list for the Namirembe Memorial Tablet and, having begun to take an interest in the subject, continued his investigations. A number of different lists appear in his note-books, the first of these corresponding closely to the Namirembe list. What is, presumably, his final list appears on page 294 of his *History* (English version). As it is not generally available, it is reproduced here in full.

INCLUSIVE LIST OF PROTESTANT CHRISTIANS MARTYRED DURING KING MWANGA'S PERSECUTION

		Tribe or totem	Place of martyrdom
1	Joseph Lugalama	Ankole	Busega near Mayanja River
2	Mark Kakumba	Civet Cat	at place of public sacrifice
3	Noe Ser(u)wanga	Black and white Colubus Monkey	called Mpimerebera

The above were the first Christians to be persecuted and martyred for the Christian religion in Buganda.

1	Noe Muwanga Walukagga	Genet Clan	Namugongo
2	Alexander Kodoko Omutebi	Sheep	,,
3	Moses Mukasa Omuzingiti	Civet Cat	,,
4	Fredrick Kizza	Bush Buck	,,
5	Elrias Mbwa	Sheep	,,
6	Robert Munyagabyanjo	Lungfish	,,
7	Daniel Nnakabandwa (Queen Mother's servant)	Lungfish	,,

The following were martyred before they received Baptism.

8	Kiwanuka Giyaza	Oribi-antelope	Namugongo
9	Mukasa	Bush Buck	,,
10	Lwanga	Monkey	,,
11	Mubi	Dog	,,
12	Kayizzi Kibuka	Lungfish	The Place of
13	Kwabafu	Lungfish	martyrdom of
14	Omuwanga of Gabunga	'nvuma'	these four is
15	Wasswa Odu of Gabunga	Monkey	not known.
16	David Muwanga	Otter	Namanve, Kyaggwe

The names given above are correct according to the information received by the writer in response to enquiries made in the various local African newspapers about these martyrs.

(There follows a list of twenty-two Catholic martyrs which tallies with the official Catholic list, except that all except Joseph Mukasa are put down as martyred at Namugongo.)

Other neophytes martyred by Mwanga for the Christian religion but of whom no mention is made anywhere in the annals of the Baganda martyrs, and the particulars of whose clans or totems and places of martyrdom are obscure :—

1) Muwanga Njigija
2) Kifamunyanja
3) Mukasa Lwakisiga
4) Sabagabo of the Department of Ekitegombwa
5) Muddwaguma (succumbed under the knife while being castrated at Mmengo)

Another Protestant convert reported to have suffered martyrdom in the County of Ssingo is chief Muwanga. He is mentioned by James Kabuga, ex-Sabalangira, as one of those that laid down their lives for the Faith at Mityana, in company with Kayizzi.

It will be noted, from the above, that Miti's investigation is independent of the lists of martyrs produced by Sir Apolo Kagwa, as Apolo lists four of the names which Miti says are not mentioned anywhere in the annals of the martyrs. In the note-books, Miti twice mentions a Mayanja Kitogo as being martyred at Mityana. He is also mentioned in a letter from Nuwa Kagyankamba, chief of Buwaya, Busiro, who gives his clan as the Civet Cat. It is not clear why he is omitted from the above list.

James Miti's contribution is valuable but it does not solve all difficulties. The multiplicity of names enjoyed by some of the victims, the nicknames and the titles, seem to have confused even the African investigators. Miti, for instance, in one of his lists of Catholics gives Antonyio Batuka Balikuddembe Lukujuju (sic) as one martyr and Joseph Mukasa as another. Apolo Kagwa, in one list, gives Kalemba and Mulumba as two separate martyrs, and Miti's Lewo Kiwanuka and Ambrosio Kizito, at first leads one to suppose that one of these is the unknown Catholic mentioned by Simeon Sebuta, until one realizes that Lewo is a shortened form of Achilles in its Luganda form, and that Ambrosio Kizito is probably obtained by omitting Kibuka from a list reading Ambrozio Kibuka, Kizito, etc.

Three independent Protestant sources of information may be considered, namely, Apolo Kagwa, James Miti and Robert Ashe (see p. 211). The Namirembe Memorial Tablet is not considered to be an independent source, as it would appear that either it is derived from James Miti, or else Miti took his first fourteen names from the tablet.

It will be seen from these lists that Miti gives no less than four Muwanga's or Omuwanga's, apart from inserting one into Noe Walukaga's name. There is probably some duplication of names. It will also be noticed that there are considerable variations in the spelling and form of Christian names. It seems advisable, therefore, to use the English form, pointing out the Luganda variations as they occur.

As the story of the persecution has already been told, and as the information available about the Protestant martyrs is very limited, the following review must take the form of notes.

210

MITI (*History*)	KAGWA (*Ebika*)	ASHE
Joseph Lugalama	Yusufu Lugalama	Joseph Lugaluma or Lugaju
Mark Kakumba	Maliko Kakumba	Joseph Nakumba
Noe Ser(u)wanga	Nuwa Serwanga	Seruwanga
Noe Muwanga Walukagga	Nuwa Walukaga	Malukaga=Nua
Alexander Kodoko Omutebi	Aligizanda Kadoko	Kadoko Alexandro Nanfumbambi
Moses Mukasa Omuzingiti	Musa Mukasa	Mukasa=Musa
Frederick Kizza	Fuledi Wigirimu Kiza	Kidza Musali Fredi Wigram
Elrias Mbwa	Mbwa Omusamula	Embwa=Musamula= Eliya
Robert Munyagabyanjo	Alubato Munyaga' byanjo	Munyaga Roberto
Daniel Nakabandwa	—	Nakabandwa=Dan
Kiwanuka Giyaza	—	—
Mukasa	—	—
Mukasa Lwakisiga	Mukasa lwa Kisiga	—
Lwanga	—	Lwanga
Mubi	—	—
Wasswa Odu of Gabunga	—	—
Kwabafu	—	—
Kifamunyanja	Kifamunyanja	—
David Muwanga	—	—
Muwanga Njigija	Muwanga Njigija	—
Sabagabo of Kitegombwa	Sabagabo we Kitegombwa	—
Omuwanga of Gabunga	—	—
Chief Muwanga	—	—
Kayizzi Kibuka	—	—
Muddwaguma	—	—

ADDITIONAL NAMES

Musabatosi from Kagwa's *Basekabaka*
Mayanja Kitogo from Miti's *Notebooks*
Kitikiro wa Nalinya from Abdul Aziz Buliwadda

Joseph (Yusufu) LUGALAMA, Mark (Maliko, Ma'ko) KAKUMBA, and Noah (Nuwa, Noe) SERUWANGA were the first Christians to shed their blood for Christ in Buganda, on 31 January 1885. The story of their martyrdom has already been told in Chapter six. Lugalama was a Munyankole, that is, a native of Ankole. The other two were Baganda, Kakumba belonging to the Civet Cat (Fumbe) Clan, and Seruwanga to the Colubus Monkey (Ngeye) Clan.

Noah (Noe, Nua) WALUKAGA, a Muganda of the Genet (Kasimba) Clan, described by Ashe as 'one of the most intelligent Africans I have ever known', was a royal blacksmith, and one of the leading Protestants. On hearing that arrests were being made, he sent into hiding his wife, children and some Christians who lived with him, and, unwilling to go into hiding himself, for fear of giving the enemies of Christianity any grounds for their oft-repeated accusations of disloyalty, calmly awaited his fate. He was condemned to be 'roasted' at Namugongo, where, while being laid on the pyre, he is reported to have joined with other Christians in urging the executioners themselves to become Christians. He was burnt alive at Namugongo on 3 June 1886.

Alexander (Alegizanda, Aligizanda, Alexandro) KADOKO of the Sheep (Ndiga) Clan, said to be a half-brother of Bruno Serunkuma but more probably his nephew, was a royal page during Mutesa's reign. Under Mwanga, he held the chieftainship of Nanfumbambi until 1885, when, according to Ashe, he was beaten by order of the Chancellor and deprived of his post because of his religion. 'He was soon given another office. He was of noble blood and was never long without some post in the king's service.' The noble blood, referred to by Ashe, was his descent from the great warrior Namunjulirwa, his grandfather. Simeon Sebuta describes the manner of Kadoko's death: 'Kadoko was seated drinking his plantain-wine from a gourd when Mukajanga told him to finish it quickly lest his friends should leave him behind. Then Kadoko put down the gourd and lay down. Then he was struck on the back of the head and died. His body was put on the pyre.' Abdul Aziz Buliwadda mentions only four as being killed in this manner, Nakabandwa, Kidza, Mbaga-Tuzinde and the Chamberlain to the Princess Royal (Katikiro wa Nalinya). Although Lefèbre does not think this identification probable, it seems safe to assume that Abdul's Katikiro-wa-Nalinya is in fact Alexander Kadoko. Other names by which Kadoko was known were Nanfumbambi, the chieftainship he held up to 1885, and Omutebi, after his residence at Kitebi. The circumstances of his arrest are given by Ashe, who says: 'Alexandro Nanfumbambi, who often gave us trouble by his inconsistencies, on hearing of the seizure of his fellow-Christians, went boldly up to the court and, when the executioners asked if any readers were concealed in his enclosure, replied, "I myself am a Christian", and was at once apprehended and made prisoner.' Kadoko died at Namugongo on 3 June 1886, being first clubbed to death and then burnt to ashes.

Moses (Musa) MUKASA, a Muganda of the Civet Cat (Fumbe) Clan, had been a page under Mutesa, in charge of the Kabaka's mosque or prayer-house (hence the title Omuzingiti). Under Mwanga, he held a minor post at court. Ashe calls him 'a bright, brave boy, who on one occasion administered a thorough thrashing to a companion who was leading some of the younger boys astray'. In view of this, it is not surprising that he should have been a special object of Mwanga's wrath. He was killed on the night of 25 May 1886, near the Kabaka's well at Munyonyo. It is said that he was first mutilated before being put to death.

It seems safe to assume that he was a victim of Mwanga's first outburst of insane fury, encountered and summarily condemned during the Kabaka's rampage through the palace.

Frederick (Fredi, Fuledi, Ferederiko) Wigram KIZZA had been present at the burning of Lugalama, Kakumba and Seruwanga in January of the previous year, in attendance upon his chief, the Mujasi or Commander-in-Chief. On that occasion he had boldly affirmed his belief in Jesus, in reply to a threat from his master to burn him also. When the general persecution broke out, Kizza's master, the Muslim Mujasi, advised him to flee and hide himself, but he refused to do so. Ashe, who calls him 'gentle, loving and brave, one of God's noblest martyrs', mentions a report that Kizza was clubbed to death before being flung into the fire. This is confirmed by the eyewitness, Abdul Aziz. It is not known why the Namirembe Memorial Tablet calls him Ferederika: the normal Luganda form would be Ferederiko.

Elias (Eliya, Eriya, Eria) MBWA, chief of Musamula and a member of the Sheep (Ndiga) Clan, or possibly of the Lungfish (Mamba) Clan, was condemned to death by fire, probably on 26 May, but later the Kabaka sent for him and had him castrated. 'He lingered a few days and then fell asleep,' says Ashe. The date of his death was probably 29 May, and the place Munyonyo, or possibly Mengo. Ashe says that Mbwa had served Mwanga while the latter was still a prince, and had been dismissed for refusing to steal some goats for his master. Later, he made his peace with Mwanga and was granted the chieftainship of Musamula.

Robert (Roberto, Lobato, Alubato) MUNYAGABYANJO, wrongly called Albert[1] on the Namirembe Tablet, was a man of about fifty and, like Mbwa, a member of the Church Council. Miti says he belonged to the Lungfish Clan, but Kisosonkole calls him a Munyoro. He was one of the palace gate-keepers and was sometimes employed as a royal messenger. The executioners arrived when he was in his house actually giving religious instruction to some boys, who managed to break through the thin reed wall of the house and escape. Munyagabyanjo remained calm and waited for them to arrest him. When his captors hesitated at the sight of a gun near the door of his house, he called out to them, 'You need not fear that I shall shoot you. Come and take me.' When they did so, he asked leave to put on his white robe and then allowed them to bind him and take him before the Kabaka. 'Are you a Christian?' asked Mwanga. 'Yes,' said Robert. 'Take him away and roast him at Namugongo,' was the summary sentence. Mackay thought that Munyagabyanjo was amongst the earlier victims, killed a week before the Namugongo holocaust, but Ashe is clearly correct in listing him amongst the Namugongo victims, because Sebuta mentions his presence on the road to Namugongo and also states that at Namugongo itself he pleaded for Abdul Aziz, assuring Mukajanga that Abdul was not a Christian. According to reports, Munyagabyanjo was dismembered, probably by order of the Chancellor, before his mutilated and bleeding body was placed on the pyre.

Daniel (Dani) NAKABANDWA, a servant of the Queen Mother and member of the Lungfish Clan, was believed by Ashe to have been clubbed to death some days after the Namugongo Holocaust. The evidence of Abdul Aziz Buliwadda and of Simeon Sebuta, both eye-witnesses, makes it certain that he died at Namugongo, and that he was clubbed to death before being placed on the pyre. The date of his martyrdom should be 3 June 1886, and not 6 June as was formerly believed. He seems to have been a relative of Mukajanga, the executioner.

KIWANUKA or KIWANUKA GIYAZA is mentioned only by James Miti and on the Namirembe Tablet, an unbaptized follower of the Protestant mission. Thomas, finding no evidence of his existence other than his name on the Namirembe Memorial, suggested the possibility of confusion with Achilles Kiwanuka, the Catholic martyr. However, as Miti is able to name his clan, the Oribi (Mpewo), and Achilles belonged to the Scaly Ant-Eater Clan, one may safely accept Kiwanuka Giyaza as a Namugongo victim, presumably burnt alive, on 3 June 1886.

MUKASA or MUKASA LWA KISIGA[1] also died at Namugongo, presumably burnt alive. Although Miti gives both these names, it would appear that this is a duplication. There is indeed, in his notebooks, some indication to suggest that the first Mukasa he lists is in fact Joseph Mukasa, the Catholic, whom Miti lists as Balikuddembe. This martyr is said to have belonged to the Bush-Buck (probably owing to confusion with Joseph Mukasa) or Lungfish clans.

LWANGA, said by Ashe, contradicting the Namirembe Tablet, to have been baptized, was a follower of the pagan chief Engobya, who showed such courage in sheltering James Miti and his fellow fugitives, arguing with their pursuers, and eventually buying them off with three thousand cowrie-shells. Nothing further is known about Lwanga, except that he died in the Namugongo holocaust, 3 June 1886.

MUBI (Mubi-azalwa, Nzalambi, and possibly also, Musabatosi), of the Dog (Mbwa) Clan, is mentioned by Miti and on the Namirembe Tablet. He is also referred to by Simeon Sebuta, who says, 'There were two friends at the prayer-house (in the royal enclosure), Wasswa and Mubi. They denied Our Lord. The rest were laughing at them but they were mourning.' Sebuta's statement that they denied Our Lord seems a little unfair under the circumstances. When the teaching of religion was proscribed after the martyrdom of Joseph Mukasa, it could only be continued in those sections of the palace which had bold and sufficiently well instructed leaders, of the calibre of Charles Lwanga, and where the catechumens could meet, free from the prying eyes of hostile companions. It seems probable that the two companions at the prayer-house had no such opportunity to continue their instructions; in which case Wasswa's statement to the Kabaka, 'I left off reading,' would have been literally true and probably not, in his eyes, a denial of faith in Jesus Christ. It should be remembered that the unhesitating and uncompromising profession of faith made by the other pages was the result of intensive preparation for this very test, by their leaders, by the priests, and by their fellow pages. Apolo Kagwa describes Wasswa as a Catholic catechumen, but Miti is more likely to be correct in stating that he was a Protestant reader. The pages seem to have followed, in general, the form of Christianity prevalent in their own particular section of the palace. Musa Mukasa had been in charge of the prayer-house, and Mubi, Wasswa's companion there, was a follower of the Protestant mission. It is almost certain that Wasswa was also. Apolo Kagwa makes no mention of Mubi, but in his *Basekabaka,* he mentions a Musabatosi, who appears in no other list.[1] Mr Thomas is probably correct in suggesting that Mubi and Musabatosi are alternative names for the same individual. Wasswa, encouraged by the example of his fellow sufferers, certainly died professing his belief in Christ; the same may safely be presumed of Mubi, not on any positive evidence, but from the fact that no outcries marred the serenity of the Namugongo scene. Also, it is impossible to believe that the enthusiasm for martyrdom displayed by his companions during the week of waiting at Namugongo was not communicated to this fellow sufferer.

WASSWA (Odu of Gabunga) has been mentioned above in connection with Mubi. Two difficulties about his identity remain unsolved. Miti calls him a servant of Gabunga, the Commander of the royal fleet of canoes, and Sebuta says he was a page attached to the royal prayer-house. Possibly he had been a servant of Gabunga before being presented to the Kabaka. The second difficulty is the Kabaka's suggestion that he was a younger brother of Isaac Kajane, himself the twin-brother of Denis Ssebugwawo. This has been dealt with in a note to page 151, where it was suggested that either the Kabaka was mistaken, or else the relationship arose out a blood-pact of which we know nothing.

KWABAFU, another Protestant catechumen of the Lungfish clan, was also a royal page and died at Namugongo. Nothing else is known of him.

KIFAMUNYANJA is mentioned by Apolo Kagwa, James Miti and by two of the Catholic witnesses. According to Aleni Ngandazakamwa, he was one of the pages serving in the outer courts and was probably, like Wasswa and Mubi, left without a leader and instructor after the death of Joseph Mukasa. Simeon Nsubuga says that, like the other two, he began by denying that he was a Christian and was given the lie by Lutaya, the Muslim Domestic Chamberlain. However he seems to have died bravely at Namugongo professing his belief in Jesus Christ.

David MUWANGA, clearly, from the name, a baptized Protestant, is said by Miti to have belonged to the Otter (Ngonge) Clan, and to have been put to death at Namanve in Kyaggwe County. Lefèbre gives his clan as the Scaly Ant-Eater, or Pangolin (Lugave), but does not indicate the source of this information.

MUWANGA NJIGIJA, sabagabo we Kitegombwa. These are given as separate names by Miti, and by Apolo Kagwa in his *Basekabaka,* but in his *Ebika* Apolo gives them as above—a name followed by a title. Sabagabo is a title belonging to one of the extensive hierarchy of minor chiefs. Bearers of the title are legion, so that there does not seem to be sufficient justification for Thomas' suggested identification of Sabagabo and Matia Gayiya, a page at Court who was beaten and imprisoned but not put to death. Kitegombwa is a district a few miles to the north-east of Mengo.

OMUWANGA of Gabunga and Chief MUWANGA, given as two separate victims in Miti's *History,* are clearly, from the Miti notebooks, two names for the same person. He is said to have been put to death at Mityana, and therefore he must have been martyred on 31 May or 1 June, when Mbugano was raiding that district. Omuwanga, follower of Gabunga, is said by Miti to have belonged to the Seed (Nvuma) Clan.

KAYIZZI KIBUKA of the Lungfish (Mamba) Clan is also said by Miti to have been killed at Mityana together with

MAYANJA KITOGO of the Civet Cat (Fumbe) Clan.

MUDDWAGUMA,[1] according to Miti, died from the effects of castration, at Mengo. In the notebooks, Miti seems to have thought that some of the last-named were Catholics, but seems finally to have settled for them as followers of the Anglican mission. This seems most probable, because Catholic enquiries about the Catholic martyrs were fairly widespread and thorough.

The following is suggested as a probable roll of Protestant martyrs:

Name	Date	Place	Method
Joseph Lugalama	31 January 1885	Busega	Dismembered
Mark Kakumba	,, ,, ,,	,,	and burnt
Noah Seruwanga	,, ,, ,,		,,
Moses Mukasa	25 May 1886	Munyonyo	Speared?
Muddwaguma	27 May 1886	Mengo	Castrated
Elias Mbwa	27-29 May	,,	,,
David Muwanga	?	Namanve	?
Omuwanga	31 May	Mityana	?
Kayizzi Kibuka	31 May	,,	?
Mayanja Kitogo	31 May	,,	?
Noah Walukaga	3 June 1886	Namugongo	Burnt
Alexander Kadoko	,, ,, ,,	,,	Clubbed
Frederick Kidza	,, ,, ,,	,,	,,
Robert Munyagabyanjo	,, ,, ,,	,,	Dismembered and burnt
Daniel Nakabandwa	,, ,, ,,	,,	Clubbed
Kiwanuka Giyaza	,, ,, ,,	,,	Burnt
Mukasa Lwa Kisiga	,, ,, ,,	,,	,,
Lwanga	,, ,, ,,	,,	,,
Mubi	,, ,, ,,	,,	,,
Wasswa	,, ,, ,,	,,	,,
Kwabafu	,, ,, ,,	,,	,,
Kifamunyanja	,, ,, ,,	,,	,,
Muwanga Njigija	,, ,, ,,	,,	,,

It is generally agreed that thirty-one, excluding Charles Lwanga who was martyred apart, died in the Namugongo holocaust. If the above list of Protestants is correct and if the unknown Catholic mentioned by Sebuta was also a victim, this would give thirteen Catholics, thirteen Protestants and five pagans.

The total number that died in the persecution cannot be ascertained with any certainty. Ashe suggested about two-hundred. Bishop Livinhac wrote, 'The number of victims is supposed to exceed a hundred.' The names of twenty-two Catholics are known for certain, those of twenty-three Protestants with considerable probability, many of them with certainty. These with the six unknown victims at Namugongo give a total of fifty-one. Even if popular rumour exaggerated the number, Mackay is doubtless right in saying that 'many were speared or otherwise killed in an endeavour to capture them in various parts of the country'. James Miti is of much the same opinion. After giving the list of those who were castrated,[1] he says, 'many other converts were arrested around Munyonyo and similarly ill-treated and put to death, whose names and places of martyrdom are unknown to us'.

It would also be unusual if an occasion like this were allowed to pass without at least some of the Christian-hunters seizing the opportunity to settle private feuds, without any regard to the religion of their victims. Dr Junker wrote that his approach to the cruel tyrant's capital, reached on 1 June, was plainly indicated by the mangled remains of fresh sacrifices to the wrath of the Kabaka scattered along his route.

It seems likely that the estimate of about a hundred victims would not be far off the mark. The death-roll was evidently heavy enough to give pause even to the cold-blooded Chancellor, and make him endeavour to dissuade the Kabaka from further slaughter.

DETAILED LIST OF THE CATHOLIC MARTYRS

CHARLES LWANGA
Age: About 25. Nationality: Muganda.
Parents: Father, Kaddu (probably); Mother: unknown.
County of Origin: Buddu (probably).
Clan: Bush-Buck (Ngabi)—Tragelaphus scriptus.
Position: Head page in court of audience hall, under Mwanga.
Baptized: 15 November 1885 by Père Giraud.
Martyred: 3 June 1886. Burnt over slow fire, at Namugongo.
Other names: Lugajju.

MATTHIAS KALEMBA, MULUMBA.
Age: About 50. Nationality: Musoga.
Parents: unknown. Adopted father: Magatto of Edible or Cane Rat Clan.
County of Origin: Bunya (Busoga)?
Position: Mulumba, assistant to county chief of Ssingo.
Baptized: 28 May 1882 by Père Girault.
Martyred: 27-30 May 1886. Dismembered and left to die at Old Kampala.
Other Names: Wante.

JOSEPH MUKASA BALIKUDDEMBE
Age: 25 to 26. Nationality: Muganda.
Parents: Father, Njuba-eseta (Muganda); Mother, Kajwayo (Munyoro)
County of origin: Mawokota.
Clan: Giant Rat (Kayozi)—Cricetomys Emini Proparator.
Position: Page and personal attendant on Mutesa. Majordomo under
Kabaka Mwanga.
Baptized: 30 April 1882 by Père Lourdel.
Martyred: 15 November 1885. Beheaded and burnt at Nakivubo.
Other names: Batuka, Lukajuju.

DENIS SSEBUGGWAWO
Age: about 16. Nationality: Muganda.
Parents: Father, Kajansi (Muganda); Mother, Nsonga (Musoga).
County of origin: Bulemezi.
Clan: Edible or Cane Rat (Musu)—Thryonomys Swinderianus.
Position: Page in personal attendance on Kabaka Mwanga.
Baptized: 16 November 1885 by Père Lourdel.
Martyred: 26 May 1886. Beheaded at Munyonyo.
Other names: Musajja-mukulu.

PONTIAN NGONDWE

Age: 35 to 40. Nationality: Muganda.
Parents: Father, Birenge (Muganda); Mother, Mukomulwanyi (Buffalo Clan).
County of origin: Kyaggwe.
Clan: White Egret (Nyonyi)—Bubulcus Lucidus.
Position: Palace guard.
Baptized: 17 November 1885 by Père Giraud.
Martyred: 26 May 1886. Speared and hacked to pieces at Ttaka Jjunge, near Munyonyo.

ANDREW KAGGWA

Age: About 30. Nationality: Munyoro.
Parents: unknown.
County of origin: Bugangadzi.
Position: Bandmaster-General, the Mugowa.
Baptized: 30 April 1882 by Père Lourdel.
Martyred: 26 May 1886. Arm cut off, beheaded and hacked to pieces at Munyonyo.
Other names: Muddu-aguma? The Mugowa.

ATHANASIUS BAZZEKUKETTA

Age: about 20. Nationality: Muganda.
Parents: Father, Kafero Kabalu Sebaggala; Mother, Namukwaya (Buffalo Clan).
Clan: Vervet Monkey (Nkima)—Cercopithecus Aethiopis Centralis.
County of origin: unknown.
Position: Page under both Mutesa and Mwanga.
Baptized: 16 November 1885 by Père Lourdel.
Martyred: 27 May 1886. Hacked to pieces at Nakivubo.

GONZAGA GONZA

Age: about 24. Nationality: Musoga.
Parents: unknown.
County of origin: Bulamogi (Busoga)
Clan: Lion (Mpologoma)
Postition: Page of the private courts under Mutesa; Page of the audience hall under Mwanga.
Baptized: 16 November 1885 by Père Lourdel.
Martyred: 27 May 1886. Speared and beheaded at Lubawo.

NOE MWAGGALI

Age: about 35. Nationality: Muganda.
Parents: Father, Musazi; Mother, Meme.
County of origin: Ssingo.
Clan: Bush-Buck (Ngabi)—Tragelaphus Scriptus.
Position: Potter to the county chief.
Baptized: 1 November 1885 by Père Lourdel.
Martyred: 3 May 1886. Speared and savaged by dogs at Mityana.

LUKE BANABAKINTU
Age: 30 to 35. Nationality: Muganda.
Parents: Father, Mukwanga; Mother, Kusubiza (Seed Clan).
County of origin: Gomba.
Clan: Lungfish (Mamba)—Protopterus.
Postition: Official under the county chief of Ssingo.
Baptized: 28 May 1882 by Père Girault.
Martyred: 3 June 1886. Burnt to death at Namugongo.

JAMES BUZABALIAWO
Age: 25 to 30. Nationality: Muganda.
Parents: Father, Sebikejje; Mother, unknown.
County of origin: Mawokota.
Clan: Black and white Colobus Monkey (Ngeye)—Colobus Polykomos.
Position: Second-in-command to Andrew Kaggwa. Bandsman.
Baptized: 15 November 1885 by Père Giraud.
Martyred: 3 June 1886. Burnt to death at Manugongo.

GYAVIRA
Age: 17. Nationality: Muganda.
Parents: Father, Semalago; Mother, unknown.
County of origin: Busiro.
Position: Page of the audience hall.
Clan: Lungfish (Mamba)—Protopterus.
Baptized: 26 May 1886 by Charles Lwanga.
Martyred: 3 June 1886. Burnt to death at Namugongo.
Other name: Musoke.

AMBROSE KIBUKA
Age: 18. Nationality: Muganda.
Parents: Father, Kisule; Mother, Ampera.
County of origin: Ssingo.
Clan: Scaly Ant-Eater or Pangolin (Lugave)—Manis Tricuspis Treminckii.
Position: Page of the audience hall.
Baptized: 16 November 1885 by Père Lourdel.
Martyred: 3 June 1886. Burnt to death at Namugongo.
Other names: Katikamu.

ANATOLE KIRIGGWAJJO
Age: 20 or more. Nationality: Munyoro.
Parents: unknown.
County of origin: unknown.
Position: Page of the audience hall.
Baptized: 16 November 1885 by Père Lourdel.
Martyred: 3 June 1886. Burnt to death at Namugongo.

ACHILLES KIWANUKA

Age: 17. Nationality: Muganda.
Parents: Father, Kyazze; Mother, Nassaza Talidda (Civet Cat Clan).
County of origin: Ssingo.
Clan: Scaly Ant-Eater or Pangolin (Lugave)—Manis Tricuspis Treminckii.
Position: Page of the audience hall.
Baptized: 16 November 1885 by Père Lourdel.
Martyred: 3 June 1886. Burnt to death at Namugongo.

KIZITO

Age: 14 to 15. Nationality: Muganda.
Parents: Father, Lukomera; Mother, Wangabira (Civet Cat Clan).
County of origin: Bulemezi.
Clan: Lungfish (Mamba)—Protopterus.
Position: Page of the inner private courts.
Baptized: 26 May 1886 by Charles Lwanga.
Martyred: 3 June 1886. Burnt to death at Namugongo.

MBAGA TUZINDE

Age: about 17. Nationality: Muganda.
Parents: Father, Katamiza Waggumbulizi; Mother, Mmumanyi (Yam-Fruit Clan).
County of origin: Busiro.
Clan: Lungfish (Mamba)—Protopterus.
Position: Page of the audience hall.
Baptized: 26 May 1886 by Charles Lwanga.
Martyred: 3 June 1886. Clubbed to death before being placed on the pyre at Namugongo.

MUGAGGA

Age: 16 to 17. Nationality: Muganda.
Parents: Father, Mazinga; Mother, Nassubwa.
County of origin: Mawokota.
Clan: Leopard (Ngo)—Felix Pardus.
Position: Page of the inner private courts.
Baptized: 26 May 1886 by Charles Lwanga.
Martyred: 3 June 1886. Burnt to death at Namugongo.
Other names: Lubowa.

MUKASA KIRIWAWANVU

Age: 20 to 25. Nationality: Muganda.
Parents: Father, Lumanyika; Mother, Maleokuvawo (Musoga).
County of origin: Kyaggwe.
Clan: Sheep (Ndiga)—ovis.
Position: Page of the audience hall.
Unbaptized.
Martyred: 3 June 1886. Burnt to death at Namugongo.

ADOLPHUS MUKASA LUDIGO

Age: 24 to 25. Nationality: Munyoro.
Parents: unknown.
County of origin: Toro-Mwenge.
Position: Page of the audience hall.
Baptized: 16 November 1885 by Père Lourdel.
Martyred: 3 June 1886. Burnt to death at Namugongo.

BRUNO SERUNKUMA

Age: 30. Nationality: Muganda.
Parents: Father, Namunjulirwa; Mother, Ndibaliza.
County of origin: Buddu.
Clan: Sheep (Ndiga)—Ovis.
Position: Palace guard.
Baptized: 15 November 1885 by Père Giraud.
Martyred: 3 June 1886. Burnt to death at Namugongo.

JEAN-MARIE MUZEYI

Age: 30 to 35. Nationality: Muganda.
Parents: Father, Bunyaga; Mother, Mukatunzi or Nnamalayo (Monkey clan).
County of origin: Buddu.
Clan: Buffalo (Mbogo)—Buffalo pumilus.
Position: Former page of Kabaka Mutesa.
Baptized: 1 November 1885 by Père Lourdel.
Baptized: 27 January 1887. Beheaded and body thrown into swamp between Mengo and Namierembe Hills.
Other names: Musoke, Muddembuga, Jamari.

NOTES

Chapter One

Note 1, *page* 5. H. P. Gale, *Uganda and the Mill Hill Fathers*, London, 1959, p. 7.

Note 2, *page* 5. Sir Apolo Kagwa, *Ebika bya Buganda*, Uganda, 1949.

Chapter Two

Note 1, *page* 9. In the latter part of his accusation, Père Lourdel is presumably referring to the introduction of commercial, as opposed to domestic, slavery. It could hardly be suggested that the Kabakas of Buganda, prior to the coming of the Arabs, had anything to learn from anyone about the disregard of human lives and property. The first Arab to arrive, Ahmed-bin-Ibrahim, is said to have been shocked by Kabaka Suna's callous slaughter of his subjects.

Note 1, *page* 11. Gale, *Uganda and the Mill Hill Fathers, op. cit.*

Note 1, *page* 13. '. . . therefore it must be false.' Mackay translates this as '. . . therefore it must be lies.' Such an expression would be alien to the natural courtesy of the Baganda; but see note 1, p. 23 for a fuller explanation of the Luganda expression.

Chapter Three

Note 1, *page* 23. '...I believe they are wrong.' The Luganda verb *Okulimba*, 'to lie', has a much looser significance than this English equivalent. *Olimba* may mean 'you are lying' but very often it merely means 'you are mistaken', 'you are pulling my leg', 'I am not guilty' (in answer to an accusation). The verb has even been heard in use at a football match in the sense of 'to trick an opponent' or 'sell a dummy'. In speaking English, a Muganda who has not thoroughly mastered the language may easily use the English verb 'to lie' in one of these meanings and unwittingly give offence. The incident related by Gale (*Uganda and the Mill Hill Fathers*, p. 263-4) is clearly an example of such a misunderstanding.

Note 1, *page* 25. The reeds mentioned are the stems of the giant elephant-grass which grows abundantly in Buganda to a height of about ten feet. When used for a royal fence, the reeds were set vertically and the tops left untrimmed. For all other fences, they were criss-crossed diagonally.

Note 1, *page* 28. '. . . neither cuttings on his body, nor gaps in his teeth'. This does not agree with Archbishop Streicher's account, that Kaggwa already bore on his forehead and chest the fire-marks of the Banyoro. It is, however, first-hand evidence which must be accepted in preference to the Archbishop's, for which no authority is quoted. Most of the East African tribes, the Baganda being notable exceptions, used to indulge in this form of ornamentation, or tribal marks, which consist of a series of cicatrices, usually arranged in patterns. One method of making these is by lifting a portion of skin with a thorn, nicking it with a knife, and then rubbing ash or some other foreign substance into the wound.

The extraction of the lower incisors was also a very common practice. It has been suggested that this practice originated as a precautionary measure in case of tetanus (lockjaw), although the explanation offered to Noni Jabavu (*Drawn in Colour*, p. 164-5) by two Banyoro students—the desire to look less like a goat and more like a cow—suggests that this extraction was a form of beauty culture.

Chapter Four

Note 1, *page* 47. 'I am getting black.' This did not, as one witness naïvely suggested, refer to the state of the Kabaka's soul, but to a physical condition. A slowing down of the circulation of the blood produces a blue appearance, especially in the extremities, of a white man, and would naturally produce a corresponding darkening of the pigment in an African.

Note 1, *page* 50. For the benefit of the reader who finds it difficult to believe that one word could possibly mean so much, it should be explained that many Kiganda names are, in fact, the first words of proverbs, or proverbial sayings. Mr Nsimbi, in an article, 'Baganda Traditional Personal Names,' *Uganda Journal*, September 1950, gives some examples of these:

'Nyonyintono (male name) from the proverb, "Nyonyi ntono yekemba byoya." This may be translated as follows: "A small bird, to appear big, must clothe itself in many feathers." Kirigwajo (male name) from the proverb, "Ekirigwa jo tekikutunuza ng'alira." Translation: "One should not cry for what will soon pass off". '

Note 1, *page* 55. The House of Eunuchs was not, at this period of history, occupied by eunuchs.

Note 1, *page* 56. Namulabira was still in prison when the priests left Buganda in 1882. Later, he managed to escape and lived in hiding in the forests around Kisubi. After the stirring times through which he had lived, he seems to have found it difficult to settle down to normal mission procedure and to have continued to act as a sort of free-lance catechist. 'A great baptizer of pagan children', he is called by one of the missionaries who, ruefully, adds that in every catechumen class he held, he had to begin the instruction of children already baptized by Namulabira.

Note 1, *page* 62. Another witness gives the names of Lwanga's parents as Salongo and Nalongo. These names mean father-of-twins and mother-of-twins, respectively. They might be proper names, but they might just as easily refer to any parents of twin children; so that the suggestion is not helpful in determining Lwanga's parentage.

Note 1, *page* 73. Perhaps the following brief quotation from James Miti's *Short History of Buganda* will bring home to the reader more effectively than anything else the status of women in the pagan world of Mwanga's day. It refers to the building of the royal enclosure at Mengo, early in Mwanga's reign:

> Each chief had to contribute his quota of labour and material. The work had to be completed as soon as possible; and for this reason, every chief, overseer or labourer who happened to come late for work, had to be fined one young girl between the ages of 14 and 20, which fine had to be paid directly to the Kabaka.

Note 2, page 73. From Mackay's journal, it is clear that he did not actually refuse a legate, but made it plain from his attitude that he would prefer to do without. After one young page had declined the Kabaka's offer of this post, Mackay did not pursue the matter any further, and left the royal presence under the impression that he had the Kabaka's permission to travel without.

Note 1, page 76. Mackay's intolerance is understandable in the light of his background and upbringing in the John Knox tradition, which regarded Catholicism as the work of the devil. In fact, hatred of what is firmly believed to be falsehood, provided that it does not also include hatred of the persons believed to be in error, is a virtue, far more admirable than the indifference to the truth which so often passes for tolerance. That even well-meaning persons would hate his Church is clearly foretold by Christ himself (John 16, 2), a prophecy that seems to apply most aptly to someone like St Paul before his conversion, and also to persons like Mackay. The reasons given by Mackay for the loss of so many of his best pupils to the Catholics, do not tally with those given by one of them, Mathias Kalemba, quoted on pages 30-31.

Note 1, page 77. Mackay states definitely that this was done on the orders of Mwanga himself, who was sleeping, and woken up by the noise of the witch-doctor's drum.

Chapter Seven
Note 1, page 86. The Kkobe Clan. In *Black Martyrs*, p. 301, the scientific name of the Kkobe is erroneously given as Cynocephalus, which is of course a Lemur. The correct scientific name of the plant, the fruit of which is the clan totem, is Discorea bulbifera. It is a creeper belonging to the yam family, of which the fruit, or aerial tuber, is edible.

Chapter Eight
Note 1, page 97. 'To eat the country'. The Luganda verb 'to eat', *okulya*, also has the meaning of 'to take over or occupy (land)'.

Note 1, page 100. Pokino. Mackay uses this title, whereas Lourdel speaks of Kyambalango. The explanation, contained in Mackay's journal, is that this individual had been Kyambalango, but had shortly before become Pokino, county chief of Buddu.

Note 1, page 102. 'English missionaries'. Of the three Anglican missionaries then in Buganda, Mackay was Scots, and O'Flaherty Irish. It is to be hoped that followers of the thistle and the shamrock will forgive the use of the word 'English': The alternative, British missionaries, although correct, sounds like a test of sobriety.

Note 2, page 102. In Mackay's journal, the Kabaka's chief storekeeper, or Treasurer, appears as Koloji. To avoid confusing the reader, this has been altered to the more usual form of Kulugi.

Chapter Nine

Note 1, page 114. The Baganda were very fond of litigation which provided one of the few forms of public entertainment. Even to-day, a workman is liable to approach his employer with the request, 'Njagala kutesa', 'I wish to discuss something.' Even though the result of the discussion is a foregone conclusion which he is quite prepared to accept, he feels cheated if he is not allowed to argue about it, the discussion being more important than the outcome. Thus they visualized even God's judgment-seat as one before which the accused would be able to argue, for hours if necessary, in his own defence.

Chapter Ten

Note 1, page 120. James Miti refers to Bwami Kirungi as a Christian but all other witnesses say he was a Muslim. The term Christian was applied loosely to anyone who had attended the instructions of the missionaries, or even Mackay's reading classes. Possibly Bwami had followed these at one time. Mackay himself states that Bwami was not a Christian, and that he was a great friend of Mwanga's, sharing with him the same hemp-pipe.

Note 1, page 128. Just as, in the early days of the Church, the Christians were accused by their pagan brethren of practising all sorts of horrible and obscene rites. To eat snakes was considered an abominable habit, as bad as if, not worse than, cannibalism; so, naturally, 'snake-eaters' became one of the popular terms of abuse used of the Christians.

Chapter Eleven

Note 1, page 130. Princess Nalumansi was killed by a rifle shot in August 1888. Her mother asserted that Kabaka Mwanga had had her killed because of her religion and because he feared that the Christians might eventually follow the English example of having a woman ruler and place her on the throne of Buganda.

Chapter Twelve

Note 1, page 139. Miti says that this was Muddu-aguma, a Catholic, a Munyoro, and a great friend of the Kabaka. The description fits Andrew Kaggwa who was Mwanga's constant companion on hunting trips and who would certainly have had the courage to stand up to and try to divert his master's ill-humour. Many of the courtiers were known by several different names or by nicknames. Muddu-aguma, the patient slave, might easily have been one of the names by which Kaggwa was known. Miti mentions a second Muddu-aguma, or Muddwaguma, a Protestant who died from the effects of castration. The possibility that this was an alternative name for Eriya Mbwa cannot be entirely rejected, although Miti gives both names, both suffering the same fate.

Note 2, page 139. This is of necessity a free translation. That given in *Black Martyrs* (p. 127) seems to be based upon a faulty Luganda text. Fr. Lefèbre, in a marginal note in his copy of that work, says: 'Cette phrase est semble-t-il la traduction du Munno, 1924 p. 123—n'agamba nti olaba ne Mwafu omwana wa Katikiro enfuyira bulago nga naye ambulako ne ntambula omu, Kitalo nno!—"Enfuyira bulago" est certainement une faute dans la texte luganda. Il faut lire "enfira bulago". Voir *Dictionnaire*, Le Veux, 1 p. 86, expression "Nfira bulago" sans traduction. La traduction serait—". . . fils de mon Katikiro, franc alleux, prêt à tout, Mwesigire qui m'est tout dévoué, lui même est absent". '

Note 1, page 140. It is generally agreed that Mwanga did not stab with the spear, but used it as a stick to strike Ssebuggwawo. Although no witness states that the martyr was struck more than once, each says that he was struck or wounded. One says, on the head; another, in the neck; a third, in the chest, etc. Miti suggests that he was stabbed in the back. None of these seems to have been an eye witness of the assault, but each appears to have derived his information from the wounds noticed on the martyr's body as he was dragged out of the Palace. Probably the only eye witness was the page, Mwafu. Taking account of Mwanga's passion—witness his hacking open the door of the store before, and his frenzied assault upon Apolo Kagwa immediately after the attack upon Ssebugwawo—and the various wounds seen upon the martyr's body, it seems safe to assume that Mwanga struck the boy repeatedly with the spear.

Note 1, page 142. Although not really related to the Chancellor, Ssebuggwawo belonged to the same clan, and had been presented at Court by the Chancellor. Either circumstance would, according to Kiganda usage, justify the use of the word 'nephew', or even 'son'.

Note 2, page 142. Ssebuggwawo was generally believed to have been killed that night, 25 May, but the account given by Musoke to Desiré Wamala is too positive and circumstantial to be lightly set aside. The two versions are simply reconciled by the plausible suggestion that the professional executioner arrived upon the scene in time to prevent the two amateurs from usurping his office. As Mwanga had ordered the immediate execution of Ssebuggwawo, the executioners themselves would do nothing to contradict the story that he was put to death that night. James Miti's account seems, at first sight, to contradict the story that the martyr was only put to death in the morning. He writes, describing his own escape from the Palace, 'The most difficult and dangerous part of our flight lay at the gates of the enclosure . . . It was only while the executioners were leading Dionizius Ssebuggwawo outside, that a number of us, Daniel Sekajja, Lule and the writer, sneaked out through the sides of the gates unnoticed and made good our escape. Arrived outside the enclosure, the prisoner was thrown down and without further ceremony had his head chopped off in the presence of us all, near a thicket upon which the Kabaka's enclosure abutted.' This account implies that Miti was an eyewitness of the execution, but it seems safe to suggest that Miti was describing what he believed had taken place, and that by 'in the presence of us all' he means 'there and then'. It is

227

unlikely that Miti and his companions, who were fleeing for their lives in a panic, stopped to watch what was happening to Ssebuggwawo in the gathering dusk. Taken at its face value, Miti's account does not agree with either of the other stories.

Note 1, *page* 143. Kato. This name is traditionally given to the second of two male twins. This particular Kato was probably not Isaac Kajane, twin brother of Ssebuggwawo, who is said to have left the Court before the persecution began, but some other Kato whose identity is unknown.

Note 1, *page* 145. This can hardly have been Musa Mukasa, the Protestant martyr, who is said to have been killed earlier that night. Mukasa is an extremely common name in Buganda.

Chapter Thirteen

Note 1, *page* 151. Wasswa. The Kabaka's words, 'his elder brother Kajane' pose something of a problem. Kajane's twin brother, Wasswa, was Denis Ssebuggwawo, the martyr, the elder of the twins. It would appear that Mwanga must have been mistaken about the relationship, or else, if it existed, it was the result of a blood-pact of which we know nothing. The younger brother of Ssebuggwawo and Kajane would not have had the name Wasswa, because a third pair of twins in the same family is not recognized as twins.

Chapter Fourteen

Note 1, *page* 163. Fr Röttgering, at Ggaba Seminary, not far from Munyonyo, has the following entry in one of his notebooks, dated 28 May 1943, which suggests that the remains of the martyr were indeed buried by some of his friends:

'On the anniversary of the Blessed Andrew Kaggwa's martyrdom, 26 May, Fr van Berkel's E.V.T. schoolboys, together with the mission schoolboys, made what was probably the first organized pilgrimage to the Blessed martyr's grave at Munyonyo . . . We found the grave, marked only by a rough cross, the left arm of which had come off, on the slope of a hill, in the compound of a Catholic. It is located behind a young Mutuba tree and, near the left, is a young orange tree. The cross stands, so I take it, at the foot of the grave. Pious hands have planted the red-leaved shrub at the head of it. Nothing else, however, showed the spot to be a grave, but there seems little doubt that tradition has marked the place verily and truly.'

Fr Röttgering also suggested to the writer that the spot where the remains of Pontian Ngondwe are buried is also known to some of the local inhabitants who have, however, so far refused to divulge the information.

Note 1, *page* 171. According to Simeon Sebuta, the group of prisoners did not follow the direct route from Nalya to Namugongo, but made a diversion so as to pass the River Lukingiridde above its source. This, he explains, was due to a Kiganda custom which forbade the execution of any prisoner who had passed through the waters of this river, and he quotes the saying, 'Lukingiridde amuganyi okufa.' (Lukingiridde rejects death).

Note 1, page 177. According to James Miti, Andrew Kiwanuka was castrated. He later became Chief Justice of Buganda.

Note 2, page 177. The spot where Matthias Kalemba was martyred is in the courtyard of the house of Aladina Visram in Old Kampala.

Note 1, page 180. The boy Arsenius was probably not the son of Matthias Kalemba, but an orphan, otherwise known as Anselm, redeemed from slavery by the priests and confided to the care of Matthias. Kalemba did have two children of his own. The elder was the girl, Julia Baleka Tibawadde, mentioned by Munaku, and the younger, a boy named Kato, who received baptism as an infant but died in 1887, the year before his sister Julia went to Tanganyika. Julia, who died in 1941, mentioned a brother of Matthias (probably a son of Magatto) named Kwabafu. According to Miti, a Protestant page of that name was burnt at Namugongo. Whether this was the Mulumba's relative (by adoption) is not known.

Chapter Eighteen

Note 1, page 200. After the plot to murder him, Nsingisira went into hiding but, unwilling to remain a fugitive, decided to face the tyrant, Mwanga, and make him declare his intentions openly. Isaac Kajane (Kato), twin brother of the martyred Denis Ssebuggwano, and another convert named Lwanga followed his example. James Miti reports:

'. . . tired of hiding and living in perpetual fear of death, the three converts . . . presented themselves before their master. The Kabaka, not finding it necessary or desirable to ask the prisoners whether they were Christian converts, simply referred to Kato's former devotion to religion, telling his audience how this boy never allowed him to sleep before he had made the Kabaka go through his day's lesson. He could not do anything against it, the Kabaka said, as his tormentor lived in the same room with him. These three were sentenced to be bound in chains and to serve their sentence without any specified date of release. They were released only in later years, after Kabaka Mwanga had been attacked and defeated.'

Note 1, page 203. Two of the Namugongo survivors, Denis Kamyuka and Simeon Sebuta were released from prison in June. From them the missionaries received an account of the holocaust and the last greetings of the martyrs. The third survivor, Charles Werabe, was freed in September. Werabe was killed at the battle of Bajja in 1889, fighting against the Muslims who had seized control of the country; Sebuta renounced his faith; but Kamyuka survived to become the main source of information about the persecution and its victims. He was present at the Beatification ceremony in 1920, when he wept at the thought of the martyr's crown which had been so nearly within his grasp.

Honorat Nyonyintono, the gallant confessor of the Faith, resisted further attempts by Mwanga to wean him from his religion. He became Chancellor during the short reign of Kiwewa and leader of the Christian forces after the Muslim coup. His death in battle, at Mawuki in 1889, was a tragedy for Buganda because he had won the confidence and affection of both groups of Christians and was the one man who, had he lived, might have persuaded the two parties to work together in harmony.

Note 1, page 204. Sir John Milner Gray gives an excellent, impartial account of the earlier troubles in his article, 'The Year of the Three Kings of Buganda', *Uganda Journal*, March, 1950.

The second chapter of Dr. H. P. Gale's *Uganda and the Mill Hill Fathers* contains a clear and brief review of the whole period. This has been severely criticized in some circles.

Margery Perham, in *Lugard, The Years of Adventure* 1858-1898, conducts a brilliant defence of Lugard's actions in Uganda, but does not conceal the fact that he acted in a most high-handed manner, or that he provoked the outbreak of civil war by distributing arms to the weaker party. The author, through no fault of her own, did not have access to the Rubaga archives.

Roland Oliver, *The Missionary Factor in East Africa*, also reviews this period of the history of Buganda.

Note 2, page 204. A sect founded in the early twentieth century by Joshua Kato Mugema. His chief apostle was Malachy Musajjalumbwa, from whom the sect obtained its name. Mugema maintained that both Catholics and Anglicans were at fault in relying upon the use of medicine, and thus not putting sufficient trust in God. He instituted his own form of baptism, and the only promise demanded from candidates was one never to make use of medicine. The sect gained a considerable following because the acquisition of a Christian name, or European name as it was called, could be accomplished without the long periods of instruction demanded by the Catholics and Anglicans. The Malachites gave considerable trouble to the medical department during the various epidemics of small-pox and plague.

Appendix I
Note 1, page 207. Honour. This, naturally, does not include any public veneration (*cultus*) which is only permissable when the Church has passed judgement and officially declared a person to be Venerable, Blessed, or a Saint.

Note 1, page 208. 'Baganda martyrs'. At least six of the martyrs were non-Baganda.

Note 1, page 213. Robert-Roberto-Lobato-Alubato-Albert. The sequence shows clearly how the mistake on the Namirembe Memorial Tablet arose. Luganda requires the addition of the final vowel, hence the Roberto. The letters R and L are interchangable, practically at will, and hence the form Lobato. For the sake of euphony, an initial vowel is desirable, and this changes the O into U; and from the form Alubato, one would naturally be inclined to anglicise the name into Albert. A similar mistake might easily have occurred, or possibly has occurred, with regard to Kidza's name. This is generally accepted as Frederick and the sequence of changes as Frederick-Frederiko-Fredi-Fuledi, but the Rev. Musoke Zimbe gives Alifuledi. It is possible that the original name was Alfred, and the sequence of alterations — Alfred-Alifuledi-Fuledi-Fredi-Frederiko-Frederick, although the reverse order seems to be the more probable. The reader may, working on these lines, find the origin of the name Alicadi, but would be unlikely to discover the origin of the charming name Zuleta, unless he knew that a popular French nun, Soeur Rita, had worked in the district in which this name is in use.

Note 1, *page* 214. Mukasa Lwa Kisiga. Musoke Zimbe gives this as Mukasa Nsiko-emira. The Rev. B. Musoke Zimbe's list of martyrs tallies fairly closely with that given by Apolo Kagwa in his *Ebika* and *Basekabaka*, the only additional name being that of Dani Nakabandwa.

Note 1, *page* 215. Musoke Zimbe also gives the name Musabatosi, but may have been following Kagwa in doing so. He does not mention Mubi.

Note 1, *page* 216. Muddwaguma or Muddu-aguma. It is possible that this was an alternative name for Elias Mbwa. Both are said by Miti to have died immediately after castration.

Note 1, *page* 217. According to James Miti,
'The following are the names of the Christian boys who were castrated.

1. Andrew Kiwanuka (Catholic). In our time, Chief Justice of Buganda now deceased.
2. Henry Nyonyintono (Catholic)
3. Ngapi (Catholic—probably as yet unbaptized)
4. Nkalubo Mirambo   ,,   ,,   ,,
5. Sanda   ,,   ,,   ,,
6. Simeon Nsubuga (Catholic)
7. Elias Mbwa (Protestant)
8. Muddwaguma (Protestant—evidently also as yet a catechumen)

Of these eight converts of the Kabaka's pages, the first six survived while the last two died immediately after undergoing the torture.' Other confessors of the faith mentioned by Miti are:

Isaya Kijambu, Gabunga or Admiral, a Protestant who was beaten and stripped of his possessions, including his wife, Bukunyisa, who was sold into slavery. Kijambu was re-instated in his post.

Sara Bweyinda, daughter of one of the gatekeepers, who was imprisoned.

Nicodemus Sebwato, who was beaten.

BIBLIOGRAPHY

A. UNPUBLISHED SOURCES

1. The *Processus Ordinarius* or *Informativus* was begun in Uganda in 1887 for the purpose of collecting the facts of the martyrdom. This most valuable source contains the statements of seven witnesses and the official report of the missionaries. The French original is in the keeping of the White Fathers; manuscript copies are in the archives of the Sacred Congregations of Rites and of Propaganda, Rome.

2. The *Processus Apostolicus* gives the sworn testimonies of twenty witnesses heard in Uganda in 1913-14. The Luganda original is at Rubaga, Uganda; the official French translation, a manuscript of about 525 pages, is in the archives of the Sacred Congregation of Rites.

3. *Mémoire Secret sur l'Association Internationale Africaine de Bruxelles et l'Evangelisation de l'Afrique Equatoriale.* Adresse à son Eminence le Cardinal Préfet de la Propagande par Monseigneur l'Archevêque d'Alger (Algiers, 1878). This document contains valuable material on the causes which led to the establishment of the Catholic Mission in Uganda. There is a copy in the Pontifical Gregorian University, Rome.

4. *Monographies sur les bienheureux martyrs de l'Ouganda* by René Lefèbre W.F. Fr Lefèbre, who spent twelve years on research into the history of the Martyrs, is probably the only writer on the subject to date who has had access to all the Luganda documents, which include the original version of the Processus and written statements by Simeon Sebuta, Abdul Aziz Buliwadda and numerous other contemporaries of the martyrs. Many of these, including Abdul, Fr Lefèbre interviewed personally. His inquiries appear to have been truly indefatigable: he attempted to trace the owners of all the names appearing on the baptismal registers of the period; made inquiries through all the clan leaders who were willing to co-operate, and sent questionnaires to anyone likely to possess information. The work was intended as a comprehensive compilation of evidence for the benefit of some future historian and as such it is of inestimable value.

5. *A Short History of Buganda* by James Miti. Copies of this unpublished MS. (in Luganda and in English translation) are available, for reference only, in Makerere College Library.

6. *Miscellaneous notes and letters* made and collected by Fr Lefèbre. These include the original of Fr Verpoorter's letter, quoted in the text, and the article by Père Le Veux, mentioned below.

233

B. PUBLISHED SOURCES

I. Diaries and letters of missionaries and others ;

1a. *The Catholic missionaries* were in the habit of sending home
extracts from their diaries in the form of letters, the most important of
which were published in their bulletin, *Missions d' Afrique des Pères
Blancs* (Algiers, from 1873), or in *Les Missions Catholiques* of Lyons. A
number of extracts from letters and diaries were published in such collec-
tions as *Extraits du Journal de Voyage des Missionnaires d'Alger aux
Grands Lacs de l'Afrique Equatoriale* (Algiers, 1879); *A l'Assaut des
Pays Nègres* (Journal des Missionnaires d'Alger dans l'Afrique Equatoriale, p. 347, Paris, 1884); *Près des Grands Lacs* (brochure, 1886).

b. Abbé A. Nicq made extensive use of the letters and diaries of all
the Catholic missionaries, and especially of Père Lourdel in his *Vie du
Révérend Père Siméon Lourdel* (Paris, 1896).

c. The most valuable of the letters from the Catholic missionaries on
the martyrs is that of Mgr L. Livinhac, addressed to the Directors of the
Propagation of the Faith on 29 September, 1886, (less than four months
after the martyrdom), and printed in *Les Missions Catholiques,* 1887,
pp. 129, 140, 148, and also in *Positio super Martyrio et Signis* (see above).

2. *The Protestant missionaries* published long extracts of their diaries
in the *Church Missionary Intelligencer and Record*. These extracts con-
tain a number of references to the Catholic martyrs.

The same is true of several books published by or about the Protestant
pioneer missionaries of Uganda: *Uganda and the Egyptian Sudan* (2
vols., pp. 372,379, London, 1882) by C. T. Wilson and R. W. Felkin;
Mackay of Uganda, by his sister (London 1890); *Two Kings of Uganda,*
(2nd edition, London 1890); *Chronicles of Uganda,* (London, 1894):
both by Rev. R. P. Ashe; *James Hannington,* by E. C. Dawson (London,
1889.).

Travels in Africa (3 vols., London 1890-2), by Dr W. Junker.

II. Further references to the Martyrs, mainly by Africans

1. *Abajulizi ab 'Ekitibwa* (The Venerable Martyrs) by Père J. Gorju,
Bukalasa, 1912. This is an extract of the diaries and letters already
referred to, augmented with some personal notes of Denis Kamyuka, the
most important witness in the canonical processes.

2. *Ekitabo kya Basekabaka Be Buganda* (Book of the Kings of
Buganda), by Sir Apolo Kagwa, (London 1912).

3. *Ebika bya Buganda,* by Sir Apolo Kagwa, (Uganda 1908, reprinted
1949).

4. *Munno* (Your Friend) the Luganda paper published by the White
Fathers, has constantly carried articles on the martyrs.

5. *Fides Service,* 1936, reports an interview of Père Raux W. F., with the mother and a cousin of Blessed Denis Ssebuggwawo.

6. James Miti's *Manuscript Notebooks* (in Luganda) are to be found in Makerere College Library.

7. *Buganda Ne Kabaka,* by Rev. B. Musoke Zimbe, (Mengo, 1939).

8. *Jeunes Héros Trop Ignorés, Mugagga et Mbaga.* A typescript article by Père Le Veux, containing an account of the holocaust by Denis Kamyuka. Père Le Veux had considerable contact with this key witness, and was able to obtain from him additional details of the martyrdoms. (This article may have been published in one of the French missionary magazines.)

III. Anthropological and historical works on the period of the Martyrs

1. *Anthropological works* frequently throw light on obscure passages in the statements of the native witnesses. *The Baganda,* by J. Roscoe, (London, 1911); *Entre le Victoria, l'Albert et l'Edouard,* by J. Gorju, (Rennes, 1920); *The Uganda Protectorate,* by Sir H. H. Johnston, 2 vols., (London, 1902); *The Customs of the Baganda,* (New York, 1934) translated by E. B. Kalibala from *Ekitabo kye Mpisa za Baganda,* by Sir Apolo Kagwa, (Kampala, 1918); *An African People in the Twentieth Century,* by L. P. Mair, (London, 1934); and, of course, the *Grammar* and the *Dictionary,* by Père Le Veux, (Algiers 1914 and 1917), and the *Luganda-English and English-Luganda Dictionary* by Ven. A. L. Kitching and Rev. G. R. Blackledge (Kampala and London, 1925); *Baganda Traditional Personal Names* by N. B. Nsimbi, Uganda Journal, September 1950.

2. *Historical Works* include *Central Africa* by C. Chaille Long, (London, 1876); *Emin Pasha in Central Africa,* A collection of his Letters and Journals, (London, 1888); *Le Père Achte,* by G. Le Blond, (Algiers 1912); Report of the Eighth International Geographical Congress Washington, D.C., 1904; *Journal of the Discovery of the Source of the Nile,* by J. H. Speke, (London, 1863); *Through the Dark Continent,* by Sir H. M. Stanley, 2 vol., (London, 1899); *Uganda,* by H. B. Thomas and R. Scott, (London, 1935); *The Year of the Three Kings of Buganda* by Sir John Milner Gray, Uganda Journal, March 1950. *Livingston's Muganda Servant* by Sir John Milner Gray, Uganda Journal, September 1949; *The Story of Uganda,* by S. G. Stock, (London, 1892); *Uganda,* by J. Richter, (Gutersloh, 1893) based on the previous work; *History of the Church Missionary Society,* by E. Stock, 4 vols., (London, 1899); *Eighteen Years in Uganda and East Africa,* by Bishop A. R. Tucker, 2 vols., (London, 1908); *Mackay of the Great Lake,* by C. E. Padwick, (London, 1917).

C. LITERATURE ON THE LIVES AND TIMES OF THE MARTYRS.

1. *Black Martyrs* by J. P. Thoonen, Sheed & Ward, London 1941. This is still the standard work upon the subject.

2. A second edition of the *Vie du Révérend Père Lourdel,* by the Abbé A. Nicq, (1906); the chapters on the martyrs do not differ substantially from those in the first edition. Third edition (Maison Carrée, 1922, reprinted 1932). The editor thoroughly revised the Abbé Nicq's work.

3. A short brochure, by Mgr L. Livinhac, in 1909, with a view to arousing interest in the cause of the martyrs.

4. A similar brochure, by the promoter of the cause.

5. *Les Bienheureux Martyrs de l'Ouganda,* by Mgr H. Streicher, Maison Carrée, 1920. Bishop Streicher was the first to use the information made available by the process of beatification. This little work has been translated into many languages, and has become the source of several other works on the martyrs.

6. *I Martiri dell'Uganda,* by Mgr Carlo Salotti, (Rome, 1921).

7. *Le Cardinal Lavigerie,* by Mgr Baunard, Paris 1922, 2 vols.

8. *Abajulizi Abesimi abe Buganda,* (Bukalasa, 1924). This short popular story of the martyrs, based on its predecessor, *Abajulizi ab' Ekitibwa* and on the Luganda dossier of the process of beatification, gives some special information, on page 28, about the clans of the martyrs.

9. *Au coeur de l'Afrique,* by Père A. Philippe, p. 191, Paris, 1928, is a free translation of Père Hallfell's work *Uganda, eine Edelfrucht am Missionsbaum der Katholischen Kirche.*

10. *Les Origines de la Société des Missionnaires d'Afrique,* (Algiers, 1929).

11. *La légende dorée au dela les mers. Les 22 Martyrs de l'Ouganda,* by Rob. Vallery Radot, Paris, 1930. A popular work.

12. *Les Martyrs noirs de l'Ouganda,* by Marie André, p. 203. Paris 1936.

13. *Uganda and the Mill Hill Fathers,* by H. P. Gale (London, 1959).

14. *The Baganda Martyrs 1885-7,* by H. B. Thomas, Uganda Journal, March 1951.

INDEX

242